THE
STRONGER
SEX

THE
STRONGER
SEX

UNDERSTANDING AND RESOLVING

THE ETERNAL POWER STRUGGLES BETWEEN

MEN AND WOMEN

RICHARD DRISCOLL, PH.D

Prima Publishing

PRIMA PUBLISHING and colophon are registered trademarks of Prima Communications, Inc.

Library of Congress Cataloging-in-Publication Data

Driscoll, Richard.
    The stronger sex: understanding and resolving the eternal power
        struggles between men and women / Richard Driscoll.
        p.   cm.
    Includes bibliographical information and index.
    ISBN 0-7615-1280-2
    1. Sex role. 2. Sex differences. 3. Man-woman relationships.
    4. Interpersonal relations. I. Title.
    HQ1075.D75 1997
    305.3—dc21   97-35044
                                                                CIP
98 99 00 01 HH 10 9 8 7 6 5 4 3 2 1
Printed in the United States of America

How to Order
Single copies may be ordered from Prima Publishing, P.O. Box 1260BK, Rocklin, CA 95677; telephone (916) 632-4400. Quantity discounts are also available. On your letterhead, include information concerning the intended use of the books and the number of books you wish to purchase.

Visit us online at www.primapublishing.com

To
NANCY DAVIS DRISCOLL,

my wife and professional colleague,
who journeys with me
while I learn so much the hard way.

May you learn to
laugh louder,
cry harder,
love deeper,
and be more reasonable.

—R.D.

CONTENTS

ACKNOWLEDGMENTS

DUE TO THE scope of the material, I have relied heavily on secondary sources. I thank Robert Wright, Helen Fisher, Christina Sommers, Warren Farrell, and Carol Tavris for organizing so much valuable gender information.

Thanks to Keith Davis and Pete Ossorio, for introducing me to ordinary language analysis.

Thanks to many friends and colleagues who offered sage comments, but particularly to: John Yates, Phil Borders, Robert Bonham, Kathy Rolenz, and Christopher Driscoll, for helping sharpen my focus, and to Gordon Burghardt and Neil Greenberg, for reviewing my evolutionary psychology.

Thanks to my agent, Lynn Chu, and my editor, Paula Lee, for the courage of their convictions.

Thanks to a small grant from the Nancy Davis foundation, which helps support our family while I write; and to Christopher, Jonathan, and Kari, for not minding too much when I was only half there.

Thanks to Harry Davis and Karen Naungayan, for editing overtime.

And, finally, thanks to my many clients who volunteered their marriages to field test my material.

INTRODUCTION:
THE OPPOSITE SEX

HAVE YOU EVER wondered if there is something basically different about the opposite sex? Maybe you sensed qualities stronger or weaker than your own, or warmer or sweeter, or cold and untrustworthy, or simply mysterious or truly unfathomable.

Why would a committed husband and loving father risk it all for a casual fling that he later says meant nothing to him? Is it a guy thing? Why would a woman who so wants warm conversations with her husband be continually upset with him, thereby pushing him still farther away from her? Is it a girl thing?

Current research shows clear differences between the sexes that are not going away. Each is a potential misunderstanding, lurking in the shadows, ready to trip us and give us something else to fight about.

Why do women want romance and conversation before physical intimacies, while men want to get past all that and close the deal as soon as possible?

Why do women want to talk through a problem, while men want to just fix it and be done with it?

Why don't men open up and reveal weaknesses, and why do women so want men to reveal weaknesses?

Gender influences what we think and feel and how we behave and misbehave toward one another. Some gender traits are just what we would expect, but not all of them. Indeed, perhaps half of what research uncovers is exactly the opposite of what society expects men and women to be. Much of it will surprise you!

Why do women typically dominate in personal arguments, as the research indicates, while we expect men to dominate and women to be subordinate?

Why do men typically bond stronger and fall harder when relationships fail, while we expect men to be more independent than women?

Why are men more inwardly troubled by casual sex, as the research shows, while obviously more interested in it?

Why are men often more concerned that women have orgasms than the women are themselves?

Why is workplace conflict more stressful when it is with women, although we consider women the "gentler" sex?

The answers, it appears, lie in human nature. While culture obviously shapes and guides us, many of our most basic gender traits seem to be innate. We shall see how the conditions of human evolution account for those traits we expect and for those we do not expect. Evolution also shows why human nature fools us when it does, accounting for our myths and illusions and exposing nature itself as a master illusionist.

Where is gender conflict heading? As social traditions lose their authority, we have more freedom than ever before to choose for ourselves. Women who were expected to raise children and hold families together are now free to seek almost any jobs they wish, spending many of their productive hours away from home. Men who once garnered respect for being providers are now expected to be sensitive companions and do a share of the housework as well.

Unfortunately, our newfound freedoms also give us more opportunities to clash over literally everything. No longer can we count on one another to meet the responsibilities that have been traditionally expected of men and women. When we both work, someone still has to taxi the youngsters. Whose career is more important? Should we take turns, or does it fall on the one who works fewer hours or earns less money? What is fair, and who is to judge? Just when every aspect of a relationship must be negotiated anew, we have fewer guidelines to help us settle our many differences. No wonder so many of us find ourselves lost in a storm amid unfamiliar surroundings.

Everywhere I look—among singles and marrieds, in the workplace, at universities and churches, and in politics— conflict between men and women is increasing. Can it be resolved, or will it blow over on its own? Or will it continue to grow even stronger, and sweep us all up in its angry gales?

Unrealistic expectations invite foolish confrontations and occasional tragedies. Now is an especially opportune time to understand gender conflict and learn to manage it, before it overwhelms us and rules our lives. I shall try to provide here the right mix of personal and professional experience, social sciences research, evolutionary explanation, and a few practical suggestions, to clarify gender conflict and point us toward friendlier relationships.

PART ONE

Love Means Resolving Conflict

Conflict is a growth industry.

—ROGER FISHER AND WILLIAM URY

W E LOOK HERE at two couples, each married ten years, and find very different relationships. In one marriage, husband and wife seem to be living in their own personal worlds, separated by an invisible barrier. They converse, when necessary, about when they will arrive home and who will pick up the children. But they seldom talk about their feelings and personal concerns. And when they do express feelings it is usually to complain and blame, out of anger, and not to understand and be understood. Indeed, neither one listens.

In the second marriage, husband and wife look forward to being together and seem genuinely comfortable with each other. Each gains strength from the other. And when they do argue, they also listen, and usually find a way to compromise and reconcile.

In spite of the obvious differences, these two relationships share a key feature in common. Like most who wed, both of these couples got along reasonably well when they courted and married, and they considered themselves very much in love. So what happened? Why does one relationship grow cold and stale, while another seems to thrive even amid adversity? What is essential for a vital relationship?

It is easy to fantasize about what we want: communication, sharing, warmth, appreciation, compliments, working together for common goals, comfort and familiarity, perhaps mystery as well, and romance. Add to that tender affection and passionate sex. If it were a picture, it might be a man and woman walking hand in hand together along the beach, as the sun drops into the ocean, painting the sky for a magic moment. Or perhaps it's an attractive couple sharing a romantic candle-lit dinner with soft music in the background.

Yet these seem to be the *signs* of a good relationship, rather than its foundations. Reviewing the course of marriages, researcher Howard Markman reaches a startling conclusion: Over the years, the amount of satisfaction in a marriage rests not on how much love we began with, how strong the attraction, or even on how much support we share. *Primarily, the quality of a marriage depends upon how well we resolve conflict when it occurs.*[1] Couples who are wildly in love but cannot resolve their differences face volatile confrontations or sullen standoffs, which break their hearts, exhaust their good will, and fill them with resentment.

After a feud about how much the vacation costs, the perfect travel plans and the walk together along beautiful Waikiki beach at sunset turn lonely and superficial. After a squabble about being late, the glimmering candle-lit dinner with fine wine and soft music becomes a poor use of your time and a waste of good food. Romance does not continue as a simple result of trying to be romantic. We must settle our differences. We can reasonably assume that those who touch each other ten years into a marriage have been settling conflicts all along, while those with the invisible wall between them are separated by many unresolved feuds.

Forget about never having to say you're sorry. Love means acknowledging our failings and finding solutions.

We do not resolve conflict by looking at only our own side of it. We need to understand one another. *Women's issues and men's issues must be viewed together, where they belong, so we can see how we fit and misfit with each other.* The clash of our individual wills is also the clash of gender temperaments that nature and culture build into us. Our own marital conflicts are small squalls in the bigger storms.

Does anyone still believe that harmony is the natural course or that conflict indicates a mismatch? Nothing could be farther from the truth. In nature, conflict is everywhere, as animals compete and prey upon one another in the struggle to survive. Modern civilization is also rife with conflict, and much of it is with those who are nearest and dearest to us.

This book is about miscommunications, where we talk past each other. It is also about stalemated wills and gridlock, where we each want opposing outcomes and neither of us gets even some of what we want. We will look at the foolishness, selfishness, and outright orneriness that keep us apart. Some of it may be hard going, but don't be fooled by the rough terrain. This is a book about friendship and love. It is about how to find love in a marriage, how to keep it and live in it, and how to get it back if you have lost it but are not ready to cancel the vows. We take the trail through the tangled underbrush of everyday conflicts because that is where we must go to understand love, to invite it home, and to provide a place for it in our hearts.

We must learn to compromise. *Any viable solutions must benefit not just one sex or the other but men and women jointly and approximately equally.* Whether we are signed up for the male experience or for the female experience, we are all in it together.

♀♂ Be content with small steps, which is all anyone ever gets anyway. You cannot reconcile opposing wills with one miraculous insight or one especially profitable night of argument. Rekindle the fire carefully, warming yourselves, without burning the house down.

CHAPTER ONE

Women As Sturdy Combatants

*There will always be a battle between the sexes
because men and women want different things.
Men want women and women want men.*

—GEORGE BURNS

IN GOVERNMENT AND industry, men hold the major positions of power. But does power in the public and economic realms translate into power in personal relationships? To find out, we tune in here on an average couple, married now four years, in the midst of a typical argument.

"All you care about is work and television," she accuses. "You are never willing to go anywhere with just me, without the children along. I'm just a convenience to you. I cook the meals. I clean the house. I'm here for sex. You take it all for granted."

In return, he says, well—nothing! She waits. "That's not true," he finally offers, vaguely, not saying exactly what is not true and offering no further argument. She feels he is *evading* her questions; he feels *invaded* by her questioning.

So what is going on here? Why is she the one doing the arguing, and why is he not arguing back? He is what used to be called the strong, silent type. But is he as calm as he appears? Is he so far above her that he can simply tune her out and not even bother to answer her complaints? Or is it just the opposite? Is he too confused and too overwhelmed by her anger to argue successfully against her? Is he simply enduring until she gets over it because he is too intimidated to do much of anything else? How can we tell?

Fortunately, social scientists are voyeurs. Researchers observe closely, trying to see us as we really are—not as we try to present ourselves or as society expects us to be. Observation has a nonchalant way of contradicting our folklore and offending our sense of how things ought to be.

EAVESDROPPING ON MARITAL ARGUMENTS

RESEARCHER JOHN Gottman, of the University of Washington, has a laboratory set up to observe and measure what goes on when couples argue. He invites couples into his lab, where he is able to record their pulse rates, heart output, skin conductance, and other indicators of stress. A video camera records their conversation as well as facial expressions and mannerisms such as fidgeting.

Gottman does not ask couples to fight, as this would not be proper. Instead, he helps couples identify a major area of disagreement, and then he asks them to discuss the issues and try to reach a resolution. And of course, they fight.

MEN ARE MORE STRESSED BY CONFLICT

Gottman finds that men tend to be more stressed by marital arguments, compared to women, who are more comfortable with emotional confrontation and better at it.[1]

In slightly different terms, men are more easily overwhelmed by emotional conflict than are women, reacting more strongly to less provocation. A typical man is seriously troubled whenever his wife criticizes him, while a woman can usually handle criticism unless her mate becomes truly contemptuous.[2] Contrary to popular expectations, men are markedly more intimidated by angry women than women are by angry men. Men tend to become confused during such confrontations, more so than women, losing track of what is said and where the argument is going. *"In the sea of conflict,"* observes Gottman, *"men sink and women swim."*[3] Men are not ordinarily blindfolded or gagged in arguments with women—it just seems that way. Overwhelmed by female anger, men forget to communicate. It's a guy thing.

Men typically *appear* calmer than their wives, who are more visibly upset, but appearances are deceptive. A typical man whose wife is upset with him is highly stressed by it, regardless of how unruffled he manages to appear.

Men stay stressed longer, too. After a caustic exchange, women's physiological stress falls off more rapidly while men's tends to remain high. Women are more comfortable with themselves after an argument, while men tend to rehash it in their minds and continue to feel trashed.[4] Men are more apt to be stressed from an argument hours, days, or even weeks after it occurs. In a poll I conducted during two presentations, about twice as many men as women indicated that they are not yet over the tension of an argument an hour or two after it occurs.[5]

We might expect those who are more comfortable in arguments to be more inclined to argue—which is just what we find.

WOMEN ARE MORE COMBATIVE

Contrary to stereotypes, women are found to be freer and more open in expressing their anger than men. Gottman observes that wives introduce complaints more than husbands, thus starting arguments more often. Once arguing, wives tend to further justify their positions and introduce additional complaints, thus expanding arguments, while husbands try to reduce the tension. Gottman concludes that *women are more willing to initiate conflict, more willing to escalate conflict, better able to handle it when it occurs, and quicker to recover from it.*[6] Men, in contrast, seek to avoid conflict, try to contain it when it occurs, are less competent in handling conflict, and take longer to recover from it.

The finding that women are more combative is substantial and robust, and has been observed by numerous researchers.[7] It is seen among couples of high and low social and economic status and in those in the middle.[8] It is found by direct observation,[9] and from reports from the couples themselves.[10] And female combativeness is not merely a product of our current era. Some of the early social sciences research conducted in the mid-1930s showed a similar pattern, with women typically dominating in arguments and men withdrawing.[11] It is also obvious to any therapist who observes even a few marriages.[12] Again and again, we see women who are quicker to complain and men who hold back.

In short, we observe that *women are generally more comfortable with personal conflict and are more combative while men, who are more stressed by conflict, tend to placate, concede, or withdraw.*

How strong are the findings? Women dominate in marital arguments about twice as often as men dominate. In the most lopsided arguments, one partner argues while the other endures in silence, immobilized by the barrage, waiting to escape. Would it surprise you that of those silenced in marital arguments, 85 percent are men and only 15 percent are women?[13] So in those totally lopsided arguments in which only one argues, *by a ratio of 6 to 1,* it is the women who demand and scold and the men who are being scolded. Gender places individuals as dominant or subordinate in marital arguments, more so than any gender-unrelated personality trait or all of them put together.[14] Gender clearly shapes the nature of intimate arguments between men and women, more so than any of us would have imagined.

How do men explain why they often acquiesce to their wives rather than arguing hard for a win? A man might say that he wants to do "what's right," or he does not want to get the wife "upset." He might say, "It is no use arguing with her because it just makes her mad." Wary of emotional conflict, men acquiesce to keep the peace.

So the man mentioned earlier who says little or nothing in an argument with his wife is surely not as totally above it all as he might appear. He is stressed to his eyebrows, hardly able to argue successfully against his more verbally combative wife.

CAN WE ACCEPT OURSELVES AS WE ARE?

THESE OBSERVATIONS are not at all flattering to men or to women. We expect men to be stronger and more independent than they appear here, and we expect women to be softer and gentler. Men ordinarily hide their weaknesses and present themselves as in charge, wanting to seem strong even when they typically lose the arguments or withdraw to avoid losing. Women find it hard to respect men who fold in arguments. And women who see themselves as mistreated underdogs, fighting for a fair break, do not want to acknowledge that they usually defeat their opposites in personal confrontations. So as men and women, *we collude to conceal how we are and to show ourselves instead as we wish to be seen.* We hide behind social masks and create agreeable myths about ourselves. And we are taken in by our own fabrications, mistaking our myths for reality. We *feel* that men are stronger, privileged, and in control of relationships, and we remember incidents that support our feelings but overlook those that do not. Social etiquette also upholds the charade. When a woman too openly dominates a man, we try to ignore it, as simple courtesy, so as not to embarrass them both.

I believe that the research findings are supportive of both men and women. Women show themselves not as weaklings, but as sturdy warriors of interpersonal conflict—comfortable with the give and take of the joust. Is that not more substantial than being the "weaker" sex? And while men are observed to be more stressed by conflict than we might expect, is it not more humane to recognize a limitation and make allowances for it, than to maintain unmanageable expectations? These findings are supportive of both sexes simply because they are true. Misunderstandings lead to unrealistic expectations, misguided actions, and failed relationships. Clear observation is a better foundation.

In any case, my aim is not to flatter but to understand. Flattery feels good, for the moment, but truth *is* good and is good for us. Or so I believe. Flattery belongs in the nebulous smoke of near misses, pleasant fictions, and wannabe realities. In relationships, as in life, it is better to reach for troublesome truth and struggle with it, than to take what feels good and pretend it is true. Remember: Opportunists flatter you, while your real friends tell you the truth.

I realize that I am beginning with a key observation that will offend some women and make machismo men blink twice. Yet we must step around a few social conventions if we are to see how gender governs our lives. I assure you it will be worth your while.

Understanding gender is like working a jigsaw puzzle. You will have to wrestle with the first pieces, which are the hardest to place and also the most important. No, they do not always fit where you might expect. Yet each piece you place correctly makes the remaining pieces easier to place. Once you have the main features of the picture blocked in, the rest tumble easily into place.

The unexpected findings beg for explanation, inviting us to grapple with some of the most fascinating and controversial questions of our time. *Why* do women so dominate in intimate arguments? If the question is confusing, it is because the findings themselves are confusing. Men are supposed to be dominant and women subordinate. We want to say that the documented observations are not really so or that they cannot mean what they seem to mean. But we would be fooling ourselves.

SUPERMYTH

The prevalent myth holds that men are dominant and women submissive in relationships, and that women, as the gentler sex, have more trouble expressing their anger. "In contrast [to men]," according to Harriet Lerner, "women have been denied the forthright expression of even healthy and realistic anger."[15] In *The Dance of Anger,* she continues: "The direct expression of anger, especially at men, makes [women] unladylike, unfeminine, unmaternal, sexually un- attractive. . . . Our language condemns angry women as 'shrews,' 'witches,' 'bitches,' 'hags,' 'nags,' and 'castrators.'"[16] "Anger is an emotion that women express far less fre- quently than do men," according to Celia Halas in *Why Can't a Woman Be More Like a Man.* "In fact, men generally feel quite comfortable with anger, express it freely, and are reasonably careless about the problems it causes in other people. . . . Women are generally afraid to express their anger."[17] Sandra Thomas and Cheryl Jefferson agree in *Use Your Anger:* "While most men have long been allowed and even encouraged to express their anger, most of us women . . . have found our anger invalidated, trivialized, and for- bidden outright."[18] These opinions are presented boldly and confidently, but with nary a hint of supporting research.

The myth is easily accepted because it is sympathetic to women and mirrors our comfortable illusions. Women want to see men as powerful, not as helpless in the face of female hostility. Men want to see their wives and mothers as gentle and nurturing, never as selfish or hostile. The more emo- tional the situation, the wilder the illusions. "My mother was a saint," proclaimed a rambling Richard Nixon—not other- wise known for his idealism—upon resigning the presi- dency. Chivalrous myths help us conceal from ourselves the awkward reality—that women tend to be more comfortable with anger and more openly combative than men.

The myth of careless men and restrained women is accepted not because it is observably so, but because it *feels* right. How can our feelings be so sure of themselves and yet so thoroughly mistaken? Perhaps nature is up to something here. Look at the previous quotes from these feminist authors, and read between the lines: "Since men are privileged and careless, and women are suppressed, women should therefore feel more justified in unleashing the force of their anger against men." Anger, of course, is a primary weapon of emotional combat. The position justifies women and encourages them to express their anger, to support their interests.

Many women do not feel powerful in relationships, and might presume therefore that men must have the power. It has even been argued that the man whose wife is scolding him has the real power, as he is controlling her by not doing what she wants. How far we will go to see men as more powerful! The man who is being scolded and not getting his way could hardly feel more powerful than the woman who is scolding him and not getting her way. All else being equal, would you not prefer to scold someone you are angry at rather than to be scolded yourself?

It has also been argued that women dominate in arguments just to be heard, because men have the real power. That sounds almost right, and it surely sounds fair. But it totally reverses the way real power works. *The one who has the real power ordinarily dominates the arguments, not the subordinate.* And human nature has never been known to be particularly fair. The drill sergeant dominates the recruit because the sergeant has the real power, and the recruit takes it instead of arguing back because he is being stripped of his power. The boss scolds the gofer but not the other way around, because the boss owns the company and the gofer is expendable. Indeed, dominance in verbal confrontation is an obvious way of gaining power, holding power, showing power, and forwarding your own agenda. One who fails to hold his own either does not have the power or is fast on his way to losing it. A teacher who has the power maintains control of her classroom, while one whose students sass her and interrupt her at will has lost her power over the class or is on the way to losing it.

Women argue strongly because they want to be heard and want to get their way, which is understandable. Yet men also want to be heard and also want to get their way. So the real puzzle is not why women argue, but why so many men do not or cannot stand up to upset women. Social expectation fails to provide much of an explanation for why supposedly stronger men buckle in arguments with supposedly weaker women. *It is as if the usual rules by which men ordinarily dominate are mysteriously suspended in these arguments, and a new set of rules applies.*

Power comes in many forms, of course. Men typically have more physical power than women, and the men who are in charge at work have more authority there, or formal power. It is in the realm of personal arguments that women have the advantage. Women seem to have more of what we might call *informal power* or *emotional power*, which counts in personal relationships. We will look closely at how such power works.

In any case, commentators who accept the commonplace myth that males dominate in personal relations—and most do—can go far afield tracking the implications of an imaginary power imbalance. Only a few bother to observe personal arguments and report what they see.[19] Beginning as we do here with actual observations takes us on a fascinating course through formerly uncharted territory.

I trust that most of us want insight and practical suggestions rather than political patronage and further justifications for our illusions. Given a clear choice, would you not choose to face a smidgen of folly rather than allow it to run your life? I will try to present what goes on in gender conflict without moral judgment. Once we see it, we can ask where it is taking us and where we want to go.

LABEL FAIRLY

From these observations, researchers draw the conclusion that women are more negative than men. Initially, I thought the conclusion followed directly from the observations. But there is a hidden bias here. The *observation* is that women are more combative and more openly hostile than men. The male researchers, who find conflict stressful, label combative women "negative." Yet conflict may establish a connection or express a problem, and the women themselves do not necessarily see themselves as negative. To be faithful to the findings, we should simply say that women are more emotionally combative, which men find quite negative.

Over the ages, women with small children have been extremely vulnerable and highly dependent upon men, so it has been vital that their needs be addressed. Given that interpersonal conflict is the usual means by which opposing wills are reconciled, is it so surprising that nature might better equip women to handle the give-and-take of emotional confrontation?

Nonetheless, the findings expose a contradiction through which we must navigate: Women, known in our hearts for their warmth and love and nurturance, are observably more combative than the men whose lives they bless.

SUGGESTIONS

THESE OBSERVATIONS suggest some direction for both genders.

Women wonder if men who withdraw in arguments are weak and inadequate, or simply unconcerned and withholding. Yet the most normal and typical men are uncomfortable with upset women, and try to avoid arguments.

♀ You should recognize that most men do not and cannot argue with upset women. Realize that a man who avoids arguing with you is not showing himself to be unusually weak or blissfully unconcerned. He is just being a normal man. It's a guy thing. You might realize that men are more vulnerable in conflict than they appear and are slower to recover from it. Be careful to accurately gauge how much stress your accusations inflict, and make allowances. Even a little anger can have more than the intended effect.

Women can be quite unconscious of how much power their anger actually has over men, who are highly stressed by it. Of course, it is natural in the midst of an argument to focus only on our own grievances, and overlook how much we are battering our adversaries. Yet this may be especially easy for women, since men often *appear* calmer in arguments and do not show themselves to be as stressed and upset as women do.

Perhaps women in earlier generations were more aware of male vulnerability. Men were said to have "big egos," or "fragile egos." Both expressions, I suspect, refer to men being more readily hurt when accused, criticized, or simply ignored. Daughters were taught to be aware of this and were advised to deal with men carefully. Women today figure that men should not be the way they are and ought to straighten up, which is grand in its idealism but hardly practical. Managing a relationship requires making real allowances for real limitations.

♂ To better resolve conflict, men must learn to be more comfortable with it. What does it take to shrug off a critical comment instead of coming totally unraveled over it? Recognize that it is normal for women to be more easily upset and irritated than men. Do not interpret it as a great catastrophe when your mate is bothered about something. Try to separate yourself emotionally from the heat of an argument, and remain as calm as possible. Stay involved, and try to talk it out.

In earlier generations, men considered women overly emotional and often unfathomable. To some extent, that attitude helped men contend with women by not taking it so deathly seriously when women were upset. Men were to uphold their responsibilities and not worry too much about emotions they could not control. Today, we are not supposed to mention that women can be too emotional. Our politically correct blinders obscure our vision and limit our ability to deal with relationships. Caught by surprise when the sweet wife turns moody or hostile, men take it far too personally.

♂ Men, recognize that women are now and always have been more comfortable with anger and other emotions. It's a girl thing. The obvious solution is to settle in and adjust to it.

ANGER AND WARINESS

The woman who argues while her husband is speechless feels justified: After all, her husband is the one causing the problem by sitting on his feelings and not communicating with her. The man who withdraws feels justified too. His wife is the one who flies at him over anything, smashes him before he knows what is happening, and then takes her win and expects him to open up and communicate with her.

Women are typically more combative, although the positions are sometimes reversed. Either way, the one who gets the best in the outburst feels it ought to end there, while the one who gets hit by the anger feels beaten up and wary.

♀♂ If you see yourself in this pattern, realize there is nothing superior about either open anger or mistrust and withdrawal. Think about changing yourself.

CHAPTER TWO

The Nature of Gender

M EN ARE FROM Mars and women are from Venus, according to a popular title by John Gray. And given all the misunderstandings between us, we might as well be from separate planets. Why are we so far apart? We are all from Earth, obviously, but we are not from the same stations on Earth. We come from the same geographic locations, but not from the same social and biological locations. Since earliest times, according to anthropologists, men and women have always performed separate tasks, living complementary but essentially parallel lives. Life in the male stations and life in the female stations required from us different qualities for our respective survival and procreation. Why should it surprise anyone that we might evolve not just different anatomies, but different psychologies as well?

Men are from Earth.
Women are from Earth.
Deal with it!

—ART BOUTHILLIER, CARTOONIST

Current research suggests that perhaps 30 percent of the differences between individuals is inborn.[1] So almost a third of what makes you different and unique is a result of the genetic blueprints you inherited from your line of ancestors. Society molds and shapes us, of course, but we must already have the stuff to be molded and shaped. Inside us somewhere are the emotions, appetites, and passions—the *oomph,* if you will, the vital juices—that incline us to fit or not fit into what society expects of us.

An extensive review in the *American Psychologist* concludes that across cultures, human evolution accounts for the overall pattern of gender differences much better than strictly social explanations.[2] Although any single evolutionary explanation can be questioned, the full pattern of explanations is highly convincing.

I present here a few such explanations, for your consideration. See these not as proven truths, but as plausible accounts. Reserve judgment. Wait until you see the entire pattern, and then make up your own mind. See evolution, if you wish, as a fascinating way to organize the information and remember it. At the least, it will help lock in your mind some of the patterns of gender conflict that so affect our lives.

The main principle of Darwinian evolution can be summarized in a single sentence: Genetic variations create variations in traits, and the more adaptive variations flourish and gradually replace the less adaptive ones.[3] It is perhaps surprising that such a simple principle should have such profound implications. We look at how gender-typical actions serve the genetic interests of males and females.

WHY MEN ACQUIESCE

WOMEN DOMINATE in marital arguments within American society, and probably in other similar Western societies as well. And it has been so as far back as the early research can take us. Through the Great Depression, the total mobilization of World War II, the popularization of television and mass advertising, the comfortable fifties and rebellious sixties, through traditional marriages and dual career marriages, before women's liberation and on past it, and into the amorphous present, the findings are much the same. However much American culture changes over the decades, women voice their feelings and men withdraw in highly personal arguments.

In peasant societies where men monopolize all positions of public power, anthropologist Susan Rogers observes that women have a great deal of *informal* influence.[4] Indeed, neither men nor women in these communities believe that men actually rule women. Rogers concludes that men and women sustain a rough balance of power, and that male dominance is a myth. Similarly, an analysis of almost a hundred preindustrial societies concludes that women often exercise informal power well beyond what is afforded them by societal rules.[5] It would seem that the informal power that tips personal arguments in favor of women is not a Western anomaly at all, but a common feature among many human societies.

We might perhaps imagine a culture somewhere that allows men to give orders but prohibits women from arguing back. Any culture obviously encourages some inclinations and suppresses others. But we can still ask about human nature. In a relatively open culture such as ours, in which men and women can argue together, and in cultures around the world, why might nature give women more clout in personal quarrels?

Solid sex differences are being found in how our brains process information and emotions.[6] Women are found to typically process emotional concerns in both hemispheres of the brain, and exchange information more easily between hemispheres, while men process emotional concerns only in the right side and reserve the left side for language and reasoning. Our contrasting brain processes surely contribute to our contrasting emotional temperaments. The advantages, suggests *Brain Sex* author Anne Moir, are that women are more adept at expressing emotions, as we observe, while men more clearly separate reasoning from emotions.[7] Magnetic imaging can now map brain activity, showing again and again that male and female brains operate differently.

Look next at why nature might program greater emotional versatility into women than into men.

WOMEN CHOOSE

Acquiescence to women can provide significant evolutionary advantage.[8] In selecting mates, women have some choice in almost all human communities. And so far as women have a choice, they will try to avoid those men who hurt or offend them or who cannot be counted upon to support their interests. The contentious young man who offends a young woman or refuses her requests will probably lose out to a man who does her favors and brings her gifts. So *men who acquiesce to women or openly support them are more likely to mate and pass their genes along to the next generations.*

When marriages are arranged, as has often been the case, parents similarly favor the man who will support a daughter over one who might exploit her. Indeed, parents and family are often more concerned about such practical matters than the daughters themselves are. An openly unsupportive man would be chosen last, or not at all. Just as populations that support women are more successful, supportive men within those populations are also more successful in mating and passing their tendencies along to successive generations.

Polygynous practices among our ancestors further restricted mating opportunities for offending males. ("Polygyny" refers to men having more than one wife, while "polygamy," of course, refers to men *or* women having more than one spouse). Of the 1,154 past or present cultures known to anthropologists, 980 of these, or about 85 percent, permitted a man to have more than one wife.[9] Although we usually judge polygyny to be unfair to women, its natural consequence is that each successful man with more than one wife can leave another man somewhere with no wife at all, and no genetic legacy.[10] A prospective husband was judged not just on whether he was able to provide, but also on whether he was reliable and could be counted upon to do so. So the evolutionary consequences of insulting females or ignoring their concerns could be terribly severe. An average man who is too quick to oppose women has fewer children, and so contributes fewer genes to the next generation.

Among our primitive ancestors, a girl was typically married by the time she was old enough to be fertile.[11] So her genetic interest was not simply to mate, which was the natural course, but to judge closely and choose a man who might provide as well as possible for her and her children.

How often do women choose men in our own society? Since men usually ask women out, are not the men making the choices? To find out, anthropologist David Givens and biologist Timothy Perper settled into singles hangouts and observed how men and women go about picking up each other.[12] Working separately, the two came up with remarkably similar observations. Women are seen to initiate about two-thirds of the courting sequences, inviting a man to approach by subtle cues such as a gaze or a smile. Women are quite aware of encouraging a man, by their attention, questions, compliments, and jokes, and by movements such as leaning unusually close or touching his arm. Later interviews revealed that most of the men see themselves as the initiators and are hardly aware that it is the woman who actually chooses her partner and then coaxes him into the chase.

Once the chase is on, it is typically the man who tries to persuade the woman to become sexually involved. He is the one who proposes dinner or a show, who first reaches out to hold hands, who initiates the first kiss, who mentions going back to the apartment, who begins necking, and so on.[13] The woman then chooses to allow the man to go forward or to slow him down and wait to see how the relationship develops. Or she opts out and looks for someone else. So after selecting the man who is to take her out, a woman then decides whether or not he gets lucky.

Similar patterns are seen among high school students. If you want to know which boys will invite which girls to the prom, why interview the boys? Look at who the girls gaze at and smile at, and stand close to and giggle with. Boys approach girls who seem approachable, and invite the girls who seem interested in being invited.

While most women understand the game, a few seem above it all and then wonder why men are not interested. A typical man will not ask a woman out unless she seems interested in being asked. He wants reasonable assurance that he will be accepted before he puts his ego on the line.

♀ To be asked, you must ordinarily show enough interest to give a man the confidence to do the asking.

♂ Recognize that you are not ordinarily in as much control of relationships as you may wish to believe. Be more alert.

Women are seen to initiate sexual liaisons in other cultures as well. While we think of men as the sexual aggressors, women are thought to initiate liaisons as much as men in about 80 percent of almost a hundred societies surveyed.[14]

CURIOUSLY SIMILAR ANIMALS

It is odd indeed that one sex should so strongly dominate our political and public life while the opposite sex dominates in personal quarrels. Yet it is not a strictly human artifact—lower animals show similar arrangements!

Observing chimpanzee politics in the Dutch Arnhem zoo, primatologist Frans de Waal is often asked who is more powerful, the males or the females?[15] He notes that in greetings, the adult males are dominant and the females show deference 100 percent of the time. In aggressive confrontations, the males win about 80 percent of the time. But in who takes objects or even food from whom, and who sits in the best spots, the females win about 80 percent of the time.

That is, a female can usually take food away from a dominant male or nudge him aside to sit in the shade! So the males dominate when public status and rank are at stake, while females dominate in situations that concern their survival and personal comfort. How curiously similar to our human society! Would it surprise you that 98.4 percent of human genetic material is absolutely identical to that in chimpanzees?[16]

We find the same dynamics in other social mammals as well, which we explore later. Males tend to dominate in confrontations over status but often give way to females over scarce food. These fascinating reversals are closely tied to our sexual natures and our very different contributions to reproduction.

CASUAL SEX VS. RELATIONSHIPS

LOOK AT our attitudes toward strictly casual sex. Young men, as most of us realize, are notoriously intrigued by casual liaisons, while young women tend to be more concerned about relationships.

In a study at the University of Hawaii, male and female students were approached by an attractive interviewer of the opposite sex, who conversed briefly and then asked the student either for a date, or to have sex.[17] Of the young men asked for a date, half agreed to go out with the female interviewer. Of those men invited for casual sex, 75 percent agreed and were ready to go. So it appears that 25 percent of college men, not interested enough to date a woman, might nonetheless agree to casual sex with her.

Of the young women asked for a date, half said they would be interested in going out with the male interviewer. There the similarity ends. Of those women invited for a tryst, virtually *none* was willing with so casual an acquaintance. Even knowing as much about males and females as we do, the 75 percent to 0 percent contrast is striking. A full generation after the sexual revolution supposedly freed us from our traditional patterns, we see ourselves here as far apart as we have always been.

Most university students are away from family and on their own, and this may be a fair sampling of what bright young adults would do in a moderately liberal society when they figure nobody is watching. Again and again, in a wide range of situations, we see that men are more interested in casual sex with a variety of partners.[18] Young men report a much stronger preference "to have sex with anyone I choose," and to have sex with no established relationship.[19] It's a guy thing. Asked if you would have sex with an anonymous partner, if there were no risk and no chance of forming a relationship, guess what? Men are four times more likely than women to say they certainly would have sex, and women are two and a half times more likely than men to say they certainly would not.[20] Is it all right for two people to have sex, if they really like each other, even if they've known each other only a very short time? A 1997 survey finds that 54 percent of college men say yes, but only 32 percent of college women.[21]

Responses would differ somewhat, of course, in other cultures. Yet the same basic contrast is found across cultures, according to anthropologist Donald Symons. It appears in illiterate tribes and in industrialized nations, and in any geographic region observed.[22] Young men are more eager for sex, while women want to be courted and are more selective.

The difference, we have every reason to believe, is in our genes.[23] The same contrast is found in the animal world, with only a few exceptions,[24] across the whole variety of species. Most of us have seen a tomcat willing to travel miles and get his hide slashed up for a "date," while a female cat stays closer to home and sees who shows up and who wins the fights. The males pursue, and females, as Darwin observed, are "coy."

Obviously, not all females are exactly coy. It is common for females to have multiple partners, and many primate females actively solicit for social and material benefits.[25] Many women enjoy sex within established relationships, and some women are as addicted to the seduction as any man. It is *relative to males*—who will typically forgo food and shelter, venture into unknown territories, battle rivals, provide resources, and risk their very lives for sex—*that females are clearly more reserved*. The observation is robust and withstands the test of time.[26]

SELECTION OF SEXUAL INTERESTS

Why the difference? Charles Darwin saw it, but was unable to account for it. The explanation was formulated by biologists George Williams and Robert Trivers just over a generation ago:[27] Since a female can bear only a limited number of offspring, she does well to choose carefully to look for optimum advantage in each mating. By contrast, a promiscuous male who sows his seed far and wide can gain a tremendous genetic advantage.[28] Even if only a small percentage of his offspring survive, his genes would spread through the population. So the accepted evolutionary explanation is that *male genes profit by being sexual opportunists while female genes, which invest more in each offspring, do best to go slowly and select carefully.* Over the generations, nature selects for sexual initiative in males and for caution in females. The explanation is deceptively simple, but has powerful implications for understanding gender relations and gender conflict.

We might profitably consider the sexes "as if they were different species," suggests Robert Trivers, "the opposite sex being a resource relevant to producing maximum surviving offspring."[29] We shall see just how often men and women act on competing interests instead of complementary ones. It can sometimes seem like we are designed to make each other miserable, which is not the case. *Men and women are designed to use one another for our own reproductive advantage. And in doing so, we happen to make each other miserable.*

Natural selection proceeds through the survival of the fittest, as those best adapted to their situations survive to produce youngsters with similar adaptive qualities.[30] In addition to surviving, we must mate and pair our own genes with those from the opposite sex to produce offspring. So evolution proceeds also through the selection of opposite sex partners who provide essential resources. *Sexual selection,* as it is called, contributes to many of our gender-typical traits.[31]

ACQUIESCENCE AND SEXUAL INTEREST

We have seen how sexual selection contributes to males giving way to females and also to males being more interested in sex. Acquiescence may seem leagues away from sexual opportunism, but note that the two evolve from the same biological circumstances: Female reproduction involves a much higher investment than male reproduction, making the female reproductive resources scarcer and so comparatively more valuable. While female genes benefit from being more selective, male genes benefit from seizing mating opportunities *and* from acquiescence and solicitous conduct, to gain access to the valuable female resources that transport them into the next generation.

Think of a young man who invites a young woman out to a posh restaurant and then to the theater to impress her, and who is attentive to her and agrees with everything she says in the hope she will spend the night with him. He is doing what he figures she wants, voluntarily, and even paying for it, in anticipation of romantic favors. If you have trouble seeing how acquiescence and sexual opportunism fit together, look no farther than your typical date.

Traits such as acquiescence to females or sexual opportunism can be only slightly advantageous and still prevail. So far as compliant men gain even a slight mating advantage in each generation, compliance would spread steadily through successive generations. Small advantages in each generation can add up to produce huge differences. We have seen substantial gender differences in casual sex and in arguments. Most of the sex differences we explore here are as obvious as these, and ratios of 2 to 1 or even more between men and women are common. Gender differences tend to be as large as findings in other areas of human behavior,[32] and those predicted from evolution tend to be especially large.[33]

Nature does not ordinarily program us by simple instinct, as occurs in lower animals. Rather, our genes help set our interest in possible activities in given situations. We have seen how human nature sets interest in casual sex higher in young men, but makes women more comfortable in angry confrontations. Variations in socialization and personal experiences further adjust the settings, yielding an extraordinarily wide range of human inclinations.

WHY WE STRAY

Women's preference for relationships and men's yearnings for casual sex contribute to why we are unfaithful.[34] Women who have affairs tend to be unhappy in their marriages, and those who are happy with their husbands tend not to have affairs. Women who stray are generally looking for the affection and companionship that is missing in their marriages. In contrast, men who have affairs are *not* found to be more unhappy with their marriages than other men! Men who stray often do so for the thrill of the sex, and not because their marriages are empty or even sexually unsatisfying.

A man whose wife is not particularly passionate might think she is seeing another man, which need not be so at all. Women have affairs not so much for the sexual excitement as for the warmth that is missing in a marriage. It's a girl thing. A woman who catches her husband in an affair might figure he is dissatisfied with her, which is not necessarily the case either. Men have affairs not so much because something is missing in the marriage, but often as a challenge and an adventure. It's a guy thing.

A woman who is angry at her husband is more apt to stray, suggesting that for women infidelity may also be a way of expressing anger. A man who is angry at his wife is no more inclined to have an affair than one who is not angry. So a woman takes her primary relationship into consideration in even the most casual tryst, whereas a man typically does not (but should).

TWO TO TANGLE

Contrasts that emerge clearly in particular situations may diminish or vanish entirely in other situations.[35] The young men who are so eager for casual sex with a young, attractive woman would not summon the same ardor for a plain woman over forty. And many of the young women who would reject strictly casual sex with a fellow student would go out with him and consider sex later as the relationship progressed. Women can be as interested in sex as men, but are choosier and consider relationship and social consequences more strongly than do men.

The findings also do not mean that men are more sexually active than women. Obviously, anytime a man has sex with a woman, a woman is necessarily having sex with a man. So surveys reporting that men begin sexual relations younger than women and are more sexually active are obviously skewed by sampling errors or responder biases.[36] Both sexes are probably fudging a bit, in the socially desirable direction. Men are overestimating, to appear more sexually successful, and women are underestimating, to appear more modest or virtuous. On average, men and women have sex with one another at the same frequency.

The higher male sex drive does mean that men are usually limited by the availability of accommodating women. It also means that men must typically court women and meet their expectations, and that women may ordinarily expect some compensation for their favors.

MALES COMPENSATE FEMALES

The custom seems to be a human universal. Anthropologist Bronislaw Malinowski observed sexual practices among the uninhibited Trobriand Islanders, who were separated from other cultures for tens of thousands of years. "In the course of every love affair," he notes, "the man has constantly to give small presents to the woman. To the natives the need of one-sided payment is self-evident. The custom implies that sexual intercourse, even where there is mutual attachment, is a service rendered by the female to the male."[37] So, too, in cultures around the world. A woman in a primitive !Kung San hunter-gatherer village tells of the benefits of affairs: "When you have lovers, one brings you something and another brings you something else. One comes at night with meat, another with money, another with beads. Your husband also does things and gives them to you."[38] Indeed, around the world, men are observed to give women tasty treats and various presents as a prelude to lovemaking.[39]

The practice also extends back to our closest primate cousins. A female bonobo (pygmy chimp) is often willing to provide sex in exchange for a fruit or a hunk of meat. She eats while he satisfies himself, and both seem quite content with the arrangement. And among chimpanzees, a male is more likely to give meat to a female when she is fertile. Indeed, when chimpanzees divide up a kill, estrous females always get a larger share of meat.[40] Some insects show similar behavior. Among hanging flies, the male catches prey and offers it to the female, who allows him to mount her while she eats it. The larger the offering, the longer she allows him to ride.[41] So prostitution rates to be the oldest profession on Earth, commonly practiced many million years before the arrival of *Homo sapiens.*

Fast forward to the here and now: Among men and women dining out together in elegant restaurants, the man pays the tab about ten times to every one time a woman pays.[42] A man who courts generally pays for the meals and entertainment, implicitly compensating the woman not just for the privilege of her company but also for the possibility of romantic favors afterward.

Among lower animals, the compensation is usually immediate and edible, although a female may also gain protection for her offspring and the benefits of friendship. Among men and women, compensation is more complex and usually more implicit. An interested man may properly give a woman any of a variety of gifts and favors, but not cash—at least not initially—for cash suggests a commercial relationship with no further obligations. The gifts are best seen as symbols of a commitment, indicating love and respect, the willingness to provide, and the resources to do so. A woman who gains a committed man who supports her and her children does better than one who gains only a box of chocolates or an evening of drinks and flattery.

CADS AND DADS

Among primates, some males mate casually and some commit and stay. Primate males who mate casually are technically termed "cads," while males who stay with their mates and offspring are "dads."[43] Among humans, men are also cads and dads, and the choice appears to be influenced more by social factors than by genes.[44] Male genes benefit from what Robert Trivers calls a mixed reproductive strategy, in which men marry and stay to raise their children *and* are interested in casual trysts with other women.[45] That is, men are inclined to be dads at home and cads elsewhere when given sufficient opportunity.

Female genes benefit from a committed man who will support her and the children, but stand to lose in uncompensated trysts. So a woman usually wants to know whether a man she is with genuinely loves her, and that he is not just playing. The ways in which women seek commitments, and the reasons men commit, are at the heart of intimate relationships.

Human nature has given to us far greater choice than to any other species of animals. We should learn to use it wisely.

BEGIN WHERE YOU ARE

IF HALF of crafting a loving relationship is changing to suit your partner, the other half is learning to accept and appreciate one another the way we are. I hope that seeing how men and women evolved helps us better appreciate the quirky ways we act toward one another. All the better if it can provide a smile or two, or even a grimace, along the way.

> *God grant me the serenity*
> *to accept the things I cannot change,*
> *the courage to change the things I can,*
> *and the wisdom to know the difference.*
>
> —REINHOLD NIEBUHR, THE "SERENITY PRAYER"

Some object to biological explanation, fearing that it sets limits on human choices. If gender is somewhat innate, then we are not free to be anything and everything we might wish to be. I see such explanation not as constraining us, but as helping to set us free. We do not master human nature by ignoring it or imagining we are too far above it to concern ourselves with it. *We become wiser, stronger, and more compassionate as we come to understand human nature and learn to work within it and work around it.*

Innate gender traits can be changed, of course, although not by merely wishing them away. Change requires conscientious attention and goes slowly. And to change anything, we must begin where we actually are and not where we wish we were or where we think we should be.

♀♂ If a journey of a thousand miles begins with the first step, get your bearings on where you are now and then venture forth with that first step. Look forward to the walk itself, and not just to your final destination.

PART TWO

The Binds That Tie

I N A MARRIAGE we commit ourselves to being involved together and to taking care of one another as best we can. Once that is said, the important questions follow. How committed are we, and how do we ensure it lasts? How involved are we, and how do we show it? How many hours and how intensely are we supposed to be together? How much do we converse? Who contributes what? Who is getting the better deal and who is being shortchanged?

Somewhere along the way we must strike a balance between individual freedom and the commitment of marriage. We search for that subtle blend of independence and interdependence—which combines air to breathe and solid ground to stand upon, the wings to soar and the warmth of the nest at night.

A man's genes gain by supporting a wife and children, but can also gain by casual sex and abandonment. A woman's genes gain by ensuring that a man stays to provide for her and her children and does not abandon them. Is it surprising that we might squabble over the required commitments? The stage is thus set for sizzling friction between men and women in the service of our competing genetic interests.

CHAPTER THREE

Pursuers and Distancers

The change women want most is for men to talk about
their feelings, and the change men want most is to be
understood without having to talk about their feelings.
—MICHAEL MCGILL

ARRIVING HOME IN the evening after work, we are all worn out and want to relax and be ourselves. But we have different ideas of what that means. We look here at an ordinary couple, into their fourth year of marriage, as they try to unwind together after a long day.

She wants to sit down together in the living room with some cheese and crackers and wine, and rehash the trials and triumphs and simple activities of the day. He wants to sit in front of the television with a cold beer and forget about the office and all that it requires of him. She wants to talk about who did what to whom, how everyone felt, her feelings about it, and what will happen next. He wants to watch the news or sports or just surf through the channels with his mind on cruise control, with no obligations.

TYPICAL MARITAL CONFLICT

THESE MISMATCHED inclinations produce what has been called *the* conflict of modern marriages. One partner wants more interaction, more involvement, and more cooperation, while the other wants more space. So the one criticizes and is upset, while the other retreats into silence. It is known as the *pursuer-distancer, demand-withdraw, or intrusion-rejection* pattern.[1]

Sharing feelings is a girl thing. A woman typically wants more conversation, more openness, more sharing, and more togetherness. In contrast, a man usually prefers some breathing space and the freedom to say what he wants or to say nothing at all. He feels awkward in conversations about feelings and in emotional exchanges. So women are often the pursuers, while men are usually the distancers. Although the gender positions are occasionally reversed, women are the pursuers and men the distancers in perhaps two-thirds of relationships.

Pursuers and distancers bring out the worst in one another. Pursuers become upset, cold, and critical when the mate is not as involved as they wish. Distancers remain passive and withdrawn, and escape conveniently into the long hours of the workaholic, the obsessions of the sports fanatic, the mindless comfort of the couch potato, or the welcome numbness of the alcoholic. The more the one withdraws the harder the other pursues, and the harder one pursues the farther the other withdraws.

The friction gives rise to typical feelings. She feels *excluded*, he feels *intruded upon*.

INFORMATION TALK VS. FEELINGS TALK

WHETHER MEN or women dominate conversations depends on the topic and the situation. Males dominate in what Deborah Tannen calls "report talk," providing information about things, while females dominate in "rapport talk" about personal feelings and social relations.[2] Men talk at length about sports, politics, social ills, economic solutions, how things work, and almost anything else on which one might show himself informed and thoughtful. Women talk freely about more personal subjects—what other people are doing, saying, and feeling, and about their own relationships. Men present opinions in public forums such as classes, lectures, and larger groups, while women relate better in the more personal atmosphere of small circles of friends. Men are seen to be generally more competitive than women, continually striving to show themselves superior, if possible, but at least acceptably adequate. In classrooms and boardrooms, men compete to offer the most accurate information and the best plans for action.

When women complain that men do not talk enough, they mean that men do not talk to them about feelings and personal concerns. Why do the same men who so thoroughly control public conversations so thoroughly vanish in the personal arena?

INTIMACY OBLIGATES MEN

IT MIGHT appear that men, wanting more personal space, are simply not as involved in relationships as are women. Yet men are found to bond more strongly than women and to take it harder when relationships fail. How do we make sense of the apparent contradiction? What is going on?

JILTERS AND JILTEES

If men were not really as emotionally involved as women, we would expect men to be freer to leave unpromising relationships and move on. Indeed, men who want casual sex with multiple partners might be expected to leave established relationships considerably more often than women. Yet that is not what we find. Surprisingly, women end unsatisfactory relationships considerably more often than do men.

Research finds that among serious couples, whether dating, engaged, or married, in any decade sampled, *women are almost twice as likely to initiate a separation or divorce as are men.*[3] Court records show that wives file divorce petitions almost twice as often as husbands.[4] And the finding is not limited to Western culture. In the former communist Soviet Union, women filed seven out of ten divorces, citing alcoholism as the primary reason.[5]

That women initiate separations more often does not always mean that they are the first to want out. A man who wants out may stay, out of obligation, waiting for a woman to hand him his walking papers. Women who want out feel freer to leave, other considerations permitting. Yet it is not simply that men are usually the ones to want out and wait for women to agree. Among dating couples, a woman is typically more able to leave an unpromising relationship, even when she has strong feelings for the man. A man with strong feelings finds it harder to let go, even when his girl-friend is no longer interested in him.[6] Some boys continue to wait for a girl who is going out with other boys, too much in love to break the bonds and go on with a life without her.

Couples separate for various reasons, of course, but one scenario is somewhat typical. The wife feels dissatisfied, pushes for more communication, is angry, and wonders if she wants to stay married. The husband resents her com-plaining, withdraws emotionally, and considers leaving her, but he feels obligated and does not want to upset her. They quarrel. When she has had enough and no longer loves him, she weighs her options carefully, makes her decision, and asks him to leave.

Many are surprised by these findings. Most of us think of men as being more independent than women and less committed to relationships. What is it that bonds men more strongly than women?

MEN FEEL OBLIGATED

Even a few brief interviews with men reveal the obvious. Any normal man experiences some feeling of obligation to a woman with whom he is intimately involved. Whether he graciously accepts it, grudgingly resigns himself to it, frets about it, ducks it but feels ashamed, or rises above it, the concern is there. It's a guy thing. A man wanting a casual relationship typically worries that the woman will take it too seriously and expect a commitment, making him feel oblig-ated to her and guilty about leaving.

The average woman seldom worries about feeling too obligated herself. Instead, she worries about whether the man really loves her and whether he means what he says. That is, she worries about whether he is really committed to her. Most women are hardly aware of the tremendous power that obligation holds over men or of its many implications for a relationship. Men are aware of it all the time.

Feelings of obligation should not be confused with love. A man may not be in love with a woman, may be bored with her, or even hate her, and still feel obligated to her.

In a student sensitivity training in Boulder, Colorado, a freshman told one of the girls in the group that he was attracted to her but he did not want her to get too involved or expect too much from him. She told him not to worry, she hardly knew him. To her, his concern seemed unflattering and inappropriate. And in a way, it was. He was trying to duck out of any responsibility for her feelings for him even before she had any feelings. Sadly, for the young man, his sense of obligation was a ball and chain.

I hope those feelings settled out for him before he tried marriage. If a guy feels so obligated before he even knows a woman, imagine how he would fare as her husband!

Obligation is the internal mechanism by which nature bonds a man to his wife and offspring. It has an obvious evolutionary advantage, in that men who stay and support their wives and children have more surviving offspring. The obligation a man feels toward his wife is usually as strong as that which he feels toward his children, sometimes stronger. In contrast, the strongest sense of obligation a woman feels is toward her children.

Why do men feel more obligated toward women than the other way around? Traditionally, a woman with children has practical reasons to stay with a man so long as she can rely upon him for support and protection. If he cannot support her or will not, she may indeed benefit by leaving him. Intense feelings of obligation to her mate would gain her no genetic advantage, and nature did not program it in.

Men are supposed to support women, most of us agree, and women have a right to be supported. So when a marriage fails, a woman feels cheated out of the support she has a right to expect. A man is troubled by having failed in his responsibility, leaving his wife hurt and upset. So women usually feel anger more than shame, while men tend to feel ashamed and responsible more than angry. Those who fit this pattern far outnumber the exceptions.

After a relationship fails, a man can be more worried about how his ex-wife is doing than he is about himself, even when the ex is managing well and he is coming unglued. The sense of obligation that holds men in relationships can severely punish those who leave.

HOW NATURE TRICKS US

WHO TAKES it harder when relationships fail? Anger helps you leave a relationship, while obligation burdens you and holds you back. So the supposedly independent man is more adversely affected when a relationship fails than is the supposedly dependent woman. Research concludes that men are more deeply hurt by separations than women. Men tend to cling longer to dying relationships,[7] and they fantasize longer about their former partners after it is over. On average, men take about twice as long to recover from failed relationships as do women.[8]

In short, men get their hearts broken more often than women and take longer to heal. Here again, many of us are surprised by the findings. We tend to think of women as being more vulnerable than men. Why do these findings surprise us?

Women express more distress, while men tend to feel more distress but not show it as much. When a relationship is in jeopardy, a woman is more likely to threaten suicide than a man, thereby obligating him to stay with her, lest he be responsible for her death. Yet three to four times as many men as women actually commit suicide after failed relationships.[9]

The general impression that males are less committed in relationships results from our selective observation. Women talk about it when relationships fail, and those around them see how upset they are. Males usually suffer in silence, and go unnoticed. A jilted woman triggers our sympathies, and we naturally want to support her. When a man gets jilted we figure he did not have the right stuff, and it is hardly a moral concern. In folklore and cinema, the tale of a sweet woman in love with a ruggedly independent man appears more often and is certainly more appealing than a tale of a sweet man in love with a ruggedly independent woman.

It may seem paradoxical that males appear aloof but bond more strongly while females, who seem more openly interested, feel freer to leave. Perhaps the explanation lies in the paradox itself. *The sense of being overly committed already makes men wary of further commitment, while women are freer to pursue intimacy because they worry less about being trapped by it.*

The common opinion that women are more emotionally dependent than men shows how nature tricks us. A woman wants a higher level of emotional involvement and is more readily upset when she does not receive it, thereby appearing more dependent. Yet she is more independent, in the important sense that it is easier for her to leave a relationship and to go on with her life. A typical man is more emotionally dependent in the important sense that he is less able to leave or to withstand the loss if the woman leaves.

The logic of genetic selection accounts for these perplexing traits. The woman who *appears* dependent obligates her mate to stay and provide for her, thus giving her children an advantage. She makes a man feel responsible for her because she could not make it without him—or so it seems. Yet when it is in her practical interest to leave, her relative independence makes it easier for her to do so than it would be for him. For men, genetic selection works the other way around. The man who *appears* strong and stable gives a woman confidence that he can support her, thereby increasing his chances of mating with her and producing offspring. Yet the sense of obligation that bonds him to his wife and children leaves him with less real independence than she has.

A parallel is seen in our romantic inclinations. Granted, women love romantic fantasies, watch more romantic movies, and buy 98 percent of the romance novels. Yet findings suggest that men accept the romantic myth that love conquers all and lasts forever, more so than women.[10] Men are more strongly attracted to their opposites than women are, and report falling in love somewhat earlier in relationships.[11] And men actually marry more for love, while women focus more on practical considerations.[12]

It is indeed ironic that men, who are more interested in casual sex with a variety of partners, nonetheless bond more solidly than do women. In spite of the wanderlust, some combination of obligation, love, and emotional neediness holds men more strongly in relationships.

ROMANTIC CONVERSATIONS

LOOK HERE at why we talk of love and what we mean by it.

SAYING "I LOVE YOU"

Women in happy marriages report more open expressions of love than those in unhappy marriages.[13] Women are far more comfortable with the language of love, and want to hear more of it than men are ordinarily inclined to produce. A straightforward "I love you" seems so simple. Why do so many men have trouble saying it?

> *In love women are professionals,*
> *men are amateurs.*
> —FRANÇOIS TRUFFAUT

So far as words of love are used to express love, their absence is naturally taken as an absence of love. Yet more is going on here than first meets the eye. Words of love can be used in so many ways. "I love you" can be used to court and seduce, to flatter, to reassure, to commit oneself, to require a commitment in return, and so on. Males and females use love words for different purposes, only barely understanding one another.

Asked if he loves his wife, a man of few words and less tact answered by saying, "I'm here, aren't I?" His wife felt he was ducking the question and was furious. Yet for many men, love translates into commitment. The same answer in a more complete version would look like this: "I know I want to be married to you. I feel good going to work every morning, because I know that I am supporting you and that we are building a life together. I need you and would never want us to part. So if that is what you mean by love, then yes, I love you." She wonders why he cannot say "I love you." But he did. In guy talk, "I am here for you" is another form of "I love you."

FEELING IT AND MEANING IT

You can think of love as a feeling or as a commitment. When love refers to a feeling, you look into your personal experiences to see whether or not you love someone. When love refers to a commitment, you ask yourself if you want to be obligated to your partner.

Two teenagers dating each other present opposite concerns about the words. "Why can't he say he loves me?" the girl wonders, especially puzzled because her boyfriend does seem to care for her and does not want to take out other girls. She wants more excitement and romance in the relationship. He asks, "How can she say she loves me and then be flirting with other guys all over school the next day?" He thinks she is being too casual about their relationship. She does not think there is anything wrong with a little flirting, especially since he won't even say he loves her.

The confusion here is in a difference between *feeling* love and *meaning* it.[14] Girls are talking about love as a romantic feeling, and when that feeling is gone, the experience is over. Considering love as a commitment, guys see expressing love as a pledge to take care of the beloved. Girls talk about love more easily because they feel it and it is interesting and involving. Boys are reluctant to say the love words because they are unsure of themselves and do not want to be stuck with such a profound commitment.

The man who says "I love you" seems to be obligating himself to continue acting in a loving manner. If he is untrue, he will be accused of being a jerk and not meaning what he says. But it is not symmetrical. When a woman says "I love you," she may be giving a compliment, but she is also obligating her partner to love her in return. So regardless of who says it, expressions of love obligate the male more than the female. Most women learn to avoid talking about love too early in a relationship, to avoid introducing an obligation and perhaps scaring a man off.

Suppose a man is trying to get out of an established relationship without causing a fight, but his partner is not going along with it. She is hurt and angry at him, tells him how very much she loves him and that she cannot believe he could want to hurt her so much. Here, her proclamation of love reminds him of his obligation to her, while her angry accusation induces guilt, pressuring him to stay.

Men have other reasons for steering clear of the love words. To the sex that is fond of the rugged masculine words like *damn* and *hell,* the love words sound squishy soft. Is it possible to combine the two into some sort of rugged masculine proclamation of affection? Could you say, "Damn. I love you, woman!"? How many women would accept it? And what about the illusion of independence that men cherish? Since love bonds, a man expressing his love is admitting that he is not as independent as he would wish to believe.

A man tends to see marriage as a tremendous additional responsibility, even today when his wife might earn an equal salary. The unfortunate consequence is that a man who communicates openly before marriage may clam up and stop talking altogether under the burden of the additional responsibility, leaving his new wife wondering what happened. How do we bridge these differences?

♀ Interpret the commitment itself as a sign of love. The everyday activities of life together are all statements of involvement, so long as we do them joyously and not begrudgingly. And be careful with your own words of love, so that you use them to connect and not to torment a mate who is uncomfortable with them.

♂ You need not retreat into silence. Talk about what being together means to you, in whatever terms you wish. Or you might try being more comfortable with conventional signs of affection. Think of flowers and sweet nothings not as silly romanticism, but as a step in mastering the masculine position in a relationship.

WHEN MEN ARE NOT OBLIGATED

Some men manage to duck the usual association of love with obligation, and can proclaim their love at considerable length to whomever arouses their feelings. When the feeling is gone, then they too are gone. The woman is left to question how the man could have loved her in the first place, if he could leave so easily. She concludes that he did not really mean what he said, and in a sense she is right. He felt an attraction for her, and called it love, but he did not mean he was committed to her.

Perhaps this is helpful to women who want more talk about love. Would you want a man who talks freely about the love he experiences but does not consider it a commitment once the rush is over?

MEN DO NOT ASK ABOUT LOVE

A man does not ordinarily pester his wife or sweetheart for expressions of love and endearment. Indeed, he may not ask his mate even a single question about how much she loves him or even about whether or not she loves him. While female genes benefit from insuring a commitment, male genes benefit from physical intimacies. As long as a woman is being sexually intimate, a man feels she is giving herself to him and that she loves him. If she is not allowing intimacies, he may wonder whether she loves him and may wonder if she is with someone else. And he may argue that if she really loved him she would want to have sex with him, to try to pressure her into it.

A boy can ask his friends whether a girl likes him, to figure out whether he should talk to her or take the chance and ask her out. He might ask a girl if she loves him, if he is trying to figure out whether to go steady with her or whether he should ask her to marry him. The average man does not ask a woman if she loves him just to reassure himself that she is there for him.

GENDER CONFLICT AS RELATIONSHIP TRAINING

SOME GENDER conflict is an inevitable result of the huge differences in what men and women look for from each other. As nature seems to have selected for some of our gender incompatibilities, perhaps it has some use for the conflict it generates.

Husbands are awkward things to deal with;
even keeping them in hot water won't make them tender.
—MARY BUCKLEY

WHY USE ANGER AND ACCUSATION?

Women who want more emotional intimacy are often upset and angry at their mates who fail to provide it. And being angry makes sense, of course, if only because it is the familiar response. But step outside the familiar for a moment, and ask an obvious question: Why use anger? It does not help a closed man feel safer about opening up and expressing his feelings. It does not help a cold man feel warmer. *As for coaxing someone to be emotionally closer to you, being upset is about as useful as a flame-thrower.* Anger is better at pushing people away than at inviting them closer. Its success rate is as close to total failure as you can possibly get. So why is it our natural reaction? Remember that nature has programmed our emotions not for the intimacy we think we want, but for the propagation of our genes. As Darwin observed over a century ago, *emotions further human survival.*[15] Look here at how nature arranges our emotions to support its own agenda.

BEING UPSET PUSHES FOR COMMITMENT

Prementrual syndrome (PMS) produces not just aches and pains but insecurity, anger, and quarrels. Severe PMS can impel a woman to relentlessly accuse her husband of not loving her and demand seemingly endless reassurances, while remaining unsatisfied with anything he says or does.

SHE: I mean nothing to you. You act like I hardly exist. You never tell me you love me.

HE: I do too tell you I love you. Over and over.

SHE (even angrier): You only say it when I bring it up. If you really loved me, you would tell me you love me on your own, without me having to ask you for it. . . .

Perhaps nature is up to something here. To make sense of the continuing accusation but without blaming, I propose an unconventional explanation: *PMS is nature's way of ensuring that any man who stays until the next fertility cycle is truly committed.* Intolerant of uncertainty, nature programs a woman to push for a solid guarantee that the man who fathers her children will stay to support them.

While I offer the comment half in jest, I have been surprised at how many people recognize in it a kernel of truth. It makes some sense out of the seemingly irrational, and invites us to laugh at our foolishness. I use it here as an introduction.

More broadly, being upset has been programmed into our natures to accomplish identifiable aims. Being upset pushes out the deadbeat who cannot be counted upon to provide and support. If he cannot hold up through a minor show of anger, a woman is better off without him. Paradoxically, once we are paired, the reassurance it requires can tighten the commitment even while driving us farther apart.

FORCING REASSURANCE

Insecurities can lead to intensely involving arguments. The following situation occurs between a couple after the first night of their honeymoon.

The fellow wakes up early and is ready to go before his wife. He tells her he is going down to get a cup of coffee and read the paper. Immediately, she is upset with him. "Without me?" she asks. "I thought I meant more to you than that." He is caught by surprise. "If you would rather I stay, I will," he agrees. But she continues. "I can't believe you would just go off and leave me the first night after we were married. If you really loved me, you would *want* to stay with me." He tries to reassure her that he does love her, that he was just going down for a cup of coffee, that he wants to be with her, that he does truly love her, and so on. She questions his sincerity. He gets angry and the conversation turns bitter, ruining the day. The two finally let it go that evening and go on with the honeymoon.

> *Before marriage, a man declares*
> *that he would lay down his life to serve you;*
> *after marriage, he won't even lay down*
> *his newspaper to talk to you.*
>
> —HELEN ROWLAND

What is going on here? Look at his repeated reassurance that he loves her. At that moment, he undoubtedly feels stressed. Realizing he is in trouble and unsure how to fix it, he could be feeling awkward and helpless, perhaps confused. He may be upset and angry at her for making such a big scene over a few minutes on his own without her. For a fleeting instant, it could even cross his mind that he made a mistake by marrying her (and that maybe he should try to get out of it). Indeed, perhaps the only thing we know for sure that he is *not* feeling right then is an intense and overwhelming sense of love for her. Yet to resolve the argument and reconcile, he must reassure her that he loves her. *The situation requires the man to proclaim in a reasonably authentic manner the one feeling we can be sure that he is not feeling at that moment!* Surely nature is up to something here.

SQUABBLES AS INCULCATION

In a Monty Python skit, which I recreate loosely,[16] a sergeant has his men lined up on the drill field.

"Any of you have anything better to do than to march up and down this field all afternoon?" he demands menacingly. "Eh? Do you?"

One man, clearly intimidated, raises his hand. The sergeant turns to him, obviously angry. "You think you have anything better to do than march up and down this field all afternoon? Eh?"

"Well, yes," the recruit stammers. "I thought I might practice the piano. If it's all right, that is, sir."

"All right, then," the sergeant barks. "Fall out." He turns again to the rest of the platoon, now furious. "Does anyone else have anything better to do than to march up and down this field all afternoon. Eh? Do you?"

A second recruit takes the chance. "I owe me mummy a letter home," he murmurs.

"All right, fall out," the sergeant commands. "Anyone else have anything better to do than to march up and down this field all afternoon?"

This time several men raise their hands, hesitantly. "There is a movie playing in town, we thought we might like to see."

"All right, fall out!" the sergeant bellows. And so on it goes, until only the sergeant remains (who truly has nothing better to do than to march).

The skit is spoofing a brutally serious situation. Normally, when your sergeant asks, you respond properly in compliance with expectations:

Sergeant: "Anyone have anything better to do than to march up and down this field all afternoon?"

Recruits, in unison: "No sir!" Any soldier who answers improperly would be dressed down in front of his unit, ordered to drop and do perhaps 100 push ups, and then asked again. The sergeant is not asking for the soldiers' feelings. The military requires compliance, and it is training the recruits to ignore their feelings and follow orders. Soldiers conditioned to comply during interminable drills are more apt to comply later on when it matters, on the battlefield.

Look again at the man who must reassure his wife that he truly loves her. Who cares how he really feels? Women's genes benefit from ensuring a committment, so nature programs women to haze their mates. The man must ignore what he feels and meet expectations. The man who complies with expectations in these ritualistic confrontations will be more apt to meet his responsibilities to his family later on, when it really matters.

Men who are slow learners will be put through the routine until they figure it out or until everyone is exhausted by the attempt. The man who feels more like swearing walks a tightrope. He knows better than to fight with his woman and make matters worse, but he is unwilling to say he loves her over and over like a trained seal barking on command. So staying silent is a compromise between an unproductive argument and what seems like unmanly acquiescence. Neither overtly opposing nor complying, he waits for the ordeal to blow over.

OVERLY SENSITIVE VS. CLUELESS

"Honey, we need to talk about where we are going with our relationship." Sound familiar? It is almost invariably the woman who initiates these conversations while the man tries to avoid them. She may see it as a chance to get closer, although it serves not to get closer but to resolve her sense of insecurity. He sees it as intimate persecution.

It is invariably the woman who wants to know everything about the relationship. It's a girl thing. She wants to know how he feels and what he thinks and what is going on in his mind, from one moment to the next. She wants to know where she stands with him. In a new relationship or in uncertain times, it is almost always a female who asks, "Does he love me?" or "Does he *really* love me?" It is too simple a question and has no simple answer, but that does not keep her from asking it. She wants to know if she can count on him to be with her and to take care of her.

Why is a woman so concerned about how her man feels? Since she has had to rely on a man for support, being sensitive to his moods and feelings allows her to make adjustments as required. Such sensitivity confers a survival advantage and has been passed to the next generation. So, *nature programs a woman's feelings to monitor a man's commitment.*

A housewife with three small children gave her opinion on why women are so emotional about relationships: "Women are more insecure," she observed. "We have to know that a man is going to be loyal and keep his promise to take care of us. We have to know he is going to do it our way."

When one member of a pair is ready to leave and the other has not had the slightest idea anything is wrong, it is almost invariably the woman who is on her way out and the man who is clueless. A woman will almost always know when something is wrong, and she will be upset and be asking questions. Because wives are upset more often than men find comfortable, many men learn to live with the emotional turbulence by fulfilling their responsibilities and trying not to take the emotions too seriously. So the husbands say, "Yeah, I knew we had some problems. Everyone does. She was upset sometimes. But I had no idea it was anything so serious." Her announcement that she is leaving comes as a bolt out of the blue.

INTIMACY VS. OUR WIRING

Realize that emotions have their own agendas and serve purposes that are not necessarily in our best interest. In the case of the honeymoon quarrel, in addition to forcing a commitment, being upset also pushes the man away from the cozy world of love and out into the world of accomplishment. By making it uncomfortable at home, an upset woman pressures a man to take on the hardships of long days in the fields, the risks of the hunt, or the dangers of battle.

Where do we go with these entangling communications?

♀ To nurture closeness, you will need to tolerate some insecurity, rather than interrogating your man to force him into reassuring you.

♂ Realize that some emotional conflicts are just gender rituals, and do not take them so personally.

Sometimes just recognizing our differences can suffice. Deborah Tannen writes of a couple who had a wonderful first night together, and were continuing with a special breakfast when he opened his newspaper.[17] Ordinarily, she would have felt taken for granted and fussed at him. But having read that men can feel intimate with less conversation, she kept the faith, and the relationship stayed on course. Of course, nature did not program her to take a chance on it. What if he really were taking her for granted?

In the sex war thoughtlessness is the weapon of the male,
vindictiveness of the female.

—CYRIL CONNOLLY

A wife may gauge her relationship as much on what her mate says to her as on what he does for her. Indications are that a woman is happiest when her husband *says* he loves her, while a man wants his wife to *do* things that show love.[18]

To avoid unnecessary hazing, express your love clearly and often enough that your wife can feel secure. If she must be sure about your love, how many ways can you tell her how much she means to you? You will be more convincing, and surely more relaxed, if you do it before she is upset enough to try to force you to do it.

THE PERILS OF BEING TOO PLEASANT

The advantages of women expressing what they want shows up clearly in marriage research. Some patterns of marital conflict are beneficial to the marriage in the long run, concludes John Gottman, even if they are upsetting at the time. *When the wife is only agreeable and compliant, a marriage tends to deteriorate over time.*[19] Although the average man cannot appreciate it when his wife demands her way or gripes at him, he may be better off for it in the long run.

Some of these uncomplaining women are annoyed inside but unwilling to say anything, and you can understand why they have poor marriages. But others are people pleasers—straightforwardly interested in making the man happy and not wanting to see him upset. Their misfortunes seem most undeserved. It is easy to idealize the sweet, compliant woman who accepts a man and goes along with anything he wants, but the average man soon tires of her and takes her for granted. I have seen some of the warmest and most nurturing women in relationships with men who take them for granted and have not the vaguest sense of what a great deal they have. *A wife usually exerts a fair amount of control in a marriage, and a woman who goes along with any-*

thing and everything her husband wants is acting more like a servant than a wife. Humankind has traditionally allowed polygyny, in our formative years. A steady regimen of affirmation at home makes a man feel he is doing so well he could have room for another woman in his life.

My heart goes out to these especially nurturing women. Some hard advice, however, will be more useful:

♀ Toughen up and expect something more from your man. By standing up for yourself, you ask to be taken seriously. Involve your husband in your feelings and concerns, and you strengthen the bond between you. The art is in being insistent enough to stay in his heart but not so overbearing that you wreck everything while you are there.

♂ My advice to men with especially nurturing women is to recognize what a totally good deal you have, and to realize that the next woman might not be so pleasant.

THE WISDOM OF SILENCE

THE SAME silence that women find so frustrating can be a sanctuary for a man in a lose-lose situation. Look at some more of its causes.

HURT AND ANGER CREATE A DOUBLE BIND

While a man is stressed by anger, tears can render him helpless. Anger and tears together make an unmanageable combination. "Being upset" usually refers to a combination of being hurt and angry at whomever upset you. Perhaps the two are logical companions in all of us. But a woman who is angry *shows* hurt much more than a man, whose usual posture is to underplay the hurt and show only the anger. It is the combination of hurt and anger together that creates a double bind and emotional gridlock.

A woman who is simply hurt invites a man to try to comfort and protect her, whereas one who is straightforwardly angry invites him to fight against her. But how does a man relate to a woman who is upset—meaning hurt *and* angry? He cannot simply support her, because she is attacking him, but he cannot openly fight her either, because she is hurt. He is damned if he does one and damned if he does the other, and unable to make sense of the situation or comment on it. The usual reaction to a double bind is emotional withdrawal, which is what so many men do when women are upset. While few men have heard of the double bind, most understand the outcome. Men know that they cannot win an argument when their wives are upset, so they stay silent to avoid provoking further anger.

To a woman, silence is unacceptable. Already upset with him, she interprets his silence as a refusal to take her seriously and an unwillingness to be involved. It further upsets her and she pushes him harder, causing him to withdraw farther, thus forming a vicious cycle.

Most women are unaware of how much emotional conflict stresses men. A man does not ordinarily mention how stressed he is when his wife is upset, and the upset woman is not looking for signs that she is upsetting her mate and ought to be more considerate.

This double bind provides women a tactical power advantage, but at a price. Nature hands the upset woman sufficient power to intimidate her uncompliant mate, and in the process blindly sacrifices the intimacy she cherishes. I suspect many women are more interested in the companionship than in the tactical advantage.

♀ You can improve the situation some by clearly separating your hurt from your anger. If you are sad and hurt and want support from your mate, you should make it crystal clear that you are not angry at him. Otherwise, given the usual associations, he will feel he is being blamed for something.

See how one couple worked through the tears:

On the night she and her fellow got engaged, the bride-to-be got her feelings hurt over a joke her fiancé made about being married, and she began to cry. He told her he could not stand to see a woman cry and went into the next room and sat down by himself. Sound familiar? She followed him in and sat down on his lap. She told him she was not mad at him but was just hurt, and asked him to hold her while she cried, which he did. She told him she loved him very much and did not ever want to be without him. Then he cried. Some years later she told me that he is still nervous when she cries, but he no longer tries to flee. She still tells him to hold her, which he always does, and they talk it through.

♀ Try asking your husband to hold you the next time you get your feelings hurt. Most men are willing to try to be helpful, so long as you seem friendly. Tell him it feels good to be close to him when you are hurt. Make it a successful experience for him, and he will be closer to you the next time.

♂ Recognize that sadness, like anger, is not nearly as serious as most men assume. Look to understand the pain behind the tears. You might allow yourself even to experience some of it yourself. None of us are in complete control of our fates—not even "real men"—and the tragedies of life are part of the human experience. Share them with someone you love, to better experience being human.

FEMALES CENSURE, MALES CENSOR

A woman who wants a man to talk freely about his feelings may incorrectly assume she will like hearing about whatever he is feeling. Most women would be in for an unpleasant surprise or two. A man who allows his mind to wander can be thinking about which anatomical features are sexually arousing, who is gross or fat or unappealing, how he is doing at faking interest in a boring conversation, and similar socially unacceptable thought fragments, along with whatever could go wrong at his job and what he can do about it.[20]

The sort of raunchy conversation that adolescent boys enjoy with one another is judged to be crude, rude, lewd, and socially unacceptable in front of females. Mothers are highly offended by unrefined adolescent male patter, and censure boys who talk too openly. Teenage boys who talk freely about their sexual thoughts and feelings with the fellows learn to clean up their acts in mixed company. Women censure offensive male language, and males learn to censor themselves to get along.

While a man may find conversation between females trivial and boring, a woman can find stock male language crude and offensive. Neither gender will be pleased by how the other judges it, but our reactions are not weighted evenly. When a man offends a woman, he is judged socially inappropriate and feels ashamed. Typically, he resolves to be more careful about what he says in mixed company.

When a woman hears that her small talk bores a man, she is offended, and she lets him know he was rude and insensitive. He will add the item to his list of what he is not supposed to reveal.

Note the important asymmetry here. When a man makes critical judgments about female conversation, women judge back, and the man hushes. When a woman is critical of male conversation, men hush or take their conversation elsewhere. The outcome in either case is that a man learns to be careful about expressing himself on gender-sensitive issues.

Men sometimes complain that the rules are continually changing and they never know when they will be censured. Some women are now offended by being called "ladies," while others consider it properly respectful. Using the generic "he" and "his" to refer to an unspecified sex individual is now judged sexist, while a generation ago it was proper grammar.

Manners and etiquette, in the best sense, are the rules that help us live together more comfortably and avoid unnecessary friction. In their practical implementation, manners often mean doing what pleases women and avoiding what offends them. Women judge men on their good manners or lack thereof, and men pick up the cues. Men suppress the sort of conversation that women judge improper, or conduct it away from women.

Any group must train its members in the shared norms and goals of the community. Women, who have traditionally required support and protection, benefit most from civilized social conduct and are most easily harmed by its absence. If women are the socializing agents in any society, as Margaret Mead argues,[21] we would expect women to exert a strong influence on male conduct across cultures. Nature seems to have assigned to women the task of civilizing males, and females as well, to the benefit of the broader community.

I can hardly imagine a civilization in which males give voice to anything that wanders through their minds and women accept or endure it without comment. Some censorship is required for comfort and reasonable propriety, and each new couple must establish its own boundaries. I offer some suggestions to make the process easier.

♀ If you must call your man on an inappropriate comment, do so gently. You do not want to hear about a good looking set of legs crossing the street ahead of you, but say so good-naturedly. Tell him you are going easy on him, and remind him to appreciate you.

♂ Realize that any relationship is a civilizing influence, and appreciate the benefits. See it as a simple rite of passage. Learn the game and conform when required, but don't let it crush your spirit.

ANGER SILENCES

A woman is upset with her husband, and is now furious at him because he will not talk to her. Indeed, she is by now so angry that she scolds him or actually contradicts him when he does speak:

HE: I really didn't mean to upset you.

SHE: Then why did you say it? Don't you know how it makes me feel?

HE: I can't talk to you when you're so angry!

SHE: You're just using that as an excuse. You don't *want* to talk to me!

She has not the vaguest clue why he will not open up and talk to her. Yet by her anger she is actively silencing him when he tries to talk. She wants him to talk, but she is too angry to listen to what he has to say.

I talk to the two of them together. I mention that men often feel intimidated when their wives are so angry, and ask him if he feels intimidated. He says yes, he feels intimidated. I ask him if he feels his wife listens when he does try to talk, or if she's too angry to listen. He says she is always upset, and she jumps on him for anything he says. So long as someone is willing to listen, our formerly silent man is surprisingly willing to talk about his feelings.

A man who will not converse when his wife is angry probably feels she is not listening. So a women can often coax her mate to open up to her by listening more and trying to understand. Indeed, most men will babble endlessly about themselves to any woman who seems genuinely interested.

♀ If your husband hardly talks to you, ask yourself how well you listen when he does talk. You cannot express your anger and listen at the same time. Which is more important?

If you want a quiet man to converse with you, you will need to show more interest and less anger.

WHY MEN CONCEAL WEAKNESS

It is well known that men do not usually reveal personal weaknesses. Passed over for a promotion and deeply troubled about it, the average man will be ashamed to tell his wife and may avoid mentioning it at all. Robert Fulghum writes of a doctor who had terminal cancer but hid it from his wife and family, who were angry about not getting to say good-bye to him before he died. As in hide-and-seek, you can hide so well that everyone gives up looking for you, and you are left alone. "Get found, kid!" Fulghum advises.[22]

As a therapist, I talk openly about my weaknesses and failings, to set the tone and to explore how personal issues might be resolved. Yet outside of my profession, I do not reveal my weaknesses much more than other men do, and I can find it terribly embarrassing when they show through. Why the difference? When a therapist shares his weaknesses, it is as a way of doing good therapy (that is, of being strong).

When I played soccer, I considered the guys on my team friends. But I would not expect any one of them to announce it if he were failing in business, if his wife were running around with another man, or if he found out he had terminal cancer. When I was younger, I occasionally mouthed off too much which, in addition to being a mediocre player, kept me off of a team I would have wanted to play on. When I got the bad news, I felt a searing sense of shame rush all the way through me and continue to burn. It was about a year before I mustered the grit to tell my wife about it. Being a mediocre player never bothered me, but I felt my breach of sports etiquette showed a significant personal weakness.

Society expects men to be strong, of course, but that does not explain why so many men take it so deadly serious. Did anyone ever tell me that if and when I mess up and lose rank, I should experience intense, searing shame, and not tell anyone? If so, I don't remember it.

Try another explanation. Traditionally, women are attracted to men with strength and position, who can be expected to support a family, while men look for women who are young and pretty. Evolutionary psychologist David Buss found that in each of thirty-seven cultures he examined, females place more emphasis on financial prospects in selecting a mate than do males.[23] Women are turned off by qualities suggesting an inability to produce, such as lack of ambition or lack of education.[24] In sizing up a man, it is not unusual for women to talk openly about his prospects as a provider. When Henry Kissinger said that power is the only real aphrodisiac, he hit close to the mark. Over the ages, the man who ranked high among other men could be expected to bring home his share of the haul and take good care of his mate. Low status males with known weaknesses were judged unsuitable as providers, and were chosen last or did not mate at all.

A good case can be made that it is quite the same today even when so many women must work to contribute to the family income.[25] While women with careers usually choose mates for personal compatibility, they typically choose among men who are ambitious and seem to be going somewhere, and not among the failures and bums. Research indicates that men who reveal insecurities too soon or too often are regarded by women (and men as well) as being "too feminine" and "poorly adjusted."[26] Thus, *the openness that a woman wants in a man can reduce his status and ruin his chances with her.* Now, as in ages past, the selection process weeds out the man who naively reveals his weaknesses. The man who conceals his failures is more successful in wooing a mate, and the inclination to be ashamed of weakness is passed along to successive generations of men.

Can you imagine a woman attracted to weakness instead of to strength? It might look like this:

HE: I found out today I was passed over for a promotion again. Smith got it. The boss said if my production doesn't improve, I will be out of a job.

SHE: Oh, you adorable loser! You make me hot! Help me get out of these fashionable clothes and take me to heaven.

Sure, it might happen—about once in a blue moon. Just as success instills confidence, weakness and failure introduce doubt about a viable future together.

So, *if a man is to mate, and his genes continue, it is in his interest to appear to be doing well and to conceal any failures and weaknesses that might disqualify him.* Nature programs a man to strive for power and, when he fails, to conceal his losses as best he can. Here, male interest and female interest collide. *It is in a woman's interest to find out as much as she can about a prospect before she hitches her wagon to his star.*[27] So, while he is programmed to show his strengths but to conceal flaws that would make him less marketable, she wants the open communication and personal disclosure that allow her to size up her man, know him intimately, and be comfortable with him.

SHE TALKS; HE SCANS, CENSORS, AND PRESENTS HIMSELF

Talking about oneself requires considerably more concentration for a man than it does for a woman. A woman who talks about herself has only to note her thoughts and feelings and express them as they come to mind. It sounds effortless, and often it is. But a man who talks about himself must orchestrate an impromptu performance. He must scan his thoughts and feelings, select those that are interesting and sound suitably manly, organize and present them in a sincere manner (but without falsehoods or exaggerations, which might expose him as a fraud), while at the same time censoring anything that could reveal weaknesses or might offend. He works to appear open and comfortable with himself while conscientiously avoiding the sort of mistakes that would cause him to lose standing. So even a few comments about himself can require considerable concentration. Not surprisingly, men who converse all day long at work are not always so interested in continuing it with the wife at home.

Some men seem not to know their own feelings at the time but then figure them out two days or two weeks later. "Do you miss me?" "Are you worried about your job?" "Do you want to have another baby?" To a man, each of these questions is a chance to mess up. Should he reveal an emotional weakness? Should he acknowledge his uncertainty about his job and worry her? Should he talk about the financial stress of another child and allow her to think he cannot handle it? Something inside him censors his feelings, even from himself, until he has had some time to think about it, weigh it all out, and arrive at an acceptable statement.

If this does not induce men to be more open, or incline women to accept a closed-off man, it does explain our differences.

♀ You might ask yourself how many flaws and failings your mate can have and still be sexually attractive to you.

♂ Ask yourself how attractive your wife would find you if your career were unraveling around you. Would she still accept you after a significant reversal? Are you giving her enough credit? And could you accept yourself?

Actually, women are not turned off by *all* weaknesses. While women are generally repelled by weakness for alcohol or drugs, and any weakness of mind, body, or character that makes a man a poor provider, a woman may feel secure with a man *who has a weakness for her.* She may be thrilled by the man who has to be close to her, to hold onto her, to love her and feel her love for him, and who would be totally lost without her. Feeling needed helps provide the sense of security that success alone cannot provide.

♂ If you have a weakness for your wife, by all means share it! It may not be the easiest thing to talk about, but it gets you further than almost anything else you can share.

Men in truly vital relationships can be quite open about their dreams and failures, and expect their wives to understand. A man who can openly share his failings with his wife has an unusual amount of trust in her and in himself, which can carry him through the toughest times. (That, or he is a total fool.)

BRIDGING THE DIFFERENCES

INDICATIONS ARE that women experience emotions more intensely and are more emotionally volatile than men. Research notes that women report more negative and troublesome feelings than men, but also more joyous and positive feelings as well.[28] So part of the reason women talk more about their feelings is that women have more feelings to talk about.

Men can see women as too emotional and too bound up by their feelings, while women see men as too unfeeling or too closed off from their feelings. Nature has programmed in this sort of friction between the sexes. Having more feelings or fewer feelings is neither good nor bad—both contribute to the richness of our lives.

Will men lose interest in sports and acquire a liking for long conversations about love and other sensitive feelings? Probably not. Will women want to talk mainly about things instead of about people? Yes, if their jobs require it, but probably not in their leisure hours.

How do we bridge our contrasting preferences for "feelings" talk? For starters, we might distinguish between our initial differences and the problems that arise from our responses to those differences. Women who are upset with their husbands for not talking are inadvertently creating further silence. Men who withdraw because their wives are upset are inadvertently creating more resentment.

♀ Women who frequently feel upset should realize that your own feelings are driving your husbands farther away from you.

Suppose a woman suggests talking about her relationship. Her husband gives her that "Oh no, here we go again" expression, and glances around for the nearest exit. Instead of being exasperated, she tries to hear what he feels.

"You're not looking forward to this?" she suggests.

"Well, no," he answers.

"Afraid I'm going to be cross with you?"

"I guess I just never know what to say."

Of course he suspects that she will be cross with him, if that has been her pattern. She addresses his concern: "I am not annoyed or anything. I just have some things I need to talk about."

♀ Try to understand the problems instead of being upset about them. Your otherwise reserved husband will be more willing to open up.

A woman who wants to be heard does not simply vanish because her husband does not want to listen. As long as she wants a relationship with him and not an outside affair, he is what she has available. The conversation he walked away from today will still be waiting for him tomorrow.

♂ Those who withdraw when feeling trapped should recognize by now that you are inviting further pursuit. Those who withdraw might look at why they do so. Is your wife so hard to talk to? Are you confused or intimidated by her seemingly relentless questions or by her moodiness? Can you tell her how it feels? If you feel too stressed and cannot manage an argument, you might as well say so! "When you're upset at me, I get tense inside. You're better at arguing than I am, so you usually have the last word."

If a man manages to say all that, will his wife listen and understand? If so, they are beginning to communicate.

But what if she feels he is blaming her, and she gets angrier? Might he do better to remain silent?

WHEN SILENCE MEANS NO PREFERENCE

Living with a partner who does not express preferences can be confusing. The upside is that you get to have everything your way. The downside is that you make every choice alone and can feel like you are living with your own shadow.

A young woman I counseled wondered if her fiancé was really as involved as he should be. He would never say what he wanted to do, which show he wanted to see, where he wanted to eat. Whatever she wanted was fine with him. With friends, he was always pleasant but had little to say. He was in upper management and worked a full eighty hours a week, every week. Most of his free hours he spent with her, and he was generous and bought her anything she wanted.

What *was* wrong with him? As we talked, it became clear that he was too worn out to find much happiness in anything he might do. Yet he was pleased being with her while she was happy, and it pleased him to make her happy. The best he could manage was a vicarious pleasure, in loving a woman who herself loved life.

Understanding her fiancé helped her realize that she was truly special to him, in spite of his silence. The two of them together chose to accept the situation and to work around it, for the time being, as he was doing well in the job and could not reschedule his hours. I would hope that his long range plans included a job change.

♀ Realize that the man who does not express an opinion is not necessarily trying to withhold himself. He may be trying to be considerate, or may not have an opinion. Or, as in the previous case, he may find more satisfaction in doing what you want.

♂ Realize that indifference can be maddening. If you do not have a strong preference where to eat, then offer whatever slight preference you have. If you mainly just want your mate to be happy, tell her that is what you want. And if it would make her happy for you to choose where to eat, by all means do so. My own solution is to state my preference, and then quickly go along with whatever everybody else wants.

SOME PREFERENCES ARE
SIMPLY PREFERENCES

When we are first in love, we want to do the same things. Men are fascinated talking to their sweethearts, hours and hours on end, and go willingly to the theater, out to dinner, and maybe even dancing. Believe it or not, some men even volunteer to go shopping with their girlfriends. Women like watching football, riding on the back of the motorcycle, even camping in the rugged outdoors miles from any facilities. The truth is that in the haze of love, we will do almost anything that the other wants to do, and love it, simply because we want to be together.

After the rush subsides, this changes. We again care about the activities themselves, at least as much as doing things together. Our individual inclinations reassert themselves. Those who want more involvement sometimes interpret this to mean that the partner does not care.

♀ Be careful! Many preferences are just preferences. Ask yourself if you are willing to do what he wants to do. Would he welcome you along with his beer and football buddies? Love is as much about respecting another's preferences as about remaking them to match your own.

♂ If you loved being more involved before you married, realize that you changed. What would it take to enjoy doing some of the things you did together before you married?

Evolution could have easily shaped our preferences for certain activities. Men seem to love sports, more than women do. Sports, as recreational combat, are about winning and losing, and the power and tactics by which men might prevail. Men, of course, have always had to judge the strength of competing groups, to figure how to make the best alliances and stay with the winners. Football involves powerful men in brutal clashes over yardage, loosely paralleling the strictly male practice of attacking or defending geographic territory. A wide range of sports including basketball, soccer, and golf, involve placing a projectile on a target, paralleling the activity of early hunters (who were almost always men).[29]

Shopping involves selecting needed items and bringing them back home, loosely paralleling the gathering activities of women in hunter-gatherer cultures. And conversing about personal matters helps women in their traditional job of staying abreast of relationships.

Marriage provides us with an inordinate amount of free time together that we did not have before marriage. Even the most accomplished conversationalists can occasionally run out of things to say. We might communicate some tolerance for the natural limitations of the situation.

MORE COMMUNICATION VS. BETTER COMMUNICATION

When several hundred psychiatrists were asked to list the major reasons that marriages fail, an impressive 45 percent said that the primary cause is the husband's failure to communicate his feelings.[30] Only 9 percent blamed sexual incompatibility. So it was the husbands who were faulted for insufficient communication, not the wives for expecting too much of it. And this is probably typical of the helping professions, where we value communication and prescribe more of it to fix relationships.

Many people believe that simply expressing feelings promotes marital satisfaction. A survey of 280 unmarried undergraduate students found that 75 percent agreed that increased self-expression, whether warm or angry, enhances marital satisfaction for both partners.[31] Watch out! People who believe this can express the whole array of angry feelings and be self-righteous about it, shredding important relationships while imagining themselves innocent of any wrongdoing.

Communication is important, but it is not *how much* we communicate that contributes to the quality of a marriage. A vast array of research finds no strong connection between the amount of communication and the level of satisfaction in a relationship, and many studies find no connection at all. We see solid marriages in which relatively few words are spoken, and marriages in which constant explosions of antagonistic feelings perpetuate the animosities.

One group of investigators observed the number of interactions between partners over the course of their relationships.[32] Interestingly, the highest levels of communication were found at the beginning and the end of a relationship. On the second date, when we are just getting interesting, we reveal ourselves and try to find out about each other—our likes and dislikes, our plans, what sorts of families we have, and so on. And the final year of a failing marriage we riddle one another with recrimination:

SHE: If you had half as much interest in me as you had in your damned career, maybe you would show some of it before we get to the bedroom!

HE: Of course Madam has to be courted for hours and hours to be properly prepared, especially when she is not particularly fond of the man she is with.

A great deal of communication usually signals that something is changing in a relationship, for better or for worse. Communication can wound as easily as it can heal, and it can create misunderstandings as easily as it can clear them up. It can solidify differences and push us apart as easily as it can resolve them and bring us closer. The productive communication that solidifies a marriage is not just clearly spoken or honest to a fault. It reflects consideration of each other, and it attempts to build bridges across our differences.

In truly vital marriages, the men are every bit as open in talking about themselves as are the women.[33] These happily married men tell about their dreams and aspirations, their weaknesses and dissatisfactions with themselves, and so on, and they feel that their wives understand. Even men in average marriages rely upon their wives to be their best friends, and men who are not close to their wives risk being isolated and lonely.

Given how much women push for more communication, you might think women were the only ones to benefit from it. Yet here we see that men benefit from it every bit as much.

♂ Open communication may be to your own advantage. If you do not like the topics your wife suggests, set your own agenda.

♀ You have a fresh argument here for more communication. Tell your man that research says it will be good for him and that he will feel isolated and unhappy without it. Then be open to what he wants to talk about.

CHAPTER FOUR

Expressers and Fixers

If women resent men's tendency to offer solutions to problems,
men complain about women's refusal to take action
to solve the problems they complain about.

—DEBORAH TANNEN

MEN AND WOMEN relate to personal problems in sharply contrasting ways. Women often share their troubles freely and openly, while men keep their problems to themselves. That does not mean that women are more insecure, of course, but only that women are more open about it.

CONVERSING ABOUT PERSONAL PROBLEMS

WE ALSO differ in how we respond when we hear other people express personal problems. Women try to empathize with one another, express sympathy, and encourage each other to continue talking about the problems. Women often share something similar from their own experience, suggesting that while life can be rough, we are all in it together. Men usually try to fix the problem, either by providing information or by conveying that it is not so important. At the extremes, same gender conversations can produce unintended humor.

Suppose an adolescent girl complains to her friends about her appearance.

GIRL: I'm gaining too much weight. I look fat in this dress.

GIRLFRIEND: I know just what you mean. I have a whole closet of clothes that I can never wear anymore, because they make me look just awful.

2ND GIRLFRIEND *(who weighs 105 pounds but joins in anyway):* I have to watch everything I eat or I gain so much I cannot fit into anything I own.

The message is that "I understand—I'm just like you, you're like me, we are in it together." The aim is to find common ground and to give voice to the common experience.

A fellow complaining to his buddies about his appearance would be met with a very different response.

ADOLESCENT BOY: I'm thin as a rail. I have no muscles.

GUY FRIEND: What do you mean, man! You look fine.

2ND GUY *(ribbing him):* You do look thin as a toothpick. Hey man, you need to pump a little iron before you blow away somewhere and I can't find you. Then who am I going to get to give me a ride home?

The message is, "Toughen up, it's not so bad, joke it off. And if something is wrong, stop complaining and go fix it." Here the insecurity itself is the problem and the friend is trying to fix it so his companion will operate properly (confidently) again. The aim among males is to support morale, maintain group solidarity, and get on with the common activities.

Same-gender groups fall naturally into gender-appropriate practices and socialize their members in these practices. Females are expected to tell about their personal secrets, and those who do not are considered aloof and remain outsiders. Males are expected to be tough, and those who show weakness are in for some ribbing. Research on friendship in North America shows that men tend to form friendship based on shared activities and do not reveal personal weakness, while women form friendships based on sharing feelings and can usually name a best friend.[1]

Females share their troubles, as Deborah Tannen suggests, to establish a personal connection, to maintain intimacy, and to avoid appearing aloof. Males rib one another not to create distance, but as a sign of respect. The message is, "Your problems are not so serious and you are strong enough to benefit from my ribbing."[2]

In mixed-gender relationships, each gender continues in the gender-typical manner. Females express the feelings; males try to fix whatever is wrong. At its best, when everything goes smoothly, expressers and fixers complement each other. A woman expresses a problem, inviting involvement and support, and a man has the solution and helps her out. She appreciates what he does to help, and he feels noble for helping. Although a few issues can be so easily resolved, most require something more.

LISTEN FIRST, THEN SUGGEST

Many personal problems cannot be fixed by simple reassurance or straightforward suggestions. So the man who offers immediate solutions to the problems typically fails to resolve anything. The woman remains upset, perhaps more so because of his clumsy intrusion, and the man feels ignored and inadequate. A typical exchange goes this way, with the fellow reassuring or suggesting a solution.

SHE: I have no real friends.

HE: Lots of people like you. But if you feel that way, you could get out and meet more people.

SHE: What do you care, anyway?

Here the man appears not to understand the seriousness of her feelings, and she judges him unconcerned. Those who express their worries want first to be understood and to feel that they are being taken seriously. Anyone who provides a quick-and-easy answer has overlooked this initial requirement, and wonderful suggestions will fall on deaf ears. The man who gives the fast answer seems not to have heard the full problem and the depth of pain. Inadvertently, he is also presenting himself as wiser and thus superior, merely by being sure of the answer while she has no clue. So his unintended message is, "You cannot figure out your problems, although you have struggled with them, but I can quickly see what you need to do to fix everything."

Men can reassure women and can offer suggestions. But it is not wise to offer them right off, as men try to do, to just fix the problem and get on with other things. It is a matter of sequencing.

♂ You must first convey that you are interested, you understand the problem, and you are a sympathetic and loyal ally. Share the experience of puzzling out the problem together. Only then are you allowed to offer a word of reassurance or a cautious suggestion. And even now, you must allow your mate to take your suggestion or not. Be patient.

In offering a suggestion, you are thereby offering yourself up as a talented leader who can find the solutions. The extent to which your mate accepts or rejects your ideas is a gauge of your importance in the relationship. When your suggestions are rejected, it feels like *you* are being rejected.

♂ Avoid taking it personally! Continue listening and trying to understand the problems, and stay involved.

How do you show that you are listening? One of the best ways is to actively reflect what your partner is saying, before you go on to comment upon it.

SHE: I have no real friends.

HE *(reflecting back what he hears):* You feel nobody likes you? Or, you feel you have acquaintances, but not real friends? Or, are you feeling lonely?

Any one of these might be the feeling. She will tell you whether you hit it, and clarify it further. And she will feel like you are genuinely listening.

♀ If you want a man to talk more, try the same thing. It has become standard stock in communications training, and it works well for anyone who is trying to listen.

MEN TAKE COMPLAINTS SERIOUSLY

Almost any man whose wife is upset feels stressed and pressured to fix whatever is wrong. When the problem does not bow to an easy solution, the pressure can be unmanageable.

SHE: I am really tired of this house and all the threadbare furniture. I am ashamed to have guests over.

HE *(angrily):* We moved here because this is what you said you wanted!

The man here takes her being upset as an accusation that he is not providing for her sufficiently, and he counters by blaming it on her own foolish choices. Here his stress translates directly to anger. He has not told her what is stressing him, and she will not understand why he is angry at her. *A man whose wife is upset will ordinarily feel she is blaming him.* It's a guy thing. A woman does not usually understand how much her being upset stresses her man.

Women often feel that their husbands do not hear them or take their problems seriously. Yet in many cases, it is just the opposite. Men take women's complaints too seriously, resulting in unnecessary stress and withdrawal.

A couple I talked with had just moved to our city, where he had a job, and she had not yet made any new friends. She was unhappy, and told him that she did not like it here, did not want to stay, and that if he did not find another job in the next year she was leaving. It got his attention. Two weeks later she had her house organized, had made several friends, was playing tennis and had been invited to go horseback riding. She told him things were better and she now liked it here. Yet he had talked to a job recruiter, which surprised her. He had it locked in his mind that she was not happy, and he told her there was no way she could convince him she was happy when she had been so miserable two weeks earlier. It took us most of a session to convince him to take her at her word.

Most men are programmed to take complaints from women at face value, while women are programmed to express their troubles casually without giving it a great deal of importance. So men tend to read more significance into women's unhappiness than women mean to convey. A man whose wife is often upset may conclude that she is permanently miserable and cannot be "fixed." Yet he will still feel responsible for her, and inadequate because he cannot make her happy. He may strive to be an unassailable breadwinner, always at work, or withdraw into the television.

♂ Remember that women are much freer in voicing complaints. You should not take each complaint so seriously. Allow the times she looks happy or says she is happy to count as much as when something goes wrong.

♀ Remember that your mate probably takes your complaints more seriously than you ever realized. Be careful how strongly you express your unhappiness. And if you are happy with him, be sure it shows. And ask him if he thinks you are generally pleased with your life with him. If you are usually happy but occasionally upset, and he thinks you are upset all the time, why the incorrect impression? Stop shooting and try troubleshooting.

NATURE PROGRAMS MEN TO BE FIXERS

WHY ARE men fixers? Evolution provides an explanation. Throughout the ages, women with small children were extremely vulnerable and required the support of the males. Men who addressed women's concerns would mate more often, support their wives better, and have more surviving offspring. So men are naturally programmed to try to fix whatever is troubling women, and to interpret complaints as pressure to work harder and provide better. Women are freer to complain, to let men know how they feel and what they need.

Imagine for a moment that it were otherwise. A man and a woman are huddled in a primitive shelter, ten thousand years ago, somewhere in middle Europe. Snow is falling outside, the cold wind is blowing through the cracks in the makeshift hut, firewood is gone and so is the food. The two converse:

SHE: Org, it is so cold in here. I'm freezing, and I'm hungry. The wind is coming through the cracks in our hut, the fire is about to go out, and we have no meat left. I'm afraid the children will starve and die.

HE: Enga, I know just how you feel. I too share the same feelings. I too feel cold, and I am hungry, as you are. I also worry about our children, just as you do. We had some really terrible winters a few years ago, when I was a teenager. I almost froze to death myself. So I really do understand.

What is wrong with this picture? What is wrong with this *man!* Any normal man would feel tremendously inadequate about not providing better. He would experience intense pressure to gather more firewood, fix the cracks in the shelter, hunt a rabbit, or do *something* to try to solve what is troubling his wife.

Perhaps ten thousand years ago a man roamed the Earth who was programmed to be completely comfortable when his wife was upset. Tragically, his wife and children did not survive the long, cold winter, and his laissez-faire inclinations perished with them. Men who are fixers pass their genes to the next generation, continuing the strong male inclination to try to fix it when a woman is upset.

It is easy for a woman to condemn a man for wanting to fix things instead of working to understand the feelings. You might make allowances. The "fix it" response has been essential for human survival for hundreds of thousands of years, and is by now strongly inbred into the normal male character. Is it fair to condemn a man for trying to be helpful, even when the way he does it is not just what you wanted?

WHO WANTS MEN WHO ARE NOT FIXERS?

Although it generates its fair share of troubles, the natural programming does prevent a few follies that could easily occur without it. I have a couple of acquaintances who, by natural temperament or by sheer acts of will, have managed to overcome any tendency to be stressed when a woman is upset with them. Both were good at listening and understanding, and both were also philanderers. One confided in me the secret of his success. "There is not a woman anywhere who cannot be seduced by a man who is willing to stay up until 3 A.M. talking about her problems."

The other fellow, who was married, talked to women at great length about their problems, including their problems with him. When a woman felt insecure, or cheated and used because he went home to his wife, he fully understood her feelings and was warm and supportive. He was so sympathetic that it was hard for any woman to stay mad at him. So a lady would tumble into bed for another round, only to get upset at him afterwward, which he also understood.

I had the opportunity to talk to one of his paramours. She found it impossible to break up with him because he was giving her the understanding she always wanted, but also impossible to continue because she could never figure out where she stood with him.

Perhaps this may help women readers. Are you annoyed with your mate because he has to "fix" everything and cannot simply listen to you when you are upset? Realize it could be worse. You could have a man who simply listens to you, on and on, and never fixes anything.

WOMEN JUDGE MEN AND EXPRESS COMPLAINTS

There is a complementary relationship between women expressing feelings and men responding to them. Nature programs women to express feelings and, thereby, to alert others to their concerns, while it programs men to hear their concerns. Women, if nature had not programmed men to try to address your concerns and work for your approval, then what would be the advantage of expressing your feelings in the first place? If nobody were concerned when you were upset, what would be the point of ever talking about what is upsetting you? Sure, it can feel good to express feelings, but nature does not usually incline us toward activities that waste our time, just to make us feel good. Clearly, something more is involved.

It is more than happenstance that women express their feelings more openly and forcefully than do men. Whether upset, angry, worried, cold, hungry, frightened, or just lonely and neglected, women profit by saying so and being heard. A woman who expresses her feelings invites her husband and her broader community to take her predicament seriously. She can gain invaluable assistance. So expressing feelings confers a real survival advantage, and is by now built into the female temperament.

In expressing their feelings, women also monitor the pulse of the community and express its concerns. Gossip, whether warmly sympathetic or harshly judgmental, is a way of sharing information about community members and of holding them publicly accountable. Why do women gossip, much more so than men?[3] Remember that through hundreds of thousands of years, it was essential to yoke the wills of men to the support of the women and children. So while women bore children and tended them, and men supported the women and children, any woman had an additional job as well: It was her job to assure that her man was doing his job. *Through gossip, women praise those who contribute and censure the egotists, bums, miscreants, and outlaws.*

In small, tightly knit communities, gossip is a powerful mechanism of rewards and punishments. An upset woman who expresses her own anger upsets those who listen and sympathize, and invites her friends to share her grievances and uphold her cause. The man who mistreats his wife or merely neglects her might be in for some harsh judgment, and quickly. She shares her pain with her kin and close friends, who talk to their kin and close friends, and so on, throughout the community. By evening, a friend or family member takes the fellow aside, informs him that he is causing trouble for himself and for everyone else, and suggests that he shape up.

In a modern society, when we live far from our families and may not even know our neighbors, gossip has lost some of its bite. But it still remains a potent force of social control.

MEN COMPETE, WOMEN JUDGE

Why are men more competitive than women? We can say that society trains males to be more competitive, and surely it does. But why? It is not just in Western cultures that males are more competitive. It seems to be so across cultures.

Men compete in various ways, according to what is important to a culture. Competition can be as overt as a foot race, or as subtle as men competing by trying to appear more cooperative and less competitive than anyone else. And male competition appears to be a human universal.[4] Among the primitive Ache of South America, the hunters share the meat in a communal pool so that all families benefit equally, regardless of who hunted well and who failed. The arrangement appears to eliminate individual advantages and create social equality, but there is more to it. Recent observations show that the best hunters are more apt to have lovers and have more children than the inept hunters. So while the men share equally, the women still go for those who produce.[5] Winning confers a genetic advantage.

Male competition is also obvious in lower primates. Male chimps work hard for status, and strife between male rivals is frequent while females settle into more stable coalitions.[6] The evolutionary explanation, recall, is that higher status usually provides additional mating opportunities, which benefit male genes far more than female genes.

Among men, competition is not simply for power over other men, although that can be a factor. Competition is for achievement and recognition in whatever the culture prizes. Men strive to show themselves well-informed, courageous, adequate to the task at hand, and willing to do whatever is required. The implicit message is, "Consider me, I understand what is going on, I am the man with the plan, and I have the courage and the muscle to carry it out. I can be a leader here or at least a major contributor." Each is striving for standing as a team player and an asset to the group pursuit. To a woman, a man is saying, "I am somebody, I have standing. Count on me, I can provide whatever you need and take care of you." In short, he is saying, "I can fix it."

Just as it is his job to support the family, it is her job to judge his contribution to see that he is doing what she requires. Women admire men who contribute, and women also condemn and scorn those who fail to support them or who treat them badly. In the face of hardships and shortages, the tendency to be upset and to judge and accuse provides a distinct advantage. The woman who condemns a man for his failings pressures him to work harder and provide more for her. Yes, women are more easily offended than men and more judgmental. See it not as a simple weakness, but as the adaptive asset that it is.

The fact that women see men as powerful and privileged, in spite of their obvious weaknesses, can be explained by evolution. *Seeing men as powerful frees women to push their*

own demands, thereby benefiting themselves and their children.
Nature selects for the woman who feels a man could and
should be doing more for her, if only he would. Conversely,
nature selects against the woman who is aware that her
anger stresses her man and wears him out. Better that she
not know her anger stresses him, so that she can push him
hard without her conscience bothering her.

Men go along with the ruse, because revealing weakness
disqualifies them as providers and limits their progeny. So
men and women accept the pretense because each benefits genetically from seeing men as stronger and women as
subordinate.

MANHOOD MUST
BE ACHIEVED

MARGARET MEAD makes an observation about primitive
societies that seems to apply to modern society as well:
"[T]he small girl learns that she is a female and that if she
simply waits, she will some day be a mother. The small boy
learns that he is a male and that if he is successful in manly
deeds some day he will be a man, and will be able to show
how manly he is."[7]

Manhood must be achieved. Young boys feel they must
prove themselves real men, and strive to do so, while young
girls grow naturally into women. In groups, boys require
strength and confidence in one another, and haze those who
appear afraid. Girls expect openness and sharing, and are
more apt to accept fears and weaknesses.

Why the difference? The key is to view manhood as the
strength, courage, honor, and success required to win a
woman and then to support her. Traditionally, a young man

must prove himself to gain a wife, whereas a young woman is marriageable simply because she is young and healthy. So young men gain by striving for manhood, and the trait is passed along, whereas young women would not gain by similar strivings.

An analysis of ninety-three cultures shows that boys more than girls are generally taught to show more fortitude and are expected to face hardships without complaining.[8] So male toughness is not simply a Western custom, but is common across cultures. Incidentally, the same analysis shows that girls are taught industriousness, responsibility, and compliance, more so than boys. Cultures typically inculcate the strengths that will benefit each gender.

LOGIC VS. FEELINGS

Men and women also clash on how we should argue and on what counts as winning. Men typically want to use logic in arguments, while women want to express their feelings and be understood. A man complains that a woman is not being rational, because she is expressing her feelings instead of listening to his logic. A woman complains that a man is not listening to her, because he is using his logic instead of hearing her feelings and trying to understand.

Men and women can be both logical and emotional, of course, but the adaptive advantages tend to favor more logic among men and more feelings among women. Men traditionally benefit from being logical, as those who can judge which plan is best tend to succeed amid the uncertainties of the hunt and perils of warfare. Men who are too emotional and not logical enough lose respect among men and women as well, limiting their mating opportunities. Being emotional does not count against women as much, and it can increase their social support.

A woman arguing against a man may appreciate his logic, but she also wants to know that he will take her concerns seriously. She is offended when he insists on using his logic against her.

NATURE BONDS MEN TO SUPPORT WOMEN

MARRIED MEN are healthier and happier than single men, and work harder and achieve more. Somewhere around 90 percent of highly successful men are married, whereas closer to 70 percent of highly successful women are married.[9] Men find meaning and purpose in supporting a wife and family, and can be lost without it.

We saw earlier how men bond more strongly to their mates and are more thoroughly shattered when relationships fold. The sex that can least manage the loss is under greater pressure to capitulate when an argument threatens the relationship. In a study of engaged couples, more than 50 percent more men than women reported frequently giving in to a fiancé for fear of losing his or her affection.[10]

So far as I can see, this trend continues solidly in marriages. Husbands are more apt to concede in arguments, fearing that their wives will be upset and angry or unbearably cold toward them. Interviews with a hundred stably married couples turned up several instances where women used rational ultimatums, often successfully, forcing a husband to choose between changing his conduct or losing his wife and family.[11] Yet none of the men had used ultimatums with his wife. Anyone can threaten in the heat of an argument. But few men are rugged enough to give a wife a serious ultimatum, and then leave or throw her out if she refuses to comply.

I have observed that men who voluntarily leave a marriage are almost invariably interested in another woman, while women who leave may or may not be interested in another man. Colleagues have reported similar observations. The paramour provides the vital connection that men require to break the connection with a wife. So men even depend on a woman to leave a marriage, whereas women can act more independently.

Men who divorce get remarried two years later, on average, while women who divorce get remarried on average six years later.[12] The quicker remarriages are often attributed to men having more opportunities. Yet a recent poll of singles finds that 66 percent of men but only 51 percent of women say they want to get married.[13] The higher percentage of men who want marriage suggests enough men for the interested women. Men are clearly more eager to get remarried, while women are usually willing to take their time and consider their options carefully.

The difference shows up in our favorite expressions of exasperation. Men say, "Women! You can't live with them, you can't live without them." Women say, "Men! Who needs them."

It has been suggested that unattached women do better than unattached men because women have more intimate friendships and talk more openly about their feelings. Maybe so. But nature could have programmed men to be more independent—or totally independent, like panthers, hunting alone and content with no need of companionship. Male dependence on women provides an obvious genetic advantage, holding men in relationships to support their wives and children.

Imagine a primitive community in which the men feel free to leave when they get offended and are self-sufficient enough to live out on their own. If their wives complain too much, these men go out to hunt, eat what they bag instead of bringing it back to camp, tell jokes over the campfire, never worry about their wives, and never come back. Their women are free to mate with other men who will provide for them, although some may starve and die. Either way, the genes for that sort of rugged masculine independence are not long for this planet.

A man whose wife dies is *ten times* more likely to commit suicide after the loss than is a woman whose husband dies.[14] Regardless of how independent he appears or how independent he imagines himself to be, *the average married man is profoundly dependent upon his relationship with his wife.*

MANAGING CHILDREN

A SIMILAR pattern is seen in how we are with our children. Mothers are usually freer in expressing their feelings, offering comfort and support when the kid wrecks his bicycle, while fathers want to fix the bicycle and get the kid on it again.

Mothers who are upset with their children usually pull the fathers into the battles as well. Suppose dad is not particularly concerned about the curfew, and the teenager is out an hour later than he agreed upon. If mom is not concerned about it herself, or manages it calmly, dad stays out of it. If mom is really worried and upset and complains that the youngster does not care about how much he worries her, then dad will probably see it as a serious offense as well. If it is upsetting his wife, it is also thereby upsetting him.

As an old saying has it, "When mama ain't happy, ain't nobody happy!" Men take their emotional cues from their wives, and can overrespond when under pressure.

SHE *(worried and upset about her son):* Where is he? He never tells me where he is going, and he never gets in when he says he will. I'll be up all night worrying.

HE *(to himself):* Damn him! Wait until I get my hands on that boy.

As is typical of fathers, he is stressed by his youngster upsetting his wife. He will jump on the son, maybe too hard, and his wife may be upset with him for overreacting.

One of the traditional understandings between father and son is, "Whatever, just don't upset your mother."[15] When the youngster does upset his mother, father acts to correct him.

JOB CONFLICT TRIGGERS MARITAL CONFLICT

WITH SO many women working outside the home, facing the usual tensions and conflicts there, work concerns are brought home and into the evening conversation. It would seem to be a natural opportunity for men and women to share their troubles, understand and support each other, look at their alternatives, and bond together against an unfriendly world. But when women talk with their husbands about their job frustrations, something goes wrong. Instead of sharing counsel as friends and allies, mates become antagonists and conversations head south. Work troubles brought home quickly turn into marital troubles. Neither men nor women understand how and why these conversations fail, or what to do about it.

SHE COMPLAINS, HE STEWS

After a stressful day, a woman wants to talk about it, share experiences, express her fears and frustration, and be listened to and understood. As usual, the man is inclined to solve whatever is wrong, and quickly. Here is the typical pattern that occurs and reoccurs in marriage after marriage:

Suppose the woman complains about her boss. "He drives me crazy. I swear, the man cannot make a decision. So I have to figure out what to do, and take some responsibility before the roof falls in. And then when he gets nervous or something goes wrong, he wants to know why I did what I did. All he cares about is covering his own ass."

Her husband tries to resolve the problem, but more quickly than is realistically possible. Initially, he instructs her on how to fix the work situation. "Just refuse to do anything to help him, and then see what happens!" Or he provides some other equally simple solutions for what are almost always complex organizational problems. "You ought to get everyone together and tell him what an awful job he is doing."

When she will not take his advice and solve the problem, he suggests more drastic measures: "Well, if you are so unhappy there, you ought to quit."

You would think the conversation should be more complicated than this. But honestly, I am not oversimplifying it. I cannot tell you how many husbands I have seen give some variation of these two responses, and nothing more. No attempt to support her feelings, understand the situation, or map out the realistic options and the consequences of each one. Nothing. The typical husband tells his wife to confront her boss or whoever is causing her trouble, and get the problem resolved. When she will not do so, he tells her to quit.

UNDERSTANDING AND SUPPORT ARE VITAL

Job situations are typically complicated, and quick solutions are seldom helpful. You rarely get anywhere telling off your boss. You cannot risk leaving the job undone so that your superior looks bad, and it is not easy to organize your fellow workers to band together and confront the boss. Is quitting a realistic option? A woman who is serious about her job and career is not going to quit over some ordinary job friction, any more than a man would.

A man needs to recognize that what his mate wants is mainly understanding and sympathy. She wants to unwind, to share with her mate, to be appreciated for the tough job she is doing. It is not strictly true that she does not want to hear solutions, but the order is important. She would be willing to hear solutions later, *after* he first shows that he understands her feelings and appreciates her grasp of the situation.

♂ Remember to understand and appreciate first, and only then look at solutions. Recognize that many irritating work situations are not easily resolved, and we do well to accept it and make the best of it.

♀ Realize how much stress your husband probably experiences from *your* hard day at work. Men are poorly equipped to hear how their wives are mistreated while they are helpless to do anything about it.

FAILED CHIVALRY

HOWEVER ANTIQUATED it seems today, a man still wants to protect his woman from the hazards of the outside world. To do so is honorable, to fail to do so is unmanly and beneath contempt. In another time it would be called chivalry. The knight would pledge to defend the lady, so that any attack on her honor was an attack upon his honor as well. How does a man feel when his wife tells him how badly she was treated at work? He must recognize that she has been out fighting the foe while he was helpless to protect her.

Much of the conflict for working women is with their bosses and supervisors who have power over them, and many of those are men. And therein lies perhaps the greatest stress. To a man, it is unnatural to have his woman away from home and subject to the power of another man. Were the conflict among women, he might figure that it is none of his business. But when another man is mistreating her, it calls forth a primal male instinct to protect. A man who cannot or does not protect his woman from other men must wonder whether she is still his woman. So far as another man can tell her what to do, and she must obey, then she is under his control. Obviously, nature selects against the man who would be comfortable allowing that to happen.

A man feels he must either support his wife within the group, so that she is respected, or rescue her and take her away from those who mistreat her. And thus the usual male response: He commands his wife to tell off her boss, and thus gain respect, or quit the job and get out from under his control. So long as a woman wants to keep her job, she cannot do either. To get along at work, she must consider what her boss wants over what her husband wants. And that is the stressor. It comes across to a man not as a simple practicality but as a major infidelity. She appears to be loyal to her boss, complaining but doing as he commands, and refusing her husband. As the husband sees it, the boss has power over his woman, whom he is powerless to protect, and she is willfully going along with it. It goes over badly. He is shamed and angry, although only the anger shows. He is mad at her refusal to change the situation. She feels he is attacking her instead of trying to help her solve her problem.

VIEW WITH SYMPATHY

Perhaps women can now understand what would otherwise appear to be a gross lack of sensitivity. Men who were unconcerned when hostile outsiders took control of the women would have hardly passed along their genes. Men are hardwired to react strongly when belligerent outsiders attempt to control or mistreat their women.

Perhaps men can better understand their own stress and frustration when faced with an upset wife who must submit to an insensitive boss. New times call for new responses. Heroism does not always mean protecting your woman from other men who seek to take advantage of her. The real heroism today can be protecting her, and yourself as well, from the nightmare of taking it all too seriously. The real enemy is not the boss but rather the sense of shame that separates and isolates you from your mate.

♂ Recognize your impulse to protect, and then avoid acting on it. Your real battle is in your own heart.

Stay compassionate and available. The rest of it will fall into place.

PERSONAL INSECURITIES

EXPRESSERS AND fixers also script personal insecurities. Women express insecurities more openly, and men try, mostly unsuccessfully, to "fix" them. Look at a prominent couple getting ready to go to an awards banquet.

SHE: I look too fat in this outfit.

HE: You look fine. You look lovely. Come on, let's go.

Perhaps the fellow barely glanced at her before he answered. So while his comment may look like reassurance, he was uninterested in her worries and his mind was on other matters. She wants him to be more understanding and more involved with her. Furthermore, although trying to be supportive, he is directly contradicting her, inadvertently suggesting that he knows and that she is mistaken. So his quick reassurance does more to confirm her insecurity than to allay it.

INSECURITIES OBLIGATE

Perhaps she looks now at the relationship, making explicit what was implicit in her initial complaint.

SHE *(feeling ignored):* You don't even care how I feel.

HE *(choosing his words carefully):* I do too care. I said you look fine.

As you can guess, such conversations soon gridlock with no way to resolve anything and no way out. This one slides from appearances to an equally unproductive rehash of who does or does not love whom sufficiently and how anyone knows it. Yet perhaps something is being accomplished after all.

Questions of appearances are more than mere vanity. As a woman considers an unappealing feature such as being overweight or growing old, the important issue is whether her mate will accept her as is. Will he love her and stay with her through it all or will he judge her to be lacking and leave her? In mentioning an unappealing feature, she is looking ahead. She is trying to be sure he will not be surprised by something later on, and so change his mind and leave her. It is a truth-in-advertising policy. She is asking that he accept her as she is, and judging him on whether he is able to do so. Each time he is patient with her and supportive through a frustrating conversation, he shows he can be counted upon. The ritual conversation, as we should recognize by now, conditions him to say what is expected, overlooking her unappealing features and accepting her as is (with no warranty).

INSECURITIES COST

Something is gained, but something is also lost. An attractive woman spends an hour choosing the outfit and coifing herself just perfectly, creating a dazzling appearance, and then totally ruins the show by pointing out her flaws. Anyone who focuses on her insecurities makes them too important, to herself and to those around her. By exclaiming her own flaws, she creates an impression that far outlasts whatever reassurance she gains. Men take their emotional cues from women, and a man will tend to see his wife as she presents herself to him. At the moment she complains that she looks fat, the man is obligated to reassure her. But afterward, the impression lingers in his mind. "Ugh. She *is* fat." Rather than talk to her about it, which would be rude, he will conceal it from her but withdraw into himself and be emotionally unavailable. So what she gains in obligating him, she loses by lowering his opinion of her.

Insecurities and reassurances can form a vicious cycle, building upon each other. She presents her insecurities, he reassures her but becomes more distant, she becomes more insecure, she repeats her insecurities, and so on.

DISCREDITING REASSURANCE

Insecurities can be stubborn and very sure of themselves. An accomplished individual who is convinced she is stupid may ignore all assurances from friends who find her bright and well informed. "I know I am stupid," she seems to be saying, "and I am surely smart enough to know that I am not as smart as my friends say I am."

We hold on to insecurities because we believe they are realistic truths about ourselves that are important to our survival. We are afraid of being fooled by reassurance, getting overly confident, and then making fools of ourselves. Paradoxically, insecurities provide a sense of security. By never reaching too high, we feel we will not have too far to fall.

The yearning for approval seems to be a human universal. Cultures vary greatly on what they applaud, of course. One values peaceful cooperation, another fierce competition; one admires the hunter with his strength and keen eyesight, another the scholar with his stacks of books and thick glasses. Yet men and women everywhere work to gain the approval of their companions and to avoid censure. Nature seems to have programmed us to find affirmation in the support of our contemporaries and to question ourselves without it. So while one surely can ignore reassurance, it leaves an important source of satisfaction untapped.

Look at the woman who complains she is getting fat, whose husband reassures her that she looks wonderful. Why should she believe him? Maybe she figures he is just being polite, saying what is expected and not meaning any of it. And since convention requires that he reassure her, she cannot know how he really feels. Maybe she figures she has him fooled for now, as he has not looked closely or cannot know how she will look when she is a few years older. She sees herself as an impostor, pretending to be more attractive than she really is.

Or maybe she figures *he* is not much of a catch himself to settle for her. This last one is captured in the Groucho Marx quip, "I wouldn't want to belong to a club that would have me as a member."[16] When we look at our mate, the attitude becomes, "I cannot respect a mate who can do no better than me for a wife (or husband)." Some conclude that Groucho had a poor self-concept, but look closer. The target of his contempt is not himself but the club, whose standards and social standing are so poor it would gladly accept him. Similarly, the man who accepts the insecure partner thereby discredits himself in her eyes—he seems to have no judgment or cannot do any better. Those who have poor opinions of themselves do not have terribly high opinions of their admirers and close friends.

Unfortunately, men and women who are uncomfortable with approval can easily pair up with disapproving and sometimes contemptuous mates. These men and women dismiss the truly accepting person as just polite, easily fooled, or insubstantial. They feel that the arrogant and critical individual knows who they really are, is more honest with them, and has higher status. So those who cannot accept approval can find themselves facing more contempt, which maintains their basic sense of inadequacy.

♀♂ Think a moment about the support or reassurance you receive from your mate, or from others who are close to you. Do you believe the compliments your mate gives you? If not, do you feel he or she is just being polite; that you have him or her fooled; or that he or she cannot be much of a prize to be satisfied to have you? List your reasons.

The insecurity-reassurance pattern is as hard on men as it is on women. The man who sees his wife ignoring his reassurance feels frustrated, angry, and irrelevant, and he has gauged it about right. She judges his reassurance to be worthless.

♀ If you feel you are not being heard, take note. Realize that he probably feels the same way. When he tries to reassure you and you ignore his comments, he will feel you are not listening to him. You cannot believe your own insecurities and his reassurance at the same time, and so must choose between them. Which is more important to you? Which do you choose?

WHY CARE ABOUT APPROVAL?

Some people are said to "care too much about approval," which is considered an undesirable trait. But is it? If you think you care too much about approval, look at another way of seeing it. Most people who worry too much about approval are really afraid of *dis*approval. If you really care about approval, you would find great satisfaction when family and friends approve of you. Every compliment would bolster your confidence and make you stronger. But if what you really care about is avoiding disapproval, then the approval you receive hardly matters. Approval means only that you have avoided disapproval, for the moment, but it may be waiting to surprise you a minute later.

If you think you care too much about approval, you may plan to rely only on yourself and disregard the support of your friends. What you will probably find is that your insecurities continue or worsen. Confidence in yourself is important, but ignoring supporters is a poor way to build confidence. Whatever disapproval you receive hurts just as much, or perhaps more, because you are not strengthened by the approval that might otherwise offset it.

If your marriage is generally supportive, the solution is not to care less about approval but to care more. Some of the most rugged individualists have solid families and close friendships, which provide the strong foundations for their independent lives.

♀♂ Support should be a staple in any good marriage. If you have a supportive relationship, allow yourself to be nurtured by it.

Approval is good for you. Investigators conclude that popular individuals tend to seek approval and find it satisfying, but are not so concerned about criticism.[17] By contrast, troubled souls tend to be overly sensitive to criticism, but cannot take a compliment. The implications are clear.

Paying more attention to the positives of your social relations should help you become more comfortable with yourself and better liked by those around you. *Caring about approval is good for you and good for your marriage as well.*

BREAKING INSECURITIES RITUALS

Since the reassuring mate is contributing to the pattern, he can help break it. It might look something like this:

SHE: I hate looking like this.

HE: I know that how you look is important to you, *(showing he is listening).*

SHE *(suddenly saddened by her own realization):* It's just that I'm getting older. And it shows too much.

HE: I think I can understand that. We're both getting older.

By simply listening and reflecting feelings, he provides an opening for more sensitive subjects. She feels he understands her, which is comforting. He leaves the issue on her shoulders, where it belongs, and shows confidence in her that she can solve it herself. The friend who has truly understood a problem is in a much better position to offer reassurances and is more likely to have them turn out to be helpful.

Those who condemn themselves may be shocked to hear the acidity of their own words reflected back at them. Someone who says "I look awful!" may not be prepared to hear someone say, "You feel you look awful?" or, "Do you really?" While she is willing to complain about herself, she is shocked to hear it echoed back at her.

CONFIDENCE IS CONTAGIOUS

Confidence in oneself translates to confidence in a future together. A study of over 220 marriages showed that having confidence in oneself contributes significantly to overall marital satisfaction.[18] Not only does self-confidence make you happier with your marriage, it makes your spouse happier with you. To have a happy marriage, Catherine Johnson suggests that at least one of the partners must have a naturally bright outlook.[19] If both are optimistic, so much the better. But if two normally dreary and temperamental individuals join forces, they have a slim chance of making each other happy.

Husbands and wives look to each other for some assurance that their life together is worth the years that they are committing to it. A marriage tethered to worries hardly seems worth the sacrifices. Optimism suggests strength to take care of whatever comes along, satisfaction with your partner, and trust in the future you are building together. Confidence is contagious, and you will see the confidence you show in yourself reflected in the eyes of your partner.

AN ACT OF CONFIDENCE
TO A WILLING AUDIENCE

We all were once small and weak, at the mercy of forces beyond our understanding and beyond our control. As adults, we have much greater power to shape our relationships. We can work to create the confidence that we want others to have in us.

To increase your confidence in yourself, act as if you had the confidence that you wish you had. "Fake it until you can make it" is good advice from Alcoholics Anonymous. "You can be as brave as you make believe you are," suggest Rodgers and Hammerstein in *The King and I*.

Pretending can seem awkward and false. Never mind—do it anyway! Those who avoid doing anything that does not feel completely natural restrict themselves to what they have always done, staying in the same old ruts. Appear to have confidence long enough, and confidence will become a familiar friend to you.

It may be surprising how strongly we sway perceptions by how we present ourselves. The individual who sees herself as warm, wise, or charming, vastly increases the chances her mate will see her that way as well. A woman who *feels* attractive projects a mysterious quality that men find attractive without quite knowing why. A man who shows confidence in himself conveys a sense of strength and security that most women find appealing.

The best reassurance involves a brighter script and some teamwork. You can invite reassurance without trashing yourself to get it.

SHE: Do I look good in this?

HE: Wow, you look great!

Good, but you can go one better, by essentially complimenting yourself and then inviting your partner to affirm.

SHE: Do I look great in this, or what!

HE: Awesome.

Here she is staging the impression, and he, as the audience, shows he appreciates it.

Many people avoid saying anything positive about themselves, for fear they will appear boastful or someone will contradict them and burst their bubble. And among supposed friends who are secretly competitive with each other, it does happen. But mates must rely on each other to fulfill romantic fantasies. Each of us ordinarily *wants* the other to be something special. So your partner is a willing audience for whatever charms you can weave from loose threads or pull out of thin air. Any normal husband will appreciate the artistry, and go along with the show. The optimism you project releases him from the burdens of providing it himself. At the least, it would be poor manners to contradict you! The longer he goes along with it, the more familiar and natural it all seems. Any normal individual appreciates a "can do" attitude.

If you want to show yourself more positively, focus on something you like about yourself and weave it into a conversation. Anything will do, although you may feel safer beginning with something unimportant. If nothing comes to mind, ask a friend or make something up:

"How about this for a wonderful suntan? Do I look good, or what!"

It would be hard to think of something less substantial than a suntan, but even that makes a pleasant impression. Perhaps you are warm and understanding, or patient with your children, or hardworking, or simply cheerful. Size up what you feel makes you interesting or special or worthwhile. Mention it, and see what reaction you get:

"Am I the greatest wife you've ever had, or what!"

If you do not get a major reaction at first, it may be that you took your partner quite by surprise and he has no clue how to respond. A good impression need not provoke an outburst of applause. The goodwill that you create pays off over the following weeks and years.

My wife assures me that she is looking forward to the fun when we are older together. I cannot say I am ready to lose my fantasy of everlasting youth or that I savor the prospect of old age. But I genuinely appreciate her vote of confidence in our future.

Although most of us appreciate optimism, nobody should expect a steady regimen of it. Life is often troubling and confusing, and we want to be able to share our concerns and find understanding and support.

♀♂ Share your fears, and appreciate your mate who maybe tries to be helpful but does not do it quite perfectly. Men especially, say what is going on and trust your wife to help. You are on the right track when you can say, "Thanks for understanding." A hug is also a good sign.

PART THREE

The Mix and Mismatch of Sexual Interests

IN THE ROMANTIC beginnings of a relationship, infatuation takes command and sweeps you along. The sweet version of altered reality called "being in love" involves yearning and fantasizing, and being easily aroused and easily pleased when you are together.

All of us wish it would last forever, many of us expect it to, and a few of us take it as a personal affront when it does not. Actually, the romantic phase can last up to a year or so after marriage.[1] Based on their own reports, married people become less romantic and less satisfied with the quality of their relationship over the first fifteen months of marriage.[2] Most would not say they became unhappy—only less euphoric. So somewhere within this span the rush subsides, leaving you becalmed and on your own in the unforeseen

115

settledness of a lifelong commitment. Sometime after the honeymoon, you wonder what caused you to be so insanely attracted to this ordinary individual who is now your spouse.

It is normal to long for the steamy attraction of the first years together, when the chemistry or pure animal magnetism made great sex so easy that you took it for granted. It is easy to be miffed when it ebbs. You might blame your mate and wonder if you made the wrong choice. But be realistic. *The romantic rush of a new relationship is a temporary blessing, not a ticket for a ride down easy street for the rest of your life.*

When the infatuation runs out, or if you were not as infatuated initially, it is time to take charge. Look to establish an understanding and a connection that can sustain some sexual energy over the many years of a lasting marriage.

Our focus here is not on the act of sex itself but on how two souls and two sets of sexual inclinations match or mismatch in extremely personal ways. The richness of sexuality comes not from the neural stimulation to orgasm, which even adolescents can accomplish on their own. Rather, it comes from the sense that you are understood, loved, appreciated, pleased, and pleasing—all intensified by the vulnerability and passion of being together.

Although sex can be seen as a vehicle for pleasure, to be practiced and perfected, it is much more than that. Sex is about attraction, bonding, commitment; about power and surrender, control and subjugation; about success and failure, acceptance and rejection; about fairness, equality, and sharing. And finally, it is about energy. Sexual energy penetrates the veil that separates you, and it connects you in ways that can leave you better aligned together or imbalanced and unsure of yourselves. Following are some thoughts on how it works.

CHAPTER FIVE

Imbalanced Sexual Interests

"How often do you have sex?" his psychiatrist asks.
"Hardly ever," the man replies. "Three times a week." At the
same time, in another office, her therapist asks the same
question. "All the time," she replies. "Three times a week."
—WOODY ALLEN AND DIANE KEATON IN *ANNIE HALL*

A TWENTY-SOMETHING HUSBAND wants sex more often, for longer spans of time, and with greater variety, while his wife wants it less and feels safer with the familiar. Neither finds the arrangement satisfying, obviously. He feels continually rejected, unloved, and sexually unfulfilled, while she feels continually pressured, unloved, and sexually inadequate. To those on either side of the bed, imbalanced interests in sex seem truly unfair.

Imbalanced sexual interests are the bread and butter of sexual incompatibilities. They make troubled marriages worse, and invite trouble in many otherwise satisfactory relationships.[1] Indeed, after a decade of marriage, it is the unusual pair who are still equally interested in each other

sexually. Most of us are better matched when we are courting. What happens?

GENDER DIFFERENCES

UNFORTUNATELY, NORMAL sexual inclinations create
mismatched sexual interests. Look here at the average and
typical patterns.[2] Individuals can vary widely, of course, so
these are only for comparisons.

ADOLESCENCE AND YOUTH

Imbalances are obvious among adolescents. When teenage
boys and girls do get together, they are miles apart in what
they want from each other. In late adolescence, males are
sexually overheated, readily aroused by anything and everything. Adolescent boys are turned on by skin that shows and
by the clothes that cover it; by the warmth of the true-blue
sweetheart and by the coldness of the stone fox; by the fantasies in their minds and by the physical touch at the school
dance; by the wiggles of girls when they walk and by their
calmness when they sit very still. Sex is an obsession for
teenage boys—intense, urgent, and pervasive. Whether
teenage boys have the boldness to act on it or the conviction
to restrain themselves, the strong sexual impulse is always
there. By one accounting, teenage boys think of sex an average of *twenty* times per hour. That is, once every three wak-
ing minutes.[3] Release is typically through masturbation,
more than with partners, and several orgasms a day are normal. Males reach their steamiest times as youths, at seven-
teen or eighteen, level off, and then face a slow but
continual decline over the decades that follow.

The pattern for females is just the reverse. Female sexual arousal is slower in youth, and teenage girls tend to experience little pressure for sexual release through orgasm. Since more variation occurs among females than among males, generalizations are not as reliable. Some teenage girls are as sexually driven as the boys, and are exceptions to the rule.

Sexual activity among young girls is often for romantic or social considerations, more than for the sex itself. In adolescence, it is usually the boys who push for sex and the girls who comply or refuse. Some girls have sex within a committed relationship, out of love for the guy or to hold his interest. Some of the more adventuresome girls gamble, to impress a boy and capture his interest. Some girls have sex out of loneliness, for the companionship it provides and the temporary sense of intimacy. Some go along with sex because of pressure and for lack of a graceful way out.

So among teenagers, *boys are obsessed with sex while girls are obsessed with boys.* It is from sexual interest that boys overcome their awkwardness and approach girls, while it is out of social considerations that girls overcome their qualms and tangle with sex.

MIDDLE YEARS

The passing of a few years reduces these typical imbalances. Sexual pressure in men usually subsides through their thirties. By their forties, orgasms per se are no longer as important, and men focus more on the sensual aspects of the experience. In their fifties, many men are absorbed in their vocations and go weeks without having sexual fantasies at all. Sexual interest also lessens when men are too stressed or overworked, or when frequent sex becomes routine.

Sexual responsiveness in females increases from adolescence and well into their forties. In their thirties, especially a few years after bearing children, women respond faster and more intensely to erotic stimulation, and they seek out and initiate sex more frequently. They may prefer longer lovemaking sessions, and multiple orgasms are common.

So somewhere in our late twenties or early thirties, sexual interest is at about the same average level in men and women. A few years after that, women are more sexually responsive than the men their own age.

THE EVOLUTION OF
IMBALANCED INTERESTS

Note that in adolescence, when boys are most obsessed by sex, the girls are cautious and sometimes unwilling, while in the middle and later years, when females are most interested, many of the men their age are over the hill and in sexual decline. Initially, this struck me as a perverse joke perpetrated upon us by nature. But it has a logic behind it. Nature has never been concerned with human happiness, but neither is it merely capricious. The imbalances in sexual interest have provided evolutionary advantages.

In every one of thirty-seven cultures studied by evolutionary psychologist David Buss, males preferred younger mates while females preferred men who were better providers and often older.[4] Our attraction to youthful women is not just a quirky Western convention but a human universal. In the mating market, a woman's value is therefore high when she is young and then gradually decreases with age. A younger woman can expect to be wanted, perhaps by several suitors who compete for her. Not overrun by sexual passions, she can take her time, size up the candidates, figure out what is and is not in her best interest, and choose accordingly.

As a woman ages and she is no longer considered so attractive, some adjustments may be necessary. By wanting sex for her own pleasure, a mature woman broadens her options. She will be more interesting to her husband, involving him in her pleasure, satisfying him at home, and perhaps reining in some of his wanderlust. If she wears him out and wants more, so much the better. A man who has more demand than he can manage at home is not as likely to be looking for a mistress or a second wife.

A woman who is sexually responsive is also easier to approach and more appealing to suitors. An unmarried woman of mature years who sets her requirements too high will not find many men trying to win her. So nature seems to have timed the female sex drive to take advantage of youth and then, as a woman ages, to compete in relationships so far as opportunities permit.

Male sexual drive, on the other hand, is at its height in youth, when status and opportunity have traditionally been the lowest for males. Adolescent boys and young adult men are not the alphas, chiefs, honchos, big cheeses, or top bananas in the typical ancestral village. So aside from making young males miserable, the inordinately strong sexual pressure drives youths to take advantage of any opportunity, and to strive for whatever status and position will increase their opportunities.

Mellowing sexual interest in the middle and later decades releases men from such intense sexual competition, allowing them to focus on guiding and supporting their children and grandchildren. An older man who goes all out for another tryst may be wasting his time or even risking his life, leaving his family to fend for themselves and thus harming his genetic interests. Typically, older men are interested enough to take advantage of an opportunity, but not so pressured that they abandon their progeny in the search of yet another mindless tryst.

A similar advantage is proposed by Jared Diamond to account for why women go through menopause, which shuts down their reproductive apparatus usually in their forties or fifties.[5] If nature selects for those who leave the most surviving offspring, would not women do better to continue to have children? Remember that the children must also survive and raise families of their own. Another child later in life would consume a mother's resources, leaving her less for her existing children. And if she were to die in childbirth, who would raise the children she already has? Youngsters can continue to benefit from their mothers (and fathers) for many years, even when they have families of their own. So somewhere in her middle years, a woman can actually increase her chances of leaving surviving offspring by forgoing further childbearing and focusing her energies on the children she already has, and then on her grandchildren. When the risk to the existing children outweighs the probable benefits of another pregnancy, nature introduces menopause as its own method of birth control.

Chimpanzee females, like those of most species, remain fertile into old age. But in contrast to human infants, chimpanzee youngsters forage for their own food as soon as they are weaned. So a chimpanzee female would gain no genetic advantage from bailing out of the baby business, and she can continue in it until death takes her out.

IMBALANCES INTENSIFY

IMBALANCED SEXUAL interests are more common than might be expected from our averages. The imbalances of our earlier years continue or grow, while relationships that begin compatibly become imbalanced.

A study of newlywed couples shows sexual rejection increases year by year.[6] While 14 percent of men complained that their wife refused sex during their first year of marriage, 43 percent complained of being refused by the fifth year. So the refusal rate among women tripled over the first four years of marriage. And women today are surely more accepting of sex than women were several generations ago. A representative 1920 survey found that two-thirds of married women wanted sex less frequently than their husbands.[7]

In sharp contrast, only 4 percent of women in the newlywed sample complained that their husband refused them during the first year, while 18 percent complain of being refused by the fifth year.

MINOR IMBALANCES SNOWBALL

Relationships go through phases. Ordinarily, in the first year or so of a marriage, sex is frequent, routine, and almost always at the initiation of the husband. He is interested in having sex whenever possible and she goes along with it because she likes the attention and wants to please. Yet a series of innocent steps can bring a seemingly well-matched couple to serious incompatibilities.

Perhaps she begins to find his continual interest too routine and no longer exciting. Maybe he insists once or twice, and she goes along with it when she does not want to, but is annoyed. So she takes a step back, and refuses when it is inconvenient. He feels rejected, pushes her further, and is miffed when she turns him down. The more he pushes, the less passion she has; the less she gives, the more he wants it.

Any relationship can go out of balance. Sex is easy to share when we each want it at the same hour and place and in the same ways and quantities. So what are the chances of that continuing in any marriage, hour after hour, year after year? About zip. Unless two partners are set exactly the same, which we never are, one will be more interested and the other less so at some point in the relationship.

REVERSED IMBALANCES

How often do men refuse women? The newlywed study suggests that almost one-fifth of women married five years are frustrated by husbands who are too tired or simply uninterested in sex. It is surely more of a problem as men grow older.

Women who would prefer to have sex more often do not therefore become the sexual aggressors and force themselves upon their husbands. More commonly, after asking a few times, women settle into being unsatisfied. Women in their thirties and early forties are the most likely to have extramarital affairs.[8]

The imbalances of youth gradually reverse themselves over the years, as women tend to become more responsive after adolescence and men become less so. Women who are courted for their favors acquire more pleasant associations with sex, while men may tire of being the aggressors.

Overworking also changes sexual interest. The constant pressure men often experience to earn a living diminishes sexual interest, which may be nature's way of limiting their children to a number they can support. Women with small children who are tired all the time are more interested in sleeping than in sex, which also helps delay the next child.

Threats to a marriage can reverse the imbalances. A woman I talked to, who had taken it all for granted over several years, became aroused and eager when she found out her husband was having an affair and might leave her. And she was not merely acting to win him back, she was genuinely more sexually aroused. Feelings of pain, fear, and anger were to be expected, but the awakening sexual interest took her by surprise. She felt awkward about wanting him so much. Yet she also felt abandoned when he was away from her, and comforted and wanted when she could arouse him and command his interest.

I have seen this happen often enough to conclude it is a normal pattern.9 If the situation remains unresolved, the pain and growing bitterness will squelch her arousal.

UNWANTED VS. WANTED TOO MUCH

It is better to be looked over, than to be overlooked.
—MAE WEST

Is it worse for those who want sex more than their partners, and face constant rejection, or for those who want it less, and face constant pressure? Men who insist do so not because sex feels so pleasant, but because being aroused and then rejected is so *unpleasant*. Blame nature, which selects for men who insist, and programs in the unpleasant feelings that push them to do so.

The amount someone complains is not a good gauge of distress. A newlywed told me about a circle of her friends who got together and occasionally swapped stories and laughed about how their husbands were always after them for sex and could never get enough of them. She told me that her husband never wanted her, and shared how totally unappealing it made her feel. And then she cried. Being wanted too much can be annoying, but it is surely more affirming than not being wanted at all.

REBALANCING SEXUAL RELATIONS

IN MANY marriages, our basic interests are not nearly as incompatible as they seem. Suppose a man wants it all the time and his wife seems to never want it. When I ask each how much he or she could accept, their answers are revealing. She says she would prefer maybe once or twice a week, while he says he would like it every night (or more), but five times might be acceptable. So even the stubborn adversaries here are only one or two away from a modest compromise at sex three or four times per week.

♀♂ Finding a compromise can be easier than it appears, as any reasonable midpoint is an improvement. If you and yours do not have equal sexual interest, what might a reasonable compromise be?

Any agreement must address the inner concerns. The man wants to be sure that sex occurs, with some regularity, and the woman wants to be sure she is not pressured and pushed.

A woman may feel pushed by a formal agreement, which can seem like more pressure. Yet an agreement can remove much of the pressure, and what you agree to willingly is often less than what you are (unwillingly) doing anyway. A woman I talked with was reluctant to commit herself to having sex with her husband twice a week or, for that matter, to doing it at all. Yet he pressured her into sex twice a week, and sometimes more, under protest. By agreeing on twice a week, she reduced the pressure without increasing the frequency.

To further reduce the pressure, the man should allow his wife to choose when they will have sex and to set the pace. He may feel that if he did not push, nothing would ever happen. But even the most wary woman might be willing to commit to a couple of weeks or so, as a trial, to see how it will work out.

Trust is tenuous in these arrangements, especially in the beginning. The whole deal is in peril the first time someone fails to comply with the letter of the contract. When she is not available on schedule, he is quick to feel betrayed. When he asks if tonight is good, she reads it as pressure and takes offense. Both must set their suspicions aside and allow the program to work.

A scheduling arrangement is a solution to an immediate problem, not a permanent program for joyful relationships. Compare it to a cast for a broken arm, which is clumsy but holds the bone in place while the injury mends. Once sexual relations improve and trust is reestablished, we can allow more freedom. He is eventually able to initiate sex some of the time, and she welcomes his invitation. And she can say no, so long as she does it warmly. Much rides on the way it is phrased. A woman does not have to perform every time he asks in order to make him trust that she wants him.

♀ You might tell him you want to, but not now. Then suggest a time: "I'm worn out tonight, but I do want to. Can we get together tomorrow? Promise?"

♂ You can overcome some of the rejection by being warm when it occurs.

When she says no, say: "Well beautiful, you're worth waiting for." Or, "I'll have to content myself with fantasizing about you."

To compliment a woman after a rejection goes against normal inclinations. But by staying sweet to her, you maintain the relationship. She is more apt to want you the next time.

Quality is more important than quantity, and compatibility can be more a matter of attitude than of perfectly balanced libidos.

CHAPTER SIX

Wish Lists

I F SEX WERE a feast and we could order whatever we wanted, men and women would choose from different menus. Typically, women want caresses and communication as a prelude to sex, while men are more immediately aroused and prefer to get to the action as quickly as possible. Sex and intimacy go together for men and women, but in opposite ways. *A woman sees sex as an expression of an already existing intimacy, while for a man, sex itself creates the sense of intimacy.*[1] Sex can be immensely reassuring, for men and women. But again, it often works in opposite ways. *A woman wants reassurance that a man wants her for more than just good sex, while a man looks to good sex for reassurance that a woman really wants him.*

Our inclinations here result from our competing genetic interests. Male genes benefit from casual sex and from commitment, while female genes stand to lose through uncompensated couplings. The woman who wants more personal involvement before sex requires something of her mate, thereby selecting for the man who is more apt to stay with her and support her children. A man who feels reassured by passionate sex bonds more strongly and is more apt to stay and support his children. So a woman wants companionship, compliments, flattery, and romantic gifts as signs of commitment, before offering her more valuable reproductive resources. A man wants to know that his woman reserves her passion for him and not for another man.

TRADE-OFFS

OUR DIFFERENCES require us to adjust to one another in ways that can actually strengthen relationships, blending the passion one wants with the intimacy and committment the other wants.

COURTSHIP BARTER

We can look at dating and courtship as a game, in which men and women have competing agendas.[2] The objective for men is to move a relationship toward sexual intimacy, while the objective for women is to move the relationship toward more involvement and commitment. To make sex acceptable to his partner, a man must convey that he finds her attractive and special, and that he is interested in her for herself and not just for sex. To keep his interest, a woman must convince him that she appreciates him and that it is going to be worth his while. In a sense then, sex and commitment are bartered as commodities. The boy who wants sexual favors is expected to romance his sweetheart, while the girl who is romanced is expected to become more sexually intimate.

Most of all, we are not allowed to say what we are after—at least not initially. A man cannot say that he wants to go out with a woman because he wants good sex with her. Saying what he wants would reduce his chances of getting what he wants to about zero. He must appear to be genuinely interested in her. And a woman cannot say that she wants to lock in a commitment or that she wants to benefit from a man's status and money—which would surely scare him off. She must appear to be charmed by him. So we each have our own agendas, which we cannot reveal, which our opposites surely understand but are not supposed to mention either. See why courtship can look like a game?

Although it can appear competitive, and often is, successful barter provides something for each of us. It produces the commitment that a woman wants, but which benefits a man as well, and the sex that a man wants, but which also pleases a woman. The combination is a good beginning.

The traditional courtship patterns include penalties for those who do not follow the rules. A fellow who makes no advances for the first few dates may be thought a gentleman, but if nothing happens after several weeks, the situation becomes awkward. She wonders, "What's wrong with him?" Or, if she takes it personally, "What's wrong with me?" Conversely, a woman who allows sexual access without requiring anything in return may cheapen the exchange, inviting him to wonder if she is too easy.

Courtship barter is no longer required in our current customs, which are freer and more versatile. In a modern version, women have sex to explore the possibilities of a new relationship, but can then feel cheated if the commitment that was not there before sex does not appear after sex, either. Some abandon the barter routine altogether, or reverse it. Some women find a challenge in making sexual conquests but do not want a relationship, and some men want a commitment but are too insecure to be the sexual aggressors. Sexually freer women are regarded more favorably by a freer generation of men, who are less inclined to consider them "fallen" or "soiled." A man can go with a woman who is eager for sex, fall in love with her, then push her for a commitment while *she* considers whether she wants anything permanent. What a switch!

Nonetheless, aspects of the traditional courtship barter continue into most marriages. When we arrive at sexual impasses, it is often because the barter is not working properly.

IMPASSES

Before marriage, the burdens of courtship traditionally fall on the man, who tenders the invitations and pays for the festivities. *Once married, a woman continues to want to be romanced, but her husband typically loses interest in doing the romancing.* A woman who is used to the attention and warm conversation prior to sex does not want it to vanish now that she is married. But the man who has taken on the responsibilities of marriage does not feel that he should have to court his wife and win her again each time. So courting carries a different meaning for women and men. To a woman, it means that her man loves her, while to a man, it means that the woman does not love him unless he continues to romance her.

Our genetic interests continue at cross-purposes many years into a marriage. Male genes benefit from the frequent sex that creates additional offspring, while female genes benefit from confirming the commitment, while also limiting the offspring to those that can be reasonably supported.

Many of our typical complaints are due to breakdowns in the barter system. A woman who complains that her husband is insensitive or just wants her for sex feels cheated and used. She is not getting the *relationship* she wants that would make *sex* feel intimate. A man who complains that his wife has lost interest or that she never initiates sex feels cheated, too. He is not getting the *sex* he wants that would make the *relationship* feel intimate.

Simple touching can become awkward. A man may feel frustrated when his wife is physically affectionate but not sexual, while she is offended when he wants to be sexual but not affectionate. He objects to her affection without sex, and she objects to sex without affection. Gridlock!

THE POWER OF "NO!"

How much communication does a woman require to respond wholeheartedly? Other considerations aside, it varies with how she feels about her man. The more appealing she finds him, the less preparation she needs to be passionate. A woman who is wildly in love might arouse herself on her way to a romantic rendezvous, by reminiscing, anticipating, and fantasizing. Conversely, the less appealing she finds her mate, the more she requires from him to be ready. A woman who is annoyed with her man may want hours of conversation and some real concessions as well.

Immediately after a squabble, a man wants sex as a way of reconnecting while a woman wants to reconnect well before sex. *A typical man believes an angry woman withdraws sex to punish him. A woman can contend, just as adamantly, that she is not trying to punish but simply does not feel like it.* A few women acknowledge withdrawing sex to punish, but many do not. I doubt most women will ever see it as a way to punish, or that men will ever see it as simply not being in the mood.

Nature produces this impasse by programing its plans. An angry woman who refuses sex does not have to *feel* that she is trying to punish. Her anger does it for her. Nature programs her to refuse sex when she is angry. So she denies her uncooperative mate, requiring him to make amends before he can have her again. How could nature have programmed us otherwise? What if the average woman still wanted sex when her husband mistreats her or acts irresponsibly? What could she use to push him to straighten up?

Traditional wisdom advises us to avoid carrying squabbles into the bedroom, suggesting that sex be a sanctuary free of everything else that goes wrong in a relationship. It is not easy advice, especially for women, who see sex as an expression of the relationship. But some do manage it, fighting hard and then loving just as hard. Those who make love after fights say that it is an unusually intense experience, boosted by the adrenaline from locking horns beforehand. And it confirms that intimacy is not harmed by an everyday clash of wills.

One recently remarried man reported that he was surprised one day when his new wife wanted to make love to him after a particularly hot argument. He was surprised again the next day, when she continued the argument just as adamantly as before. With his first wife he usually slept on the couch after arguments. He became more comfortable in arguments with his new wife, and more apt to state what he really felt, rather than holding it inside and resenting her for it. And he was more willing to listen to her and to compromise. Feeling secure that she loved him, he could admire her independence rather than feel threatened by it. He considered her spirited. She too was comfortable arguing for what she wanted, assured that she could push her case without jeopardizing their connection.

AGE REVERSALS

As sexual interests change with age, the traditional arrangements lose their hold. By middle age, men are in better control of their less intense sexual impulses, finding it easier to slow down and take time to get acquainted. Yet age has its handicaps. Many men in their forties are simply unable to respond sexually to women whom they perceive as cold, critical, or overly demanding. Now it is the man who feels too vulnerable to participate in an intimate act with a partner who seems to care not about his feelings but only about herself. Since he is less interested in sex, he may be the one who is unavailable for sex after an argument or whenever he is annoyed, while she sees sex as involvement and wants more. He can withhold sex until she makes up to him, or do without. Such arrangements run against the traditional expectations, and against masculine expectations, but occur nonetheless among older couples.

For both genders, physiological responsiveness changes with age. Arousal for men becomes slower and more tenuous, while it becomes quicker for women. By their fifties, many men require manual stimulation to achieve an erection.[3] Yet for many women in their thirties and after childbearing, vaginal lubrication occurs almost instantly upon arousal, making them physiologically ready.[4] So older men must rely on their partners to slow the pacing and provide the physical stimulation to prepare them for sex, while the more mature women are physiologically ready almost from the outset. Age thus reverses our physiological requirements.

Such changes seem uncomfortable and often remain unspoken. At a basic level, men continue to believe that a real man should be ready wherever and whenever and that their own failure to perform indicates sexual weakness and inadequacy. And women continue to believe that they should be courted for their sexual favors and should not have to take charge themselves and do the courting. The older woman who wants sex more than her husband may still expect him to win her interest and she may be annoyed at him when he does not.

An attractive woman I counseled in her late thirties wanted sex more frequently than her husband, and was understandably miffed that he would not initiate. Yet when he did initiate, she refused him. She was mad about his indifference, and wanted him to make up to her *before* going to bed with him. Not surprisingly, he lost whatever arousal he had toward her, which hurt her more. She was used to men being sexual aggressors, willing to do whatever she wanted, and did not understand the new arrangement.

Perhaps we identify too strongly with the familiar patterns of our youthful years and assume that they should continue, even when simple observation indicates that they do not. Or perhaps nature has so strongly programmed women to expect to be courted that it feels too unnatural to cut men some slack or to do the courting oneself.

BETTER BARGAINS

WE CAN benefit here by simply understanding each other better.

♂ Recognize that women usually see sex as an expression of existing intimacy and not a way to become intimate. Hear requests for more connection as a way to make sex better, rather than as an attempt to manipulate or delay.

♀ Realize that for men, sex itself can establish a truly special sense of intimacy. See requests for sex as an attempt to be close.

These differences would be understood better and more easily remembered if we talked about them.

♂ If you feel a warm glow after sex you might tell your wife about it. Were there some special times when she wanted you physically, when you felt truly and deeply loved? Tell her. Sharing connects your hearts together.

♀ Remember times when your fellow was especially soft and sensitive, that turned you on. Tell him what he does or might do to give you a buzz. Give him an exciting reason to do it again.

We all have some leeway in what we want and what we can accept, which suggests room for negotiation and compromise. Women can adjust to briefer preliminaries and can fantasize to get in the mood, while men can adjust to lengthier preliminaries and even learn to like it. But where is the balance point?

WHO SHOULD CHANGE?

Customs in what men and women are supposed to do vary from culture to culture. Even the advice of the sex and marriage manuals changes over the years. The predominant philosophy of the 1950s and 1960s was that women are not simply slower to become aroused than men, but are naturally passive, requiring guidance.[5] Cast as leader and teacher, the man was seen as fully responsible for the experience. He was advised to be more patient in his pacing and more artful in his techniques. The philosophy of manuals from 1975 to the present, by contrast, is that women are self-sufficient agents, perfectly capable of managing their own responses and responsible for their own satisfaction. The woman is advised to learn better ways to arouse and satisfy herself, with or even without a man.

The manuals from the earlier era ask husbands to better meet the conditions their wives set, while the more recent manuals suggest that wives forego their usual conditions and learn to take the initiative themselves. Men may take heart that much less is asked of them now compared with the earlier era, when initiating sex was entirely their responsibility. Women may appreciate being an active participant, and have fewer disappointments.

ROMANCE AND PASSION

Suppose a woman would be passionate if her fellow talked to her more, and he would be more involved if she were sexually interested. Sounds like a good place to say what you want and strike a bargain. You can link the romance one wants and the passion the other wants, so they merge together as a single activity.

A woman who wants more closeness before sex might assure her fellow that the two really go together. Suppose he tenders a proposal for right now, and she does not feel close. "I'm not in the mood," can come across as a rejection. "You only act interested in me when you want sex," is obviously much worse. "Why don't we just spend some time together, and we will see what happens?" is more neutral, but the man who worries about rejection would not be reassured.

Offer a real bargain: "Let's talk and get really close, then make love." Or, "It would be nice to make love, but I want to be really close first."

Try linking more talk to better sex: "I want us to spend some time together and talk and hold each other so that I will be really aroused when we make love."

How could he refuse?

It is probably easier for a woman to set up the arrangement. You know what you want, and you know when you are in the mood for romance.

Do you feel that your fellow should be more thoughtful and considerate on his own? Of course. But if he is a typical man and not a fantasy, he is probably more the way he is than the way you want him to be. So your practical choices are to coach him to become more romantic, stew over his failures, give up on romance altogether, or to look for it elsewhere. So coaching may not be the worst of all possible worlds.

A man can learn to appreciate the preparation. The attentiveness and closeness a woman wants should feel like a sensuous beginning, not an unpromising frustration.

Allow yourself to experience the communication and caresses, and enjoy it. Just because nature pushes you toward immediate sex does not mean that it is necessarily more satisfying. Men who adapt to the slower pacing tend to find it more satisfying than quick sex. Nature is interested in its genes, remember, and not in your happiness.

Most women want to know that when passion takes a night off, the warmth and love stay on. A man who stays close to his wife when sex is off is saying to her that closeness matters to him too.

♂ See accepting her wishes as an investment in the future. Security ought to come not from scoring every time, but from knowing that your mate is really pleased with you.

A man who is troubled by closeness that arouses but does not lead to sex should talk about his feelings. Is it simple frustration, or more than that? Is it a sense of rejection, of withdrawal of affection, of abandonment? Does it include feelings of isolation and loneliness or incompleteness in ways that are hard to describe? Such feelings usually stay underground, not because they are unusual or abnormal but because they seem awkward, impolite, immature, or selfish.

♂ Share your feelings. Sharing says your feelings are normal enough to share, and establishes a connection.

CHAPTER SEVEN

The Politics of Pleasure

S EX IS A shared experience, in which two sets of feelings team up and blend together in a sort of alchemy. You find the experience most pleasing when you know it is also pleasing to your mate who, in turn, wants to know it is pleasing you. And so on. At its best, sexual intimacy makes a good relationship richer and two separate individuals more connected and more complete. At its worst, of course, it is dreadful, and whatever goes wrong seems more important because someone else may judge. When one considers sex unsatisfactory, the chances are that the other will soon find it unsatisfactory as well.

SENSITIVITIES

WHY IS sex often fraught with so many complications? Some people blame society for creating unnecessary inhibitions, while others blame overinflated expectations. Liberal marriage manuals advise us to become more adept at sex, improve our techniques, and venture out into new and more stimulating variations. Conservatives counter that sex has been oversold, so that expectations are now too high and everyone is too quickly disappointed by what should be accepted as average, satisfactory sex. Obviously, no relationship can live up to the mythical standard of intensely pleasurable multiple orgasms (hers), brought about by a masterful and properly paced performance (his), culminating in a grand finale (simultaneously), followed by blissful calm and a spiritual rejuvenation that leads naturally to a repeat of the whole wonderful sequence.

But the problem runs deeper than a puritanical culture or wild, runaway expectations. We humans have quite mixed feelings about sex—we always have, and will continue to into the foreseeable future. Cultures may be loosely permissive or terribly strict, and Western culture seems to go through phases, now strict, now bawdy, now somewhere in between. Yet all cultures, even the most accepting, have rules and prohibitions on when, where, and with whom sex is permitted. And most cultures take what seems to be an inordinate interest in the sexual activities of their members, sanctioning some pairings but condemning others. To survive, individuals must look for the cues that say "yea" or "nay," "acceptable" or "prohibited," and respond accordingly.

We are programmed to take these cues extremely seriously, as though our very survival is at stake. And indeed, it always has been. Prohibited liaisons have carried severe penalties—up to banishment or execution. So sex can be easily associated not just with pleasure but with shame, guilt, envy, jealousy, judgment, and obligation. Like a sponge, it seems to soak up whatever attitudes and emotions surround it. Our sexual selves seem to be highly sensitive to affirmation or condemnation. If you doubt it, think for a moment about setting the table incorrectly and having someone notice and publicly ridicule you for your mistake. Then imagine you have an illicit tryst and are found out and ridiculed for it. What a difference! The sexual arena feels so much more personal. Is there any way a breach in table manners could carry the same emotional impact as does a sexual transgression?

The surge of shame and guilt triggered by sexual indiscretions can be far out of proportion to the amount of actual harm done. And our minds can convince us that everyone is watching, or that God himself judges and condemns. Nature programs our brains to play this trick on us, so that we take our sexual conduct seriously. I cannot imagine how God or angels could be nearly as concerned about human sexual transgressions as we ourselves are.

Our natural openness and sensitivities make us care about how our partner feels. Is he or she pleased, or unsatisfied and condemning? Men and women look to different signals for personal affirmation.

MEN WANT WOMEN TO WANT THEM

What do men want most in sex? Men want a woman to be interested and aroused, active in the lovemaking, passionate, and satisfied by the experience. In a broad survey of some four thousand men, a woman's passion was rated as the most important factor in the man's sexual satisfaction.[1] The majority of the men—60 percent—said that they were most irritated by women who seem cold or uninterested while having sex. A mere 5 percent said they were put off by women who make the first advance, who make demands, or who seem "too easy." Asked what their partners could do to make sex more exciting, the most frequent suggestion— from 34 percent of the men—was "Be more active!" The typical male fantasies involve a woman who is eager for sex and goes wild.

The appeal of female passion is more than just the additional noise and thrashing about. The passionate woman acts to satisfy herself, making her a vested partner in the joint adventure. Passionless sex suggests that the woman is doing it to console or placate the man, as a favor, or because he talked her into it or pushed himself on her when she was not interested. Men, of course, object to seeing sex as a gift for which they will be beholden. Suppose a woman's signals say, "Personally, I am not interested, but if you insist . . ." He then imagines she finishes with "then you are inflicting this unseemly and inconvenient act upon me, you owe me for it, and I will hold you accountable as I choose." Men do not want to feel so responsible.

Today, amid so many male sexual insecurities, it is interesting that men claim they accept the sexually demanding woman but are put off by the one who wants nothing for herself. The man who has performance anxieties is not afraid of missing out on some pleasure himself. He fears that he will fail to provide sufficient pleasure for the woman and that she will, therefore, see him as inadequate. So the woman who knows what she wants and goes after it sets a man at ease, contrary to expectations, simply because she herself wants something he can provide. It feels flattering to be wanted and honorable to please. The feeling that the woman loves sex provides a comforting answer to a man's unspoken sexual confusions and insecurities. More than any other form of compliment, it is the woman's pleasure that a man reads as genuine love and appreciation.

As quirky as it seems, many men are at least as invested in the woman's pleasure as she is herself. "Did you do it, honey? Was it good for you?" The woman who lies quietly and simply receives sex somehow offends, while the passionate woman is infinitely more exciting. The lady who occasionally fakes it does so not for her own pleasure, but to keep her gentleman satisfied.

Women can take advantage of men's interest in women's satisfaction. A woman who wants to generate some excitement might talk to a man about what sorts of sex she enjoys, watch his imagination go wild, and then still require him to court her before closing the deal. It works the other way as well. When a woman says she puts up with sex but does not enjoy it, any man should know she is not flirting with him!

TRADITIONAL VS. MODERN

SEXUAL ATTITUDES may be loosely classified by whether sex for the woman is considered a favor for a man or simply a pleasure in itself. It can be both, and it often is, but the distinction remains. In the traditional view, a proper woman accepts sex to begin a family and maintain a marriage. Lust, like money, is not a proper reason. Sex is a favor a woman provides to a man, for which she should be properly compensated through marriage and family or improperly compensated through hard cash. In the modern view, a woman seeks her own pleasure in sex, or feels she ought to, so that sex, like virtue, is its own reward. Sex is not merely pleasant, but normal and healthy, and the woman who cannot love it is considered backward.

An uneasy trade-off between the modern view and the traditional one remains. If the modern woman loves sex strictly for her own pleasure, is she no longer entitled to special consideration? Just because a woman enjoys sex does not make her necessarily willing to give up the entitlements that traditionally go with providing it.

Such concerns can be seen in some of the earliest Western literature. In ancient Greek mythology, Zeus and Hera, the king and queen of the gods, were quarreling, as Greek gods were prone to do, over whether the male or female gets more pleasure out of lovemaking. Men want to believe women love sex, so you can guess which position each of them argues. As their umpire, they chose Teiresias,[2] a young herdsman. By extraordinary circumstances, he had once been changed into a woman, experiencing lovemaking as a woman for seven years, and then was changed back into a man. Teiresias ruled that the greater pleasure was given to the woman:

> *Of ten, the man enjoyeth but one part,*
> *Nine parts the woman fills, with joyful heart.*[3]

Hera, infuriated, punished Teiresias by blinding him. Later, Zeus compensated him by giving him the gifts of prophecy and a long life.

We are not told the circumstances of the quarrel, but they are easy enough to imagine. Zeus, like most men, wanted to believe that his lovemaking was greatly satisfying to his wife (and to many women, as he was a freewheeling philanderer). Hera wanted to control his raging ego and gain some credit for the many sacrifices she made as his wife, sharing his bed. He boasted that women gain great pleasure in sex. Nonsense, she countered—women accept sex merely to satisfy men.

Because Greek myths were told by men, Zeus' favorable ruling from Mount Olympus is not too surprising. A female authority could easily arrive at the opposite conclusion, as Joyce Brothers does to support her suggestion that when young women live with their boyfriends, they are being used. She believes women should hold out for marriage: "If a woman is willing to move in with a man and provide . . . sex without expecting anything much except an orgasm in return, that is all she is going to get. And since most women only reach orgasm about half the time," she argues "there is no way she is going to get as much out of it as he does."[4] So it is not just men who count orgasms. Joyce Brothers is also counting. A modern woman who enjoys sex can still argue that it is for her fellow, either as a way to justify marriage or as a tactical advantage in an argument. And since only she knows her own experience, the Greek gods now silent, it is her option to call it as she wishes.

Males are expected to compensate females for romantic liaisons, not only among humans, but in other animal species as well. Enjoying sex need not change the arrangement. Among bonobos, considered the most sexual of all the primates, females are not just willing but truly wanton. Bonobos communicate constantly, and females have at least twenty postures and calls to indicate willingness to copulate. Yet here too, sex is bartered. An adolescent female might approach a male, making it clear that she wants him, and then afterward she helps herself to some of his food stash.[5]

THE EVOLUTION OF THE FEMALE ORGASM

While male orgasm produces ejaculation, the female orgasm has no parallel function and is not necessary for reproduction.[6] So why did nature build it into the human female? It is the sort of question that only a biologist would ask, but it leads somewhere. When nature wires us for some serious pleasure, it is not just a favor, as though nature is benevolent and cares for our happiness. It is because the pleasure response helps get the genes passed along. It is easy to speculate about its function, and many have. I offer here some of the more plausible possibilities.

The female orgasm can be fickle. In a recent survey, women reported having orgasms about two-thirds of the time in sex with a male partner, either before, during, or after the intercourse itself.[7] That leaves about one-third of lovemaking sessions in which women do not experience orgasm. Intercourse may be insufficient by itself, and manual or oral stimulation is often necessary to achieve orgasm. Some understanding and patience may be required from a man to make it happen. The sensitivity needed to bring about the effect may have helped our ancestral mothers distinguish between the conscientious suitors who would stay and make good dads, as opposed to the here-today-gone-tomorrow cads who were thinking only of themselves.[8]

Remember that men tend to be at least as interested in female passion as are the women themselves. Obviously, female orgasm strokes the male ego.[9] Men who want female passion would have preferred the more passionate woman over her more passive competitors, as so many men do today. So mate preference would tend to select for women who can be passionate and can be brought to climax. And once mated, the man must still work at it if the passion is to continue. A woman who is annoyed at her mate may submit to sex, if pushed, but she can hardly be forced to climax. So to share his lady's pleasure, a man must support the woman, try to please her, and generally accept doing a few things her way. In so doing, he involves himself more fully with her feelings and concerns. The additional attention and commitment required to achieve the mystical "O" thus strengthens the pair bonding and improves the survival chances of the children.

We should also look at why men are so fascinated by female orgasm. Men look for cues to approach a woman, as pushing oneself on an uninterested bystander is not the wisest thing to do. Sensitivity to female interests would be adaptive, as males who respond to the cues would mate more frequently, make fewer mistakes, and thus pass along their response sensitivity. Signs of female passion serve as a sexual trigger for the typical man, while the lack of passion leaves him unsure of himself or unaroused. Female orgasm, of course, is one of the more objective signs of female passion.

Perhaps this can help the woman who wonders why her man needs sexual reassurance. Nature has selected for men who look for approval and try to avoid condemnation. See it as a way to balance out his raw passion and maybe arrive at a more civil relationship.

The concern for female sexual pleasure varies between social groups. It is more pronounced among the more educated and less apparent among blue-collar communities. And not all cultures share our Western obsession with female sexual responsiveness. Many cultures, Margaret

Mead observed, do not even recognize that women can enjoy sex, much less have orgasms. Or perhaps people in these cultures sense it, on an intuitive level, but do not talk about it even to one another, much less to the visiting anthropologist lady who is so nice. Some cultures expect women to accept sex passively and not participate in it. But why? Out of a man's fear that the lady who wants passion might find it with another man? Because he fears the way female passion controls him, causing him to care too much about her sexual experience? Because he is insecure about quick ejaculation, which is quite acceptable when she wants him to just get it over with anyway? Or because she wants to remain morally superior to him? Does she subtly condemn him for using her to quench his animal appetites? Does she require him to compensate her for it? Your guess here is as good as mine.

Recent research now suggests a biological function for the female orgasm. The spasms, when orgasm occurs during or shortly after male ejaculation, seem to transfer the contents of the upper vagina into the cervix.[10] Female orgasm would thus increase the probability of conception from a pairing. So by her orgasm, or lack of it, a lady might influence whether or not she is impregnated and by which partner.

Symmetrical features are a sign of good genetic health, and biologists note that females of various species normally choose for more male mates with symmmetrical features over their less symmetrical competitors. Biologist Randy Thornhill and colleagues at the University of New Mexico found that women tend to have more orgasms with men with more symmetrical features, who may appear stronger or healthier. Women may thereby select the presumably better genes over those of less symmetrical men.[11]

The sperm selection function provides one more explanation for men's concerns about female orgasm. A man may be more apt to pass his genes along when his partner has an orgasm, especially if she has opportunities to be with another man as well. And while most of our ancestors were married and many were faithful, an ample amount of infidelity has been found across cultures.[12] Thus, women would have had opportunities to select one set of genes over another, by having orgasms with one man but not with another. It follows that men, in turn, would eventually adapt to this sperm selection function. Nature would select for men who feel secure and flattered when a woman has an orgasm but are troubled and perhaps suspicious of her when she does not—which is exactly what we find. The typical man is reassured when his mate goes wild, but wonders if she is withholding from him when she is passive.

Why are men often *more* concerned about women having orgasms than the women are themselves? Women sometimes want to enjoy the warmth and closeness of sex without having to push for an orgasm, which men seldom understand, and may find objectionable. Sperm selection may explain the puzzle. Female orgasm would almost invariably benefit a man's genes, especially when a woman has another lover, and nature would therefore select for men who covet it.

Given that the typical man is innately fascinated by the phenomena, it adds whole new dimensions to the sexual adventure. A man can do everything a woman wants to coax more passion from her, or he can try to demand it and be hurt if she does not comply. A woman can impress a man with her passion or demand more from him if she is to experience it—and she can withhold it if he neglects or offends her.

Female orgasm can be a source of shared pleasure and intimate satisfaction for both men and women. Or, it can simply give couples something else to fight about.

PLEASURE IN AMBIGUITY AND PARADOX

A few notable inconsistencies have shown up so far in our sexual attitudes. The message given by men who push for more sexual passion is, "I want you to love sex and go wild about it, not because I am insisting on it but because you yourself love it and want to." But if it is for her and not for him, why is he the one who is requesting it? The message given by women who do enjoy sex is, "I love sex but I still expect you to court me and appreciate my doing for you what I want to do for my own pleasure anyway." OK, so maybe it's not supposed to all add up and make sense. I will limit myself to a few words about how to live within the ambiguity.

♀ Be especially sensitive to how much your man looks to you for sexual reassurance. Even a casual remark that sex is not as important to you as it is to him can hurt more than it should. When and in whatever ways you *do* enjoy sex, communicate it. Involve him in your experience. The "ohs" and "ahs" and cooing of love-making connect you together. If it feels good, say it. At least try saying it, and see if saying it feels good.

Those who do not like to talk during sex can talk about it before or afterward. As in any of the performing arts, you look for the reviews the next morning to see how well you have done that night.

If you feel selfish seeking your own pleasure, turn your thinking around. Being pleased is a way to be generous, while being dissatisfied, or remaining so and not trying to change, can be stubborn and selfish.

Obviously, the complaints should stay out of the bedroom as much as possible. A professional woman I talked with worked too many hours and then came home to manage the housework, while her musical husband taught a few lessons and played odd gigs at night. She appreciated his joy in living and his gentleness with the children, but wanted him to take up the slack around the house. When he wanted sex she was worn out, and steadfastly refused. He accused her of not liking sex, but she never let him get away with it. She argued back that she loved sex but was simply too tired for it. Or she said that she loved sex but was too mad at him to do it. He complained that he missed having a sex life, and she countered that she missed it just as much as he did. Once, seeming flirtatious, she said she liked sex, but she was not sure she liked him. He took her anger in stride and continued talking with her. I was fascinated with her way of holding firm and still staying feminine. The two weathered some hard times but came out the other side still in love with each other.

♂ Try to broaden your views of what women actually appreciate in bed. Men tend to overestimate the importance of multiple orgasms, assuming it has the same significance for women that it has for men. In the face of expectations that she go wild with sex, your woman may appreciate the leeway to slow down sometimes and relax.

You take an orgasm as proof of pleasure, but is she content when she does not have one? Ask her. In the absence of any proof otherwise, you might as well believe what she says.

How does a man say he appreciates the sexual relationship? Simply wanting her sexually is not the same compliment to her as her wanting you is to you. Can you tell her what it really means to you? It is easy to joke about sex, but you may find it awkward to say much about your actual experiences.

Surprisingly, women seem considerably more comfortable talking about the specifics of their own experiences than do men, reversing our usual impressions. Sex therapist Dr. Ruth Westheimer observes that many women speak shamelessly about intimate experiences "as though talking about cookie recipes at a church social."[13] Seldom do the men I talk with volunteer to tell me much about what they do in the bedroom.

♂ Do you like how she holds you during lovemaking? Do you like what she says, what she does, how she smells? What do you most like about how she looks? The most important things may be vague and hard to formulate. Perhaps sex makes you feel calmer, more comfortable with yourself, better connected. Does her giving herself to you make you feel she loves you? Does she seem warm and sensitive to you when you make love? Do you count on her wanting you more than you think you should, and would you be lost and lonely without her? Do real men say things like this? Try it out, and see if it brings you closer.

CHAPTER EIGHT

Fantasies

A MARRIED ACCOUNTANT FOUND himself infatuated and in an affair with a nude dancer. The bubble burst when his fantasy love went on to fresh adventures, leaving him on his own to figure out what went wrong.

He was back with his wife and was trying to work on his marriage when he came to see me. The wife was accomplished, attractive, comfortable—a people-pleaser. Not that long ago, he had thought she was everything he wanted. When they married, and in the years when they were going out together, *she* had been his fantasy. What happened?

Aside from a few ordinary squabbles, the marriage was a good one. He and his wife grew familiar and comfortable with each other, as is normal. Fantasies of other women began to cross his mind. It was not that he would actually *prefer* another woman to his wife, and surely not in the beginning. But new fantasies were more arousing, simply because they were new, and he continued with what gave him the surest rush. Over the years, he forgot about his fascination with the woman he had wanted most, who was now his wife.

We looked for a way to regain some of the spark he had felt for his wife earlier. It was either that, or he could continue to live with the formal shell of a marriage while his deepest yearnings were for someone else.

I suggested he try fantasizing about his wife. He thought it a stupid suggestion, and objected. Aside from considering it pedestrian, he felt it an unwarranted restriction on his freedom to do what pleased him. By now, he thought of his wife as the bad cop who kept him from his fantasies, and as the judge who condemned him for them.

He would not have to change all his fantasies, I conceded, but only perhaps half of them. Finally, after considerable conversation, he agreed to that much, if only to get me off his case.

It took some concentration, but he was able to resurrect a few fantasies about his wife. Gradually, it became easier, and the fantasizing became more pleasant. Over the following weeks, he felt more involved with his wife, and more comfortable at home with her. He was better able to tolerate the times she was upset with him or simply hurt over the recent affair.

A few years later, the wife phoned me. She reported that she and her husband had grown closer again, and had remained close since our sessions.

EXTRACURRICULAR FANTASIES

HOW FAR should we allow ourselves to fantasize about the appealing beauties and brawn we see in television and movies, commercials, romance novels, or even with close friends and casual acquaintances? It can be fun, of course. But is it innocent fun or does it carry further consequences?

It is by now a secular truism that sexual fantasies are normal and healthy and that we can indulge ourselves so long as we do not act on them in inappropriate ways. "Do whatever feels good," it is said, "so long as you do not hurt anybody."

Most people fantasize about sex with new partners. Indeed, the appetite for fantasies is so commonplace that perhaps it is only the most unusually controlled or especially dull individuals who do *not* fantasize. Even in supposedly intimate relations with a spouse, most of us occasionally fantasize about being with someone else. The rush of imagining another partner is highly involving, providing a sweet lift on a rainy night when there is too little warmth at home or we are too lazy to open our hearts to it.

It is better to accept normal feelings than to condemn oneself for them. Yet appetites normally work to satisfy themselves and not to assist your balance or personal fulfillment.

OUTSIDE FANTASIES COST

Imagining sex with other partners is even more prevalent in troubled marriages. Spouses who have grown apart have few pleasant thoughts of one another, and are too filled with grudges to entertain pleasant thoughts of each other. You do not argue that an inconsiderate mate gives you nothing at all and then secretly treasure memories of how well he or she satisfies you in bed. Yet daydreams about new partners are a cause, as well as a consequence, of poor marriages. Yearning for someone else carries our heart away from home, and along with it our wishes for intimacy and our tolerance for the everyday hassles of being together. Yearnings to roam contribute to conflict and alienation between us.

In the usual sequence, imagining sex with other partners is simply more interesting at first and provides a stronger rush than thoughts about the familiar spouse. What harm is there in a little imaginative fun? As a marriage matures and becomes less arousing, outside fantasies become more important, providing relief from the monotony and boredom without having to change anything in the marriage. Down the road, you begin to measure your spouse against the rush of the fantasy. And how often does a real person compare favorably to the thrill of an erotic fantasy? You may resent the spouse for not doing everything that the fantasy lover does, or for not *being* the fantasy.

By now, it is easy to feel cheated by the marriage and no longer willing to invest as much as it takes to resolve conflicts and stay close together. And as the marriage fails, from neglect, the fantasies become even more appealing. So a troubled marriage and outside fantasies reinforce one another.

Men who were shown pictures of *Playboy* nudes were found to later describe themselves as less in love with their wives than men who saw unarousing pictures.[1] Perhaps you can guess why. In primitive times, how often would a man be confronted with such a youthful and appealing temptress, already undressed, smiling warmly, and ready to give herself to him? How many men would refuse? A color glossy is only an illusion created by modern technology, and the actual woman is as far away as your imagination can reach. Yet your neurology responds to the fantasy picture as though it were the real thing. And to prepare for the new offering, your mind minimizes the love with the current mate. So as you yearn for the riches of the fantasy, you leave yourself a smidgen poorer in your reality. Erotic movies are appealing, but many of the men whom I asked tell me they feel more scattered and unfocused afterward.

♂ When you take in a few beautiful nude fantasies, track where your mind goes with the one you married.

Female sexual fantasies involve romantic tales rather than nude visuals, but have much the same impact. At least 98 percent of the those who read romantic novels are women,[2] and women are also the main consumers of romance stories in magazines, TV, and the movies. Romance novels place the heroine with a hero who is wealthy and powerful, and perhaps talented or sensitive, who falls in love with her for her beauty, opens doors, and takes her into a world she could not go to by herself. The romance provides a vicarious adventure complete with power, wealth, love, and passionate sex. It makes an everyday husband or boyfriend seem truly pedestrian by comparison. As with men who see nudes, women who experience vicarious romances with powerful men would probably find themselves less in love with their actual mates. So the same advice holds:

♀ When you go on your romantic fantasy adventures, track where your feelings go with the one you married.

BIOLOGY SEEKS VARIETY

Sexual variety has appeal, especially to males, in numerous species as well as our own. The tendency to be bored with the familiar and fascinated with a new partner is referred to as the Coolidge Effect,[3] after a story about the former president and his wife. On an official visit to a farm, the first lady passed the chicken pens and inquired about a rooster who was vigorously mounting a hen. "Does he do that more than once a day?" she asked. "Oh yes, dozens of times," answered the guide. "Tell that to Mr. Coolidge," she replied.

When President Coolidge passed the pen, he asked the same question, and got the same reply. "Same hen?" he asked. "Oh no, Mr. President, a different hen every time." He paused, and said, "Tell that to Mrs. Coolidge."

A bull enthusiastically copulates with a cow five or ten times, and then completely loses interest in her. If a new cow walks along, he will copulate with her about the same number of times, and then lose interest in her as well. Nature programs the bull to be eager long enough to get the job done, and then to lose interest so that he saves himself for the next job that happens to walk by.

Humans can remain fascinated with the same partner anywhere from a single tryst to as many hours as we can fit into a year or two together. Yet the fascination does wear off eventually. And as it does, new possibilities become more appealing.

Men and women who have multiple sex partners do not do so for the same reasons, so it is easy to misunderstand one another. Men usually seek multiple partners for the simple satisfaction of the sex, while women are often looking for something more personal. Women tend to think that men who seduce and abandon do so to hurt women, which is seldom the case. I have talked to women who seduce and abandon men out of anger toward a particular man or toward men in general. But men typically seduce women out of sexual interest, and those who abandon do so not to hurt the woman, but to avoid entanglements and remain free for the next adventure.

MEN ARE MORE TROUBLED BY CASUAL SEX

MALES FANTASIZE about casual sex more often and more intensely than do females, and they are more willing to have casual partners. Young men now state that they would ideally like to have sex with more than eighteen women in their lifetimes, whereas women state they would be happy with four to five.[4] You might assume therefore that men adjust better to casual sex and find it more satisfying. But, you would be wrong. Surprisingly, research indicates that males typically have *more* trouble dealing with casual relationships than do females.

The contrast shows up strongly in two separate studies of mate swapping, done a generation ago when it was still popular.[5] Among swingers, it was almost invariably the husband who was first interested in the adventure and who talked his wife into it. Yet once involved, the tables turned. The wives became the enthusiasts, while many of the men found themselves dazed and confused.

Note that for men and women, imagination and experience work in opposite ways. Men imagine sex with multiple partners to be truly extraordinary, but then experience it as overwhelming. Women imagine multiple sex partners would be quite unsatisfactory, but then adjust reasonably well to it.

Men are handicapped in casual relationships, psychologically and physiologically, compared to women. Men are more troubled by feelings of obligation, as we have seen, and worry more about their partners than do women. Men are more attracted to women than women are to men, fall in love somewhat earlier in relationships,[6] and bond more strongly. Men fall harder when relationships fold, fantasize longer about the former partner, and take about twice as long to get over it.[7] And the male rigging, unlike the female all-weather counterpart, seems engineered to fail in high stress conditions. With new sex partners, performance worries are the norm rather than the exception.

MEN FEEL MORE REMORSE

Men, who are less experienced at saying "no" and not good at it, are more easily pulled into troublesome involvements. A 1988 study of sexually active college students found that 63 percent of the men, compared to 46 percent of the women, reported having had unwanted intercourse.[8] That is, almost 50 percent more men than women have sexual relations that they later regret. Men, who feel more responsible for their partners, also experience more guilt and remorse after casual intimacies.

Breaking up afterward is always troublesome. I have talked to men who say they feel guilty about literally every woman they slept with and then broke up with. And they also feel hurt by the women who jilted them. Here again, the research totally confounds our myths of gender typical experiences.

Men confess affairs out of guilt, women out of anger.
—ATTRIBUTED TO THEODORE REICH

Married women I talk to who are having affairs have typically told at least one close friend, and many have told their whole office. Married men having affairs typically do not tell a soul, and worry that someone will find out. Surprisingly, men seem to be much more secretive about their illicit activities than do women.

THE ILLUSION OF INVULNERABILITY

Why is it that we *feel* women are the ones who are more easily harmed by casual sex, while close observation shows just the opposite? The woman who is hurt by a casual man is quick to say so, calling the man a jerk and a scoundrel and garnering sympathy. The man who is hurt by a casual woman feels inadequate, and tries to conceal his failure. A typical man does not even want his paramour to know that he is troubled by sex with her—she might lose confidence in him and jilt him. So we hear about women being harmed by casual sex, while men appear to come and go with no pain. Human nature makes men more troubled by casual sex but creates the illusion that men find it as natural as breathing.

Maybe "real" men are expected to be comfortable with casual sex and untroubled by its complications. And a few men are that sturdy, serving as inspiration for folklore and stereotypes. But obviously, the real experiences of most men are a long, long way from myths and expectations.

Even men who should know better continue to believe they are invulnerable. A handsome lawyer spent a few wild years with a seemingly unlimited supply of willing women, followed by six months of self-imposed chastity to get his head together, and then found a wholesome woman and married her. A few months married and now fantasizing about every babe who gave him a second look, he wondered why he ever threw it all away for a marriage. He was wiser now, he figured, and would avoid the mistakes he had made

the last time. Hope springs eternal. The thrill of new opportunities completely overrode the lessons of how a few casual
relationships had once trashed his mind. Confident again
and feeling his oats, he assumed he would go through his
next adventures unscathed.

Blame it on nature. Male genes benefit by casual sex,
and male genes synthesize a pleasurable fantasy and give
men the illusion that the next casual adventure will be as
good as the fantasy. It is not, in that insecurities and the
sense of obligation interfere. But the deed gets done, and
the genes may get transmitted.

Perhaps more men are catching on. In a 1994 survey,
71 percent of men said they felt it would be difficult to have
sex without emotional involvement—up 12 percent over the
previous decade, when only 59 percent felt it would be difficult. Experiences with a generation of more available
women may be introducing some reality. Of women, 86
percent felt sex without emotional involvement would be
difficult—the same as a decade earlier.[9]

BE REALISTIC

Our moral qualms about philandering men come from our
natural concern for women, who have traditionally been
exploited by casual sex. Now medical technology lowers the
threat of pregnancy, leaving women freer to do whatever
they wish. Perhaps the qualms about casual sex are still
valid, but the rationale should be turned around: *It is men
who are more harmed by casual relations, who should be more
careful.* The fantasies that are so exciting in the imagination
can be more trouble than imagined.

♂ So some sound advice (as if anyone ever listens): Realize you benefit from a committed relationship! *See*

marriage not as frustrating your adolescent sexual fantasies but as keeping you safe from them.

Men who are hurt by casual sex with fast women do not get any sympathy. You are on your own.

The flip side here is that many women find it surprisingly easy to get in and out of as many casual relationships as they wish. We still feel that women are exploited by casual sex, even though many women now take it in stride and some acquire a taste for it. Yet many of the basic gender preferences still remain. Even women who do not want a commitment still expect to be courted for their favors.

RETURN YOUR
FANTASIES HOME

WHAT MAY seem like a small shift in your imagination can introduce a richer emotional connection between you and your partner. A simple intervention typically benefits unhappy couples who fantasize frequently about sex with other partners.

♀♂ Try to focus on being with your partner during sex. The climax is most crucial, so if your mind wanders beforehand, refocus on being together as you climax.

Over several weeks, most people who try are able to rechannel many of their fantasies toward their spouses. And among those who can do so, the results are consistent: They are calmer and more comfortable with one another, quarrel less, and are not as hard and bitter when they do quarrel.[10]

♀♂ The challenge is to re-channel your sexual fantasies toward your mate, being gentle and patient with yourself as you do. Make ample allowance for human nature, which delights in arousing you as it runs new adventures across your imagination.

Can you fantasize about your mate? Choose an especially sweet time when you were making love together, hold it in your mind, and see if it arouses you. Can you hold it for several minutes, and get a mellow buzz from it? If so, make a practice of it. It will be pleasant and help reconnect you with your mate. A meditation need not be boring to be beneficial.

Do you get bored or find your mind wanders? If so, what does that tell you? Are you irritated at your mate about something? Identify the obstacles and see if you can overcome them.

I have talked with men and women in unhappy marriages who were willing to have sex with their spouses but were unwilling to think about the spouse while doing so. These individuals were too annoyed with their mates to share themselves in that way, although they found the sex act pleasant or at least tolerable enough while imagining other partners. *The personal experience of being with your partner seems to be considerably more intimate than simply engaging in the physical sex while imagining being with someone else.*

♀♂ Do you question whether fantasizing about each other can help your marriage? Why take my word for it? Try it out for yourself. Try fantasizing about your spouse for two weeks, and check your feelings. Then give yourself some slack, as you might normally, and allow your mind to wander into whatever you wish for the next two weeks. Track how you feel about your mate.

RE-CREATE YOUR FAVORITE MEMORIES

Remembering a pleasant memory increases its importance.

♀♂ Think about the first time you and your mate kissed, or the first time you made love. Think of the times when you felt most strongly attracted to each other. The specifics re-create the feelings. Remember where you were, the weather, what you did together, how you were dressed or undressed, the sights, sounds, smells, and so on.

How well do you and your mate connect? Can you feel his or her love for you? When do you feel it most? When do you look for it and try to feel it? When do you miss it? Talk about it together.

A sexualized connection can be especially intense. Can you feel when your mate is attracted to you? Share your thoughts.

Agree on a time when you will each fantasize about each other. Afterward, share your experiences. Can you feel anything? Is it pleasant simply knowing your mate is thinking about you?

Variety is intriguing, although the continuing search for it can itself become a routine. Men can get aroused watching erotic videos, but the average woman does not want her fellow to turn on watching another nude on the video before he makes love to her. Not to worry. Couples find greater excitement when they rely on their own imaginations and share their fantasies, according to one study, than when they introduce erotic books or pictures to arouse themselves.[11] Talking together about feelings and fantasies invites a special and personal connection that is completely missed while watching erotic material.

♀♂ We need to talk more about our sexual feelings toward one another, so that we appear as real people interested in being together in that way.

Some people do not have sexual fantasies. Yet since fantasies are only make-believe anyway, you are free to make up whatever you wish. Talking about a fantasy can create some of the feelings that naturally go along with it.

♀♂ Use your imagination and spin the sort of fantasy that you wish you were actually experiencing. Have you ever told your mate that you had a sexy dream about him or her? Do you tell your mate that you wake up warm and mellow after making love? Just a few such comments can go a long way. Learn to talk about loving sex, and you are more likely to find that you really do love it. Share your interests, and it will make you more interesting to your mate.

PART FOUR

Genuine Understanding

W E SOMETIMES EXPERIENCE one another in ways that seem to go well beyond our biological composition and social programming. It is not too unusual for intimates to report seeing into one another and intuitively reading moods and feelings that go unnoticed by outsiders. Such intimacy can feel so genuine and so complete that it makes the many compromises needed to maintain it worthwhile. We look next at what intimacy can and should be, and at how to truly understand one another.

CHAPTER NINE

Soul Mates

To love another person is to see the face of God.

—*LES MISÉRABLES*

MANY ROMANTIC FANTASIES include a sort of perfect understanding between two individuals who are truly meant for one another. And immediate and intuitive understanding does occasionally occur in reality, in special circumstances.

WHEN SOULS CONNECT

WE USUALLY think of our feelings as contained inside of us and invisible to anyone else, which is generally the case. Yet most of us can remember a few special times when we were infatuated, when we could "see" or feel the attraction in the other person.

How much of this is merely our imaginations, and how much is a genuine connection? The vibes we "see" can be just figments of our yearnings that leave us looking foolish once we realize we are mistaken. Yet I have seen such connections verified, not just once or twice but often enough to have confidence that they are real. Some of us can tell when one we love feels close to us, and also when he or she *stops* being close or when something is wrong. People report "knowing" when a mate is worried, ill, in trouble, or involved with someone else, well before anyone says anything.

In *Lucky in Love*, Catherine Johnson looks at couples who have vital, thriving relationships after many years of marriage. These intensely involved men and women report understanding one another in an intuitive way that is not easily accounted for by visual or auditory cues. Each may know when the other is pleased or appreciative, sad or worried, and sometimes even what the other is thinking, without being told. "Where it is axiomatic among couples' counselors that no spouse can be a 'mind reader,'" notes Johnson, "these couples do precisely that: they read each other's minds, and on a regular basis. It may well be that people's 'fantasies' of what a good relationship would be— fantasies of 'perfect' understanding, of needs being met without the need to *ask*—are not so far off the mark. . . . As far as the long term thriving couple is concerned, the messages are getting across, with words or without."[1]

Yet those in vital marriages do not keep their thoughts to themselves and expect their mate to read their minds, becoming upset and angry when it does not happen. Most of them are reasonably good communicators and say what is on their minds. They push themselves to understand each other's thoughts and moods, as a way to be closer and to love more deeply. When their own feelings are deeply understood, it's a bonus.

EMOTIONS SUPPORT AND SUSTAIN

The connection between us can comfort and sustain. I talked with a recently married woman who spent her free moments daydreaming about her husband, loving him and feeling his love for her. On a terribly busy day she worked straight through lunch and past dinner, concentrating completely on the tasks with no time for her own thoughts. When she got home her husband was uncharacteristically moody and sad. "Do you still love me?" he asked, pleadingly. She was puzzled, but reassured him she did love him. Ordinarily he could feel her love for him, and he felt abandoned when she was not sending it to him. Only after several such incidents did she finally realize how directly he experienced her love and how quickly he could feel it missing.

Couples can and do support each other in an unseen realm, living richer lives because of it.

♀♂ Those who can intuitively "feel" each other need to communicate more, not less. It can be especially troubling when you sense things but cannot get your impressions confirmed. If you feel out of sorts, say what is going on! Otherwise, you generate confusion and worry.

WHEN LOVE CANNOT CONNECT

Not everyone who is loved can *experience* being loved. Some individuals with genuinely loving partners are too troubled, untrusting, or egotistical to experience the love. This is confusing for the more loving partner. When you love someone and he or she feels it, that completes the transaction. You feel satisfied in your loving and good about yourself. But when you love someone who places walls between you, are you still giving your love? If you send a gift to someone, but it is lost in the mail, have you given that person a gift or not? Well, yes and no—yes, in that you sent it, but no, in that he did not receive it. So it is also with giving love. If you love someone, and he or she cannot feel it, then are you giving that person your love? See why it is so confusing to love someone who is closed to it?

♀♂ Love is not pushy. Infatuation casts a powerful spell, but love in the compassionate sense does not force itself upon you. You must be open to it.

EMOTIONS CAN ALSO HARM

IN THE same way that emotional energy can uphold, it can also undermine. In my work on mental shielding, I ask people how they experience incoming hostility. Without any telltale scowl or grimace, can you tell whether someone has angry feelings toward you or is just thoughtful or complacent? Many felt they could see hostility in another person, in the face or coming from the eyes. I recognize the tremendous leeway here for false impressions. We can easily introduce our own insecurities and "see" someone as antagonistic when the person is actually only perplexed or indifferent. Yet I believe we can and do feel antagonism.

As an undergraduate student, while explaining something to a graduate teaching assistant, I found myself feeling like such a total idiot that I could barely continue talking without tripping over my words. I was no paragon of confidence then, but such a severe reaction with no apparent cause was unusual. The fellow himself never said anything to me, critical or otherwise. Later, however, I heard that his classmates considered him intolerably arrogant, and had ganged up on him over the contemptuous way he treated everyone around him. In retrospect, I concluded that my reaction was an intuitive response to the contemptuous feelings he probably had toward me and what I was saying. Since then, thankfully, I have become better able to sense when contempt is coming from someone else, and I do not take it so personally.

How does it feel to be close to someone who is in a rotten mood? Maybe you can manage it so long as you know where the feelings are coming from. What about someone who you feel has no respect for you but will not acknowledge it? Is your impression coming from your own insecurities, or from your companion? Impressions that remain unsubstantiated remain confusing.

♀♂ Recognize that your emotions can impinge on others, and theirs on you. Be careful with those you love, and admit it when you are having a bad day.

WHAT FEELINGS DO YOU WANT TO SHARE?

A woman wants more from her husband, who she feels does not understand her feelings. Yet her husband reports, rather accurately, how she feels, and is especially keen at sensing when she is upset or annoyed with him. She wants him to be more sympathetic and involved with her, of course, and not just to understand her feelings. He is overwhelmed by her feelings, and so withdraws from her when she is upset.

♀♂ Before asking whether you can connect emotionally, ask if your usual feelings are something both of you would find pleasant to share. Many relationships are limited not by our inability to sense feelings, but by the unpleasantness of the feelings themselves. Want your mate to be more intimate? Make sure that the feelings you contribute are comfortable enough to draw him or her closer.

Those in truly intimate marriages merge their hearts together, and work to stay that way, so long as the connection remains warm and meaningful and can be trusted. Each cherishes the connection enough to tend to it conscientiously and to invest to preserve it.

When we feel how our actions affect someone, we are more careful not to injure. And when we are careful, we make it safe to be close, to open up and share our hearts, to truly love one another. We expand our sense of ourselves to include whomever we love, experiencing the happiness of another soul and some of the sadness as well.

ARE YOU SOUL MATES?

Soul mates are individuals who are presumably meant to be together for mutual comfort and support, and also to learn from one another. Yet even linking up with your soul mate may not set you on easy street. So far as one or both are proud, wounded, or just not tuned in, even soul mates can cause one another a great deal of trouble. I imagine that my wife and I are soul mates, which is not to say that everything has been easy. I have at times considered her to be the most impossible person on the face of the earth, and I have been told this is also how she felt about me at those times.

It is easy to wonder which couples are well matched, which are really meant to be together and which are not. At one time or another, most of us have wondered if we were with the right person and if it was worth trying to right a wobbly relationship, or even possible. I see no easy answer to these questions. Each case has its own logic. Yet a simple rule of thumb may be of some help:

♀♂ In most cases, it seems reasonable to try to do what you can to improve a relationship, see what happens, and then go from there. Those with children have additional responsibility to hold a family together, while those without children have mainly themselves to consider.

CONSCIOUSNESS IN A BIOLOGICAL MACHINE

SURELY WE can accept evolution and still see ourselves as fully human. Yes, our brain activity clearly contributes to what we feel and think and how we relate to one another. Yet there must be more. Our intuitive sensitivities tell us that we are more than physiology, and they suggest we are spirit as well. I figure that within the biological machine that is us is a spirit or soul, along for the journey, which is also us. Our souls are somehow mated with our physiology for the span of our lifetimes.

Our higher selves must wrestle with our primate brains, which try to make monkeys out of us. The challenge is to manage our biological tendencies instead of being managed by them.

There is nothing new about seeing ourselves as spirit and flesh, of course. What is new here is the expanded understanding of how flesh—our biological nature—affects our relationships.

How does biology govern action? Some behavioral inclinations are clearly programmed into the human brain, to promote our survival. Were this not so, our species would have perished long ago, leaving Earth with no curious humans to ponder human nature.

The brain is indeed a biological machine, built to assess situations and respond in an adaptive manner. Artificial intelligence can be programmed into computers, to assess situations and produce adaptive responses, similar to what a simple animal might do. But computer intelligence is not conscious and is merely a mechanism, whereas human intelligence is not just a mechanism but also a conscious entity.[2] How do mind and body join together? It is an old question, of course, but I offer a few thoughts.

NATURE ACTIVATES EXPERIENCE

Nature draws our conscious minds into its service. Sex, for instance, is a genetically engineered program for creating a viable copy of our genes. This does not mean that we have sex in order to replicate our genes. Typically, we have sex simply because we want to and *feel* like it. Exactly! *Nature programs into our conscious minds the feelings and the will to do what promotes our genes.* Biological requirements trigger conscious yearnings, and we act on our yearnings without ever considering what nature accomplishes through our actions.

Seeing how nature uses sex to reproduce gives us a tremendous advantage. By using our wits and medical technology, we can find perhaps a dozen ways to circumvent nature's mechanisms. So too with our innate emotional programming. Understanding how nature programs us invites us to step back and smile at ourselves, and to adjust our reactions to better suit our own purposes.

Our biological nature has served us well over the eons, contributing to the survival of the human species. And in many cases, our automatic and emotional responses still serve us well. Fear, which impelled us to flee lions and be suspicious of outsiders, now pressures us to study for tests and to prepare for a cold and unknown future.[3] The apprehension that many of us live with is a remnant of this adaptive mechanism.

Our natural reactions may be in the best interests of our genes but not in our best interests personally. Shame and guilt pressure individuals to conform to group expectations, and so inhibit reckless transgressions and maintain socially expected conduct. Yet the experience of shame and guilt can be truly painful. The same goes for a sense of inadequacy and low self-esteem, which hold individuals safely in subordinate positions.

THE EVOLUTION OF SIN

Even inclinations that are intensely pleasing need not be in our own best interests. Expressing anger, for instance, can be immensely satisfying when we feel justified and self-righteous. Yet it can wreck our lives. Consider a honeybee, mad as a hornet, that attacks and stings an intruder, losing its own life in the process. Its anger impels it to sacrifice its own life, for the protection of the beehive, and the unwitting bee goes along without objection, to its death.

The same goes for human anger. Anger can go on the attack and sacrifice those you love, for its own agenda, filling you with self-righteousness to enlist your cooperation. Your anger is not concerned about whether you yourself are hurt along the way.

Anger aims to punish. More specifically, anger acts to *warn* your adversary you mean business, to *intimidate* him or her into compliance, or to *retaliate* as payment for wrongs already done to you.

Evolution has no interest in human happiness. Human traits were selected through the ages not to provide us with loving relationships, but because they helped pass our genes into the next generation. Infidelities, anger, and ordinary selfishness can and do promote our genes at the expense of understanding and love.

Biological inclinations can undermine our higher aspirations. In the traditional Christian listing of the major sins, each is clearly useful for biological survival. *Pride* strives for social position and refuses to acknowledge wrongs or accept loss of status. *Envy* seeks to improve your relative position by trashing your rivals.

Anger warns, "Don't mess with me!" and, "Do it my way or suffer my wrath!" *Avarice* tries to accumulate provisions and hoard for hard times ahead, and *gluttony* stores up calories for the winter. *Lust* is the father of each new generation. *Sloth* is the only apparent exception (but even that conserves energy while others do the work). So here is a biological explanation for those human qualities that are labeled "sins." Each contributed to survival and propagation, and so was passed along from our ancestors.

Evolution does not have to work in the best interests of an entire species, argues Robert Trivers, but merely to advance the interests of each set of genes. The same goes for sin, which promotes the genetic interests of an individual while undermining cooperation and fellowship among the broader human community.

It is not the mere occurrence of these primitive emotional states that takes us off the path, but their excess. To the extent we allow ourselves to indulge in them, we merge into them, go where they take us, and dwell in the consequences they create for us.

Many of our innate inclinations are considered moral and right, such as the strong sense of obligation a mother typically feels toward her baby or a father feels to support his family. Yet even these must be managed and can be troublesome in the wrong circumstances. Think of a new mother who feels terribly guilty leaving her baby to go back to work, or a boy who still feels he should take care of "his" girl even after she has jilted him and is going out with someone else. The sense of obligation can continue to haunt us, even when we have done all we can.

♀♂ Recognize that your biological nature looks out for its own genetic survival, and not for your personal fulfillment. You will do well to override some of its inclinations. The challenge is not strictly to control your nature, but rather to understand human nature, enjoy it, reign it in when you must, and guide and channel it to your own better aspirations.

CONSCIOUSNESS GUIDES ACTION

A computer can be programmed to play brilliant chess, but artificial intelligence fails to produce anything even remotely resembling common sense. Computer intelligence will improve, of course, as the technology advances, and perhaps the next generation of machines will be more sensible. Yet the human mind is incredibly complex, and computers are not apt to catch up to human experience anytime soon. What gives us our advantage? It would seem that consciousness itself provides an adaptive advantage, over what might be expected from a strictly biochemical machine without it. Being conscious helps us understand our surroundings and act more sensibly.

Consciousness guides our physical action. We can choose to act, consciously, and our arms and legs move to implement our choices. Whatever we think or feel or do involves brain activity, of course. So consciousness affects brain activity inside our heads just as surely as brain activity affects consciousness. Unfortunately, we do not even vaguely understand how it all works. The communication between conscious mind and biological machine remain as deliciously mysterious as ever.[4]

SCIENCE AND SOUL

Unfortunately, popular positions on evolution versus spirituality clash so strongly that they appear irreconcilable. Creationists adamantly oppose evolution, and favor literal interpretations of early biblical stories. Biologists tend to be strict naturalists, seeing no place for the hand of God. Yet nothing about the known process of evolution precludes the possibility of a soul or spirit within each of us, or of a higher realm that touches our lives. If a spiritual realm does exist, nothing would have prevented God from allowing our human species to acquire its present form through the long and tedious process of evolution. As a way of understanding human nature, flesh and spirit fit together splendidly. Evolution, as we have seen, even provides solid explanations for selfishness and sin, which are only vaguely explained without it. Surely nothing about evolution should prevent those who believe in a higher realm from continuing to do so.

Various spiritual traditions identify a more primitive and selfish side of oneself, which we might call *ego*, in contrast to our *higher consciousness* or spiritual side. Ego includes pride, fear, lust, anger, thirst for status and power, fear of loss, shame, guilt, and all the appetites and insecurities that promote biological and social competitiveness. Higher consciousness introduces compassion, intuition, sensitivity, callings, and passions. Insofar as spiritual training has a common goal, it is to take us away from our narrow egos and put us in touch with a higher consciousness and the realms beyond. Yet ego is concerned with its own survival, and is not easily vanquished. Amid threats or temptations, ego takes over and governs in its own interests.

We get scared, mad, or too concerned with our pleasures, and our sense of peace and goodwill vanishes.

Ego, it would seem, is the psychological face of our biological inclinations, shaped by our experiences.

CHAPTER TEN

Listen To Me!

The unexamined life is not worth living.

—SOCRATES (469–399 B.C.)

In many ways the saying "Know thyself" is lacking.
Better to know other people.

—MENANDER (342–292 B.C.)

OW WELL DO most of us listen? Within what is broadly termed "trouble communicating," most of the problems stem not from failure to say what we want but from failure to listen and understand. The most common marital miscommunication, known as "cross-complaining," is at least 98 percent talk and less than 2 percent listening.

CROSS-COMPLAINING

IN *CROSS-COMPLAINING*, also called *counter-complaining*, each partner ignores the other and voices his or her own complaints. One expresses a grievance, the other responds by expressing a grievance of his own, and so on. Here are some typical "he says, she says" snippets.

HE: You're going through the money I earn faster than the federal mint can print it.

SHE: You think you're really funny.

SHE: You never get home when you say you will. How can I plan supper?

HE: You always find something to complain about. If it's not one thing, it's something else.

HE: You never act like you want sex. You never initiate anything.

SHE: Nothing I do is ever enough for you. I quit trying.

SHE: You never talk to me.

HE: Remember what the marriage therapist said? You should never say "never."

These conversations may seem normal enough to the participants. But just reading them can bend your mind. Do you find them confusing? In each case, the response is close enough to the initial comment to almost pass, but completely disregards its concern. Yet we become so comfortable with cross-complaining that we hardly notice what is going wrong.

LISTEN FIRST

Why do we pay so little attention to what someone else says? Blame it on natural egotism, which wants to put oneself first. Most of us want to speak first and be heard. Then, perhaps, we are willing to listen as well. There is, however, an advantage in reversing the natural order.

♀♂ Listen first, and repeat back the essentials, so that your partner really knows you have really heard him or her. Then, in all fairness, you can ask to be heard in return.[1]

In most cases, it works. By patiently listening and showing you understand, you dramatically lower the tension. Surprisingly, being heard and understood is often as important as having one's own way. And you need to understand the opposing position to figure out whether to agree, bargain, compromise, or hang tough. *Most arguments fail not for lack of rhetoric but for lack of an audience.*

♀♂ Work to be sure your audience stays on your side, and you will be astonished how much power your arguments will carry.

If resolving conflict is the key to happiness, then listening is the key to conflict resolution. Really listening means more than just watching the words go by, waiting for the chance to jump in and counter with our own opinion. It means listening attentively, and accepting what is said, even critical comments, without being offended or stressed by them.

> *O divine Master, grant that I may not so much seek*
> *To be consoled as to console,*
> *To be understood as to understand,*
> *To be loved as to love.*
> —PRAYER OF SAINT FRANCIS OF ASSISI

IF YOU NEVER THOUGHT ABOUT LISTENING

Many have never tried listening because they never thought it was important.

♀♂ If that is all it is, you are in luck. Yours is the easiest problem to fix. Realize how important listening is. Reread the comments section on cross-complaining. Talk to your partner about whether you add complaints upon complaints, and how often.

Think of one or two times you spoke before you listened. Ask yourself what you missed by not listening. Need help? Ask your partner what you missed by not listening.

Arrange with your partner for each of you to check to see how well you are listening. Converse about something—anything. As you do, rate yourselves not on how much you say but on how well you are listening. Who is listening better? Who rates "most improved." Do you know why your partner rates you as he or she does? Are you listening?

WHEN YOU WANT YOUR OWN WAY

Some people do not listen because they have more important things on their minds—like expressing their own feelings and pushing for what they want.

♀♂ Be practical. If you say what you want and are not getting it, then saying it again and again is unlikely to help. To get your partner to listen, you will have to listen as well. Listen first, then introduce your own opinions.

Pushing for your own way is also boring. Since you focus only on your own feelings and your own arguments, you never see the full picture. Perhaps you think you are tired of the relationship and lonely because your mate does not understand you. But by listening to yourself repeat yourself, you are boring yourself witless. Listen to your partner, and see what you have been missing. Even if you do not get your way, you will surely find the conversation more interesting.

LOW STRESS QUARRELS

RESEARCHER HOWARD Markman concludes that the quality of a relationship depends on how well you are able to handle negative feelings, particularly your partner's expression of negative feelings about you, the relationship, and life in general.[2] Obviously, feeling injured, angered, and stressed limits your ability to handle your partner's feelings. Remaining calm in conflict is vital to staying focused and resolving grievances.

Some couples argue forcefully for what they want and still remain relatively unstressed in conflicts. These pairs usually fight fairly, stating what they want without accusation. Just as important, they also understand how much stress the other can manage. Each person wants the argument to work out well all around and tries to ensure that it will. Just as the tension becomes unmanageable, one may crack a joke, concede a point or two, offer a compliment, or acknowledge that he or she goofed. Partners are aware enough to see when they are doing harm and concerned enough to try to mend it.

Suppose he has been pushing too hard, and she has gotten her feelings hurt and starts to cry. "You aren't listening again," she says. He sees he has hurt her feelings, and that she is about to stop talking to him. So he smiles, and then concedes. "I do have a problem listening. Could you repeat what you just said?" And this time, he listens.

How many of us are sensitive enough to see when we are taking an argument one step too far?

RULES FOR COMMUNICATION

Howard Markman and collaborators suggest rules for talking and listening, and ask couples to handle sensitive communication "by the rules." In the *speaker–listener technique,* only one partner speaks at a time while the other listens. The speaker presents his concerns, and the listener then paraphrases what she hears. It helps the listener to better focus on the message, show she is listening, and correct any misunderstandings. The two trade off having the floor, alternately expressing their own concerns and trying to understand the other. The more volatile the subject, the more important it is to adhere to the rules. Markman's *Fighting for Your Marriage* is an excellent introduction to managing conflict in relationships.[3]

Some of the rationale for using rules is based on gender differences. Research indicates that when conflict occurs in games, girls are more likely to break off the game while boys are more likely to clarify the rules or make up new rules to keep the game going.[4] Among the girls, the relationship is more important than the game, whereas for the boys, who relate primarily through activities, the game *is* the relationship. The rules that allow boys to manage conflict in sports and games are obviously missing in most marriages, setting the stage for men to withdraw when conflict occurs. Women can manage the unrestricted emotional exchanges that men find unmanageable. So introducing rules into heated conversations levels the playing field. Rules allow men to participate instead of being over-whelmed, so that women can have a partner who talks and listens instead of withdrawing.[5] Markman's conflict-management training is unusually successful in stabilizing marriages, suggesting that we do indeed get along better when we argue by the rules.[6]

HIGH STRESS MEANS POOR LISTENING

Men and women have different ways of listening or, more importantly, different ways of failing to listen. Look here at some of the obstacles that stand in the way of our hearing one another. Several of these occur more in one sex than the other, although any of us can stumble over them.

Researcher John Gottman observed couples to see how they handled conflict, and then looked in on these couples again three years later, to see how they were doing. He found that the level of stress experienced in the earlier arguments, particularly by the husbands, clearly affected the future of their marriages. Those who were highly stressed tended to have deteriorating satisfaction over the next three years. Couples who could argue calmly were more satisfied with their marriages three years later. That much might be expected. It was the *strength* of the findings that is so surprising. Gottman found that the level of stress the men experience in conflict accounts for *80 percent or more* of the subsequent changes in marital satisfaction.[7] A connection that strong is quite unusual in social sciences research. The conclusion is clear: Being comfortable during conflict suggests a bright, rosy future, while high-stress conflict means foul weather ahead.

It is the husband's stress level that is most important, and by now we can guess why. Men are more easily stressed by conflict, taking it too seriously and turning angry themselves or withdrawing into silence and brooding.

TAKING IT TOO PERSONALLY

Those in vital relationships are usually able to accept criticism without taking it too personally. When we are overly sensitive and unwilling to accept criticism, we limit what our partners can say to us without causing harm. Oversensitivity to criticism suffocates communication.

I talked with a pediatrician, who wanted to find out how his marriage had gone so wrong and patch it up. His wife judged him to be emotionally unavailable and was considering leaving him. He told me that he had felt close to her when they were first together, and she had been attracted to his charm and his joy of life. How did things change so much? He identified a critical incident, just after they were engaged. She told him he was not a good kisser, and she proceeded to instruct him on how she wanted him to kiss her. He took her comments as broad condemnation, seeing her as controlling and something more—perhaps "vicious" would not be too strong a word. He remembers mistrusting her after that, and he withdrew emotionally from her. He went through with the wedding but this incident, and a few similar ones, severed what had been a warm bond of affection. And she grew increasingly unhappy with his aloofness.

I had occasion to talk to the wife. Yes, she was bossy. But she was also intelligent, organized, attractive, and sexually responsive—which was what attracted him to her in the first place. Were he to have been comfortable with her occasional criticisms, and maybe even have agreed to kiss her as instructed just to please her, he could have been more happily married. Overreaction to occasional criticism is lethal. Easy acceptance of contrary opinion is necessary for understanding and compromise.

The man had been genuinely injured when his fiancée told him he was not a good kisser, and he failed to recover from it. I doubt that many women would be that hurt by such an ordinary comment or that unable to shake it off.

♀♂ Are you oversensitive when your mate is upset or critical? How does your mate rate you? Check with him or her, and ask some of your friends or other family.

Try this one item test. Read the following statment, and rate whether you agree, disagree, or are not sure:

When you speak in anger, you say what you really mean.

If you believe a few words spoken in anger reveal a broader inner malice, you are taking anger far too seriously. *Words spoken in anger need not be any more or less important than words spoken out of appreciation or concern.* Someone making an angry comment may be just blowing off steam.

♀♂ See a moment of anger as a mere blip on the video screen. You will be more comfortable with your mate and with everyone else as well.

BRUSH OFF HOSTILITY

The implication is that to better manage conflict, we do well to become more comfortable with it. Unfortunately, the advice itself does not usually help. Stress reactions are mainly autonomic and not under conscious control. I engineered a stress-reduction training, called *mental shielding,* to help you stay calmer in conflict situations. In the training, you stretch and relax, construct a shield in your mind, and then practice using your shield to deflect hostile comments. Those who practice shielding stay calmer later on, in hostile situations. A solid 80 percent of those who read the booklet and listen to the training cassette are clearly calmer in conflict over the next several weeks. Lower stress allows you to listen better, think more clearly, answer cordially instead of angrily, and resolve conflict instead of being swept along by it. *Mental Shielding to Brush Off Hostility*[8] includes a booklet and a thirty-two-minute training cassette.

INSISTENCE AND MISUNDERSTANDING

THE MAN who does not talk much about his feelings poses a challenge to the woman who wants to understand him. Yet this obstacle is not insurmountable. Most men will respond to a good listener, and they will provide enough personal information to splice together a general sense of what is going on. The challenge is to be a good listener.

With so many women wanting more communication, you might think that women would be primed to listen to and understand whatever men manage to say. Alas, such is not the case. I am surprised at how often I hear a woman complain that her husband never talks, and then observe that she does not hear the first word he says when he tries to tell her something. Any woman who can out-argue her husband can easily get too involved with her own winning argument to take much interest in his losing argument. The same holds for the man who can out-argue his wife, although it is women who are typically more comfortable arguing.

I DON'T UNDERSTAND WHY . . .

We sometimes complain about not understanding something, as though we want an explanation, when what we really want is a change. Both genders do this, although women seem to do it more often. Look at some examples:

"I don't understand why you can't remember a card for Valentine's day."

"I don't understand why you can't talk to me about your feelings."

"I don't understand why you have to watch football all afternoon."

The ambiguity is in what we mean by *understand,* which has two meanings. It means "to comprehend with your intellect," as when a teenager says, "I don't understand why the sun comes up in the East." He wants an explanation, so he can pass the science test. It also means "to accept, condone, or tolerate," as when the same youngster says, "I don't understand why I have to go to bed at ten o'clock." The last thing he wants is a sufficient explanation. He wants to stay up. And he is saying that unless you can give an acceptable explanation—and no explanation will be acceptable—then he should get to stay up. He is trying to harass you into conceding to what he wants.

Saying, "I don't understand why you can't remember a Valentine's day card" sounds like a question, but is really a complaint. You are irritated that your mate did not remember! You are grilling him for not remembering, and you want to see him squirm. No man is going to score points trying to explain why he cannot remember a card, and he knows it.

Unfortunately, a complaint masquerading as a question can produce resistance rather than compliance. The man loses the immediate argument, but the woman loses in the long run. Confused by her tangled accusation and annoyed about being grilled, he is not going to remember it the next time either.

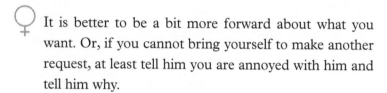

It is better to be a bit more forward about what you want. Or, if you cannot bring yourself to make another request, at least tell him you are annoyed with him and tell him why.

YOU JUST DON'T UNDERSTAND!

A similar analysis applies to "You just don't understand," which is also the title of a book on gender dialect. "You just don't understand" is a woman's expression, meaning not that men never use it but that women use it considerably more often. An exasperated woman who says, "You just don't understand" might seem to mean that you are not comprehending the problem, but it means more than that. She is also saying that the issue is important to her and she means business. She is saying that you are not taking her concerns seriously enough and, until you do, she is fed up with your insensitivity and is not interested in talking to you further. "You just don't understand" puts you on notice that the issue is no longer negotiable, and that it is your job to concede or else face a continuing standoff. A man may "understand" her position but not agree with it, or not want to comply with what is expected. The admonition pits one will directly against the other, and the sturdier combatant has the advantage. "You just don't understand" is a woman's expression because men try to stay out of battles they cannot expect to win.

OVERBLOWN ACCUSATIONS

We have all heard that we should not say "always" and "never," but we all do so anyway. One who feels neglected and wants more conversation says, "You never want to talk to me!" One who feels left out and wants more consideration says, "You always think of yourself first!" Why do we so mindlessly create such overblown accusations?

Anger usually expresses itself as an accusation against whomever we feel mistreated by. Anger says that we are justified, and that our opposite is wrong and ought to concede. Of course, anger wants to hurl the strongest accusation possible. So anger tends to focus narrowly on what someone has done wrong and to present it in the worst possible light, exaggerating the case and ignoring the opposing arguments entirely.

Angry confrontations are intensely involving, as we uphold our own justifications as if our very survival depended upon it. Unfortunately, we are taken in by our own arguments. It is said that a press secretary tells wild tales of convenience to gullible reporters, sleeps soundly, then comes to believe his own tales when he reads them the next day in the newspapers. Similarly, an angry person presents overblown justifications to strengthen her own case, but convinces herself as she argues them so convincingly. Attitude research confirms that as people prepare a position and argue it aloud, they become more convinced of its merits.[9]

A woman who yells tearfully at her husband that he does not love her anymore is not merely expressing her feelings. She is scripting and participating in an intensely involving experience. As she accuses, she *experiences* the misfortune she is portraying. She feels the emptiness and the terrible injustice of it all. While her accusation is aimed at her husband, it afflicts her as well, leaving her as injured by it as he is. The more she repeats it and the more convincingly, the more she wounds herself with her message.

Why so much anger? Women often feel that their husbands do not really hear them until they get really mad.

Overblown accusations create a vicious cycle that is self-maintaining. We feel unfairly treated, we express our grievances as overblown accusations, we believe our own propaganda, we feel more mistreated and more deeply injured than ever, we become angrier, and so on. By strengthening its sense of justification, angry accusation fans its own flames.

The Gottman research finds that women tend to escalate arguments while men try to defuse them.[10] So women are more apt to use overblown accusations, be taken in by their own propaganda, and feel yet more justified. Many men cannot even follow the points of the arguments. In angry confrontations, women tend to feel justified while men get confused.

We use "always" or "never" in an argument because these words seem to make an accusation stronger, more forceful, and more final. One who *always* does something is obviously the culprit and has no leeway to squirm out of it by claiming that it was just a few times, or inadvertent, or not very important. Yet the *always* or *never* words usually make an argument weaker, not stronger. Since these accusations are usually not true—or not completely true—your mate can easily dismiss them as simply false, overlooking the important issues contained within. Because they are unfair, overblown accusations offend, generating counter-accusation (instead of understanding) and resistance (instead of cooperation). It would not help to be more clever, more forceful, or more persistent. You need to be more fair.

Perhaps the best way to moderate anger is to gain a clearer and fairer sense of the grievances that produce it.

♀ ♂ Try to state your grievances carefully and fairly, without exaggeration. In doing so, you do not weaken your position but make it stronger and more credible. You might also try to balance your own concerns with those of your mate, which makes it more likely that you will be heard.

Instead of saying "You never talk to me," say "I realize that you do talk to me, and I appreciate it, but it has been a while. Could we spend some time together and just talk?" Your more civilized request is likely to get a much more civilized response.

When you are careful with the truth, you also clarify your own thinking. You rebalance the mental scales that you use to weigh your relationship. You come to see your grievances for what they are—sometimes important but not the catastrophes you were blowing them up to be.

Those who make the most outrageous accusations may have trouble making the simplest and most reasonable requests. They may feel they should not complain about small matters, so they reach too far and make everything all too important. Lacking confidence in amateur boxing, they take up nuclear weapons.

♀♂ Are you able to state your position, and argue for it, simply because you want your way or feel strongly about something? Or must you turn it into an intolerable injustice before you can say anything? Better to stay with the simpler issues and argue them with confidence.

Can you argue on your own, or must you call forth your anger to argue for you? Better to argue it yourself. Anger is an overzealous ally that stirs up more trouble than it is worth.

Overblown accusation can slide easily into paranoid accusation. Feeling mistreated, we blame someone for *wanting* to hurt us and doing so on purpose. Sound familiar? He works late without calling and shows up late for dinner. She is worried and upset. She says, "Why do you want to hurt me like this?" He may be working late to get ahead, and maybe because he dreads going home as well. But men do not work late for the explicit purpose of upsetting their wives. By personalizing the offense, she makes her grievance more forceful.

UNDERSTANDING AN
OVERBLOWN ACCUSATION

We usually object to an exaggerated accusation and argue against it.

SHE: You are always late!

HE: I am not *always* late. You are being ridiculous!

She does not recognize that by exaggerating, she has made her case false. He does not recognize she has said anything that is true or worth saying. She can do better, of course, but he can too!

♀♂ When you answer an accusation, even an overblown one, it is important to address the actual feelings. So when your partner gripes that you are always late, try to overlook the "always" and focus instead on the legitimate concern.

"Well surely not *always*," you might say, "but you are saying that I am frequently late, which is so. And that it bothers you. Let me think about it for a moment and figure out why I am having trouble being on time."

People tend to repeat themselves until they feel understood. By hearing the message, you lower the pressure your partner feels to continue forcing it upon you. You may move past the accusation and go on to negotiate and perhaps resolve the concern.

COMPASSION

Romanticism involves seeing the best in your partner and cherishing your idealized image. Compassion lets us see someone as he or she really is and love him or her in spite of the flaws—or perhaps even more so because of them. You can be infatuated with someone and love your idealized vision, without really knowing that person at all. But it takes compassion to listen, gently and without judgment, until you truly understand someone. Over time, it is the amount of compassion rather than the romantic flavoring that makes or breaks a marriage. We tend to focus on the wonderful qualities when we fall in love, but each of us has our shadow sides as well. We do well to push past our idealized images and learn to love the whole package. White bread looks fine, but the whole grain has more substance.

PART FIVE

Where To from Here?

A NY PLANS FOR social progress must take human
nature into account. Those who try to create utopias
but ignore human nature have produced not better
societies, but chaotic relationships and the occasional totali-
tarian nightmare. We do best to understand human nature
and make allowances for it, so that we can take advantage of
our recurring qualities instead of being ambushed by them.

Gender surely influences the organization and fabric of
any human society. We look next at how gender contributes
to our moral values, our work relationships, our culture, and
our very understanding of ourselves.

CHAPTER ELEVEN

Surprisingly Chivalrous

W E SO NATURALLY expect that men *should* support women that it operates almost invisibly, in the background, as a standard for moral judgments. Sure that men should support women, we are quick to judge men who fail to meet their responsibilities or who harm women. Those who act improperly are called "cads," "rakes," "jerks," "animals," "bums," "scum," and more recently, "sexists" and "chauvinists." But what do we call men who act as they should? "Gentlemen," perhaps? Or, "good men"? What do we call the arrangement by which men ordinarily support and protect women? The word that comes closest seems to be *chivalry,* which refers not just to the quaint customs of medieval knights, but also to generosity and courtesy toward females. I use the term here in its broadest sense, for lack of a better word, to indicate a concern for the welfare of females and the tendencies of males to support females and to sacrifice for them.

EARLY ORIGINS

A LOOK AT lower animals suggests that human chivalry comes to us by way of our primate ancestors.

CHIVALRY AMID FAMINE

How do social animals apportion scarce resources? Investigators at the Calcutta Zoological Garden severely limited food rations for a mixed-sex troop of rhesus monkeys. Given that male monkeys are larger than females and more often violent, what would you expect? The male monkeys are surely strong enough to shove the females aside and hoard the food themselves. Yet the males did not use their strength against the females. Rather, it was the younger male monkeys who lost weight, so much so that two adolescent males almost starved and had to be removed from the troop and rehabilitated.[1] It seems that when vital interests clash, females and ranking males feed while lesser males starve and must eventually die.

At Rutgers University, mixed-sex colonies of rats were underfed and then given food where only one could eat at a time. Adult male rats are about 30 percent larger than the females, stronger, and more aggressive. So again, you might expect the stronger males to dominate these scarce resources. Yet the females got an equal share and more. In four separate colonies, the females monopolized the feeder almost 60 percent of the time.[2] Milk chocolates, considered a special treat, were eaten by females in fifty-six of eighty trials, or 70 percent of the time.[3] Such findings are startling, indicating not just parity between stronger males and weaker females, but the subordination of male survival to female survival.

We do not ordinarily judge animal behavior as either moral or immoral. Animals simply act as nature programs them to act. Yet were these human societies, a similar bent to sacrifice males so that females can survive would be considered chivalrous. Clearly, in understanding competition for food among these hungry animals, *chivalry is more important than size, brute strength, or general aggressiveness.*

So too in human communities that face starvation. Perhaps the most famous is the Donner party, which set out across the Sierra Nevada mountain range in October of 1846, headed for California. Stranded by unexpected snows, these pioneers passed the entire winter together, exhausting food supplies and eventually resorting to cannibalism. Of the eighty-two pioneers trapped in the snows, thirty-five died of starvation and hypothermia.[4] All but one of the first fourteen to die were vigorous adult men, who had exhausted themselves wrestling the wagons across the mountains and managing the more strenuous tasks.[5] In all, 52 percent of the males died (twenty-five of forty-eight), compared to 29 percent of the females (ten of thirty-four). Girls and younger women fared the best. Of the nineteen females in the party aged five to thirty-nine, all but one survived. Even if rations were evenly distributed, the men did not take enough food to compensate for their harder workloads and higher susceptibility to the cold.

Pioneer girl Laura Ingalls writes of a terrible winter with provisions running out and the family near starvation.[6]

"Pa," facing demanding physical labor and losing weight, insisted that the others share the food. This should not surprise anyone. Any community may have a few scoundrels. But the normal man does not hoard the provisions while his wife and children go without. Where survival is concerned, a chivalrous attitude toward females seems to be embedded in humans as well as in other animals.

It has been argued that more women die in famines because men can use their strength to monopolize the resources.[7] We might imagine an odd tribe somewhere, ten thousand years ago, in which the men freely hoard as much food as they can eat and the women and children subsist on the table scraps. Inevitably, when food runs low, the men eat everything and the women and children starve, leaving our imaginary tribe with no next generation. Among our actual ancestors, men surely supported their women and children, which is why they are ancestors and not the last of a now extinct race.

Male chivalry protects females, but at a price. *The same inhibitions that cause males to concede rather than shove females aside for food also cause men to withdraw emotionally rather than argue with women who are upset with them.*

MALES FIGHT MALES

Most of us have seen pictures of bucks locking horns in life and death struggles for dominance, and so naturally assume that the males dominate everyone. To reconcile the observations, we must look at the pattern of male aggression. *Males who aggress usually do so selectively, not against females but against other males, to maintain their territory and for sexual access to the females.* Males fight other males. The bucks fight against other bucks but not against the doe, who graze contentedly and then mate with the winners. So while we observe that males are usually dominant in social animals, we must recognize that it is other males that are being dominated, more than the females.

A roughly similar pattern is seen in human society, although it is not as tight as we might wish. Men are more aggressive, but the most severe male aggression is against other men. In fatal confrontations, three-quarters of those killed by men are other men.[8]

Feminist writers have objected to parallels between animals and humans, concerned that male domination among lower animals could be used to justify continued male domination in our own society. Observations that females often dominate take us away from those earlier concerns and on to challenging new concerns.

Of course, male conduct often goes beyond simple acquiescence. Males actively support females in numerous animal species in addition to our own. Dolphins identify a pregnant female by sonar, and will swarm around her to protect her from possible predators. If a pregnant woman swims with them, these mammals cluster around her and ignore anyone else in the water.

MALE COMPETITION
AND FEMALE CHOICE

Why are males programmed to concede to females where vital interests are concerned? Male acquiescence might be considered generous, and perhaps it is, but its origins lie in the brutalities of genetic selection. Look at an evolutionary explanation.

Males who assault females and hoard vital provisions would seriously imperil the next generation of offspring, thereby harming their own genetic interests. In competitive situations, the stronger males prevail at the expense of weaker males, but *the dominant males cannot benefit genetically by harming the females*. Indeed, dominant males benefit instead by supporting the females, preventing peripheral males from taking their food. Obviously, the females must survive to carry the dominant male genes into the next generation, while the peripheral males are irrelevant.

Among lions, a reigning male may claim the kill for himself, which is decidedly unchivalrous. But it is the adolescent males he chases off and banishes from the pride, while the females remain and benefit from the association.

Most groups of mammals have more than one eligible male, giving females a say in which males mate and which are rejected. Female choice of mates is apparent among many species of birds and mammals, including most primates.[9] Among chimpanzees, for example, lower ranking males are observed to give way to females during feeding, to win their cooperation later for clandestine matings.[10] A young male monkey who pushes a female aside and steals her food is not going to be her first choice for a mate.

So regardless of whether males or females control mating, male genes benefit from supporting females. A dominant male benefits by favoring reproducing females over subordinate males, while an average male benefits by supporting females who might choose him as a mate.

Recall that among chimpanzees, male chimps ordinarily have higher rank than females, but nonetheless give way in squabbles over food. Male genes gain from higher status, more so than female genes, so the males fight harder for respect.[11] But when vital interests are concerned, these same males defer to the females, whom they must rely upon to propagate their genes.

In our own species, as we shall see, men generally support women and try to protect them against rogue men who would harm them. A typical man tries to provide well for his wife and family.

DAMSELS IN DISTRESS

One of the most wickedly effective pick-up lines I have heard plays upon chivalrous sympathies. A woman walks up to an interesting man, takes his arm, and asks for his protection: "There's a fellow following me who I'm trying to lose. Act like you know me, and just talk to me for a few minutes, will you? I'd be ever so grateful." My guess is that it does the job just about every time. She casts her pick as a real man who can protect a woman who prefers him to another man. He feels like her champion and hero, and she takes it from there.

Note that the ruse does not work with the genders reversed. Imagine that a man walks up to an interesting woman, takes her arm, and runs the same line on her: "There's a woman following me who I'm trying to lose. Act like you know me, and just talk to me for a few minutes, will you? I'd be ever so grateful." He thus casts himself as a lowly cad, who gets involved with a woman and then tries to lose her. What woman would feel an overwhelming urge to protect him from his mistakes?

Chivalry compels men to support women, to champion their causes, to uphold their honor, and to protect them against other men who might harm them. Interestingly, something similar is seen among chimpanzees.

In one incident, a threatened female chimp called upon a male friend for assistance. Using high-pitched barks, she pointed toward her assailant with her whole hand (rather than just a finger), at the same time kissing her friend and patting him. As her pleas became more insistent, he charged out to battle her antagonist, while she stood by and watched approvingly.[12] Thus another damsel in distress is rescued, and her champion becomes the hero of the hour.

Ordinarily, the male chimp who protects a female can gain opportunities to mate with her later, while one who refuses his support will also be remembered and treated accordingly. The same applies to humans. Men who uphold women against offending men gain their respect, and perhaps their favors, while men who ignore women lose out. So nature programs men to support women in distress, and to battle against men who threaten women. While men are stronger physically, women who enlist men as allies can be every bit as formidable.

THE CHIVALROUS MONEY TRANSFER

Over the ages, women who were busy tending to children did not have as many opportunities as men to forage for provisions. Men whose production went to support their wives and children surely provided a survival advantage over men who did not, especially in the colder climates. In today's society, where do the resources go?

Overall, it appears that men and women share equally in the material benefits of Western society. Men work considerably more hours outside the home and earn about twice as much money as women.[13] Yet much of their earnings goes to support their wives and families. Would it surprise you that in several areas where figures allow comparisons, more of the resources go to women?

The *Statistical Abstract of the United States* notes that about 50 percent more is spent for apparel and services for women, such as clothes and hair care, as is spent for men.[14]

A similar pattern is seen in health care. While the medical establishment is often criticized as sexist and unfair to women, the overall figures present a more sympathetic picture. Women consume about two-thirds of the health care dollar—receiving twice as much medical care as men.[15] I see the same pattern in mental health services. About two-thirds of those who seek psychotherapy are women—not because women are worse off but because women tend to be more comfortable asking for help.[16] The government spends about twice as much to research female-only diseases such as breast cancer, as male-only diseases such as prostrate cancer.[17] A similar pattern appears in retirement benefits. Men as a group pay twice as much into Social Security,[18] while women live six or seven years longer on average and receive about 50 percent more than men in total benefits.[19] Overall, the figures suggest that women gain considerably from the resources men provide (as men gain obviously from the companionship and families that women provide).

Most people assume that women as a group are worse off financially than men, and so find these figures astonishing. This too can be explained. Men do not always support women out of the simple goodness of their hearts. Women complain to pressure men to provide for them. The squeaky wheel gets the oil, and the female wheels are more vocal than the male wheels. Women thus publicize their own grievances more often and more vigorously, creating the *impression* that women are worse off than men. So the same social pressure mechanism that transfers financial benefits from men to women also causes us to misunderstand our economic arrangements. *The illusion that women are worse off is an integral component of the transfer arrangement:*

shaming men to continue providing. Would it be possible for women to acknowledge that women are as well off as men, and then still to push men to provide better? It would be a much harder sell.

Some women are quite poor, of course, especially unmarried women with children. Of the truly destitute—the homeless—about 85 percent are males, only 15 percent are females.[20] Yet we are normally more concerned about homeless women than homeless men. Homeless women remind us that we are failing to provide for our women, whereas homeless men are considered losers who are presumably responsible for their own sad fates.

These resource allocation figures resemble those seen in rat colonies, where the females consume somewhat more of the resources than the males. Our homeless figures resemble the pattern found among rhesus monkeys, where females and positioned males eat while the marginal males starve. With regard to how we allocate resources, our human community looks suspiciously similar to bands of lower animals. The difference is that lower animals presumably are not aware of resource allocation by sex, whereas we have the mental capacity to be aware of our arrangements but are programmed to misunderstand them.

You may know of at least a few men who are total bums—drinking beer, watching television, and collecting dust, while their wives support the family and clean up after them. Our near-universal attitude of contempt toward such men sets them apart as examples of what men should *not* be. You may also know of a similar number of women who do not work or raise children, who watch television or shop all day, while their husbands work hard to support them. We usually accept the attractive woman who finds a rich man to support her, while we are uncomfortable indeed with the smooth man who lives off a rich woman.

The question of exactly how men and women share in our financial resources will not be answered anytime soon. My point here is merely that we transfer to women a considerable share of what men produce. So in spite of feminist ideologies that argue otherwise, men continue to materially support women.

♀ Those who take it all for granted should recognize how much you rely upon men for so much of your standard of living.

♂ Those who are beginning to feel irrelevant should recognize that men continue to support women and that it would not be done without you. Take satisfaction in how much you contribute.

WOMEN COMMAND OUR SYMPATHIES

CHIVALRY SHOWS up not just in our conduct, but in our moral sympathies as well.

MEN USING WOMEN

A man who continually berates his wife is misusing his power, and we want to stop him. Most of us would judge him a bully and a verbal batterer. Were I her brother or her father, and not a sensitive psychologist, I might take him aside, tell him that I expect him to straighten up, and let him know I mean business. Family and close friends might try to talk the woman into leaving him, and help her if she is willing to go.

Now switch it around. What about the woman who continually berates her husband and adds to his stress? She can make us uncomfortable, but we are not so sure about him, either. What did he do to make her so upset? Is he not treating her right? Anyway, what is he—a wimp? Real men are expected to take care of themselves and to take care of their wives as well. How many of us would jump in on his side and argue his case against his upset wife? Surely not many. How many would try to get him to leave her? Again, not many. See the contrast? We feel we ought to protect women from men, while we expect men to take care of themselves (or lose out).

Complaints that men mistreat women arouse our moral sympathies, while complaints that women mistreat men are considered whining. We are morally outraged by men who are cruel to women, but we tend to stay out of it when women are cruel to men.

Traditionally, in most cultures, a woman seeks a commitment in a sexual relationship. And if she does not or cannot get it, her family and friends stand ready to help her. Emotions run high. We are outraged by the man who sleeps with a woman but refuses to commit, especially when she is upset about it. He is using her, and we want him to shoulder his responsibilities or be gone.

Family and friends can be more concerned than the woman is herself. Interested parties may try to convince her to leave the jerk while she complains about him but stays because she has feelings for him. The woman who cannot get a commitment is being exploited, and if she willingly goes along with it she is allowing herself to be exploited. Note the asymmetry here. The man who cannot get a commitment from his lover is not a moral concern. We may feel sorry for him, but so what? We see males as exploiting females sexually and not the other way around, regardless of which partner refuses to commit.

Our sympathies go with upset females, who must be supported whenever children might be conceived. These same sympathies persist even when no children are expected, suggesting assistance from our genes.

The norm among human cultures is for men to support women and children, and families without men are at a comparative disadvantage. So to be competitive, nature and culture must yoke the wills of the men to the interests of their mates, their offspring, and the broader communities.

SELECTION OF CHIVALROUS SYMPATHIES

It seems reasonable to be concerned about men using women, while it would be odd indeed to crusade against women using men. However commonsensical, we should still ask the obvious question: What makes us feel this way? Why should we be more concerned about protecting women from men than protecting men from women?

Family considerations undoubtedly contribute. Just as a boy who marries a girl and stays to raise their children thereby benefits her family genes, a boy who impregnates a girl but fails to provide has exploited the resource and cheated her family out of the necessary assistance. A pregnant girl may fall back on her family, but she thereby stretches their resources and reduces their competitive advantage. So parents, siblings, and the whole clan have a genetic interest in a daughter being treated properly. The family wants to see that any boy who is with their daughter is good to her and can be counted upon to support her. The cost of taking advantage of a girl can be severe. The anthropological archives contain ample instances of fathers or brothers who slay a false suitor who betrays a daughter or sister.[21]

Families are not so concerned about a son who has a casual romantic adventure. He is just sowing some wild oats. *Male genes can benefit from casual liaisons as well as from committed ones.* Nor is the family always so concerned about whether the girl is treating him like a prince or not. It is better that a son be with *some* girl, even if she is mean to him, than with no girl at all. Any girl can transport the family genes into the next generation.

So the inclination to protect our women from bad men provides a genetic advantage, whereas protecting our men from bad women would be genetic folly. By selecting those sensitivities that promote our genes, nature programs us to be outraged by men exploiting women but not by women exploiting men.

The traditional double standard that allows casual sex for males but not for females applies only to those within your clan. For outsiders, it reverses itself. That is, the double standard allows a girl from elsewhere to have casual sex with a son, but stands adamantly against a boy from elsewhere who wants casual sex with a daughter. I would hardly accept the young man who rings my doorbell, shakes my hand, smiles, and says, "Hello, Mr. Driscoll. I'm here to have recreational sex with your daughter." How many fathers would?

Chivalrous sympathies can provide additional genetic benefits. A man who stands up for a mistreated woman against her husband may gain favor with her or with her women friends, any of whom can transport his chivalrous genes into the next generation. A man who stands up for a mistreated man against his wife can lose favor among her women friends, reducing his chances of mating and imperiling his genetic future. Men are programmed to avoid such huge genetic risks. Women who stand together also set the standards of conduct for their communities, thereby protecting themselves.

Today, with modern birth control, many accept when a woman friend sleeps with her lover or even lives with him, so long as she is content with the arrangement. The moment she is upset with him and complains, she triggers our chivalrous programming. We are outraged, and we want to help her get rid of the jerk.

The implication is that our natural human concern for the welfare of females is not a haphazard social convention that could just as easily have been otherwise. It is not as if the founding forefathers wrote into the constitution that men should support and protect women instead of the other way around, and we have acted that way ever since. Our concern for females goes much deeper. It resides in our innate natures, and surges up when females are mistreated or distressed.

Chivalrous sympathies guide gender socialization as well. We expect men to be dominant, but we feel men *ought* to support and protect women rather than fight against them. So at least in that sense, the man who defers to his wife rather than fighting against her is doing what he ought to do.

In *The Moral Animal,* political scientist Robert Wright argues that evolution shapes not only our actions but our feelings and moral sympathies as well.[22] Our sympathies are programmed not for any abstract notion of fairness, of course, but for the survival and propagation of our genes. We see here how *genetic selection sensitizes us to men mistreating women but leaves us oblivious to women mistreating men.*

MEN TAKE THE RISKS

WE NOW admire plucky women who work in macho fields, as undercover police officers or jet-fighter pilots, but we are all more comfortable when men take the actual risks so that women remain safe. Recent figures show that *94 percent of on the job fatalities are men, while only 6 percent are women.*[23] Even adjusting for more men working than women, that is almost a 10-to-1 ratio of male-to-female fatalities.

Men are much more willing to take risks than women, in our own culture and around the globe.[24] And we all expect men to face the sorts of job hazards that we would be unwilling to push upon women. Chivalry is also evident in our unquestioned acceptance of these practices. Would any of us want to argue that women should take more of the perilous jobs so that men might be safer? I have not heard any women argue for equal risks, and it would be hard to respect any man who is foolish enough to argue for it. *We see human nature not just in those positions we argue, but also in those positions that are so solidly accepted that it makes no sense to argue either for them or against them.* We feel so strongly that men should sacrifice themselves to protect women that it would be literally unthinkable to turn the arrangement around.

WHY MEN SACRIFICE

Why do we feel so strongly that men should take risks? Life for our ancestors was often perilous, and men frequently risked their lives to hunt game,[25] battle nature, and battle other men. Men favor comrades who share the sacrifice, and demote or exclude those who do not. Women also favor men who are willing to sacrifice for them, now as always. As a result, courageous men tend to mate and pass along chivalrous traits, while known cowards lose out. Even a man who is injured or dies in action might gain honor among his clansmen, who would continue to support his family.

In contrast, women would gain no genetic advantage by risking their lives for men, and, therefore, are little inclined to do so. Women sacrifice themselves to protect their children, which is in their genetic interest. So the simple process of genetic selection, working over millions of years, accounts for why men risk their lives for women and not the other way around.[26]

WAR IS A GUY THING

Military battle surely involves more injury and death than any other human activity. We might assume that soldiers have traditionally been male because men have the superior upper-body strength that combat requires. But there is more to it. Men risk everything in warfare, but can gain from it as well. Traditionally, those men who won battles acquired more territory and also gained access to additional women, whereas the losers were subjugated or killed. Among women, the reproductive consequences of warfare were smaller. Women who won could gain only marginally, while those who stayed out of it might nonetheless mate with the victorious men and bear children. So warfare is more important to men's genes than to women's genes. It is reasonable to assume that men acquired more upper-body strength than women because men with superior strength benefited in combat with other men, while the weaker men lost out.

Warfare occurs among our chimpanzee cousins. Groups of male chimpanzees have been observed to form raiding parties, intruding into adjacent territories and killing the neighboring male chimps, thereby gaining the territory and access to the females as well.[27]

In modern warfare, physical strength and aggressiveness are not the principal features of a good soldier. Strength is an obvious asset, but it has not been as critical since firearms leveled the playing field. Most adults could learn to fire an assault rifle or drive a jeep through a barrage of exploding shells. The essential quality is the willingness to submit to military authority, out of honor and loyalty to comrades. *A soldier must be willing to follow battlefield orders at the risk of being shot up, blown apart, incinerated, gassed, drowned, speared, stabbed, stoned, or bludgeoned to death.* Soldiers are men because men can be trained to sacrifice themselves in ways we would ordinarily not expect of women.

Today, where America has vastly superior weaponry and no significant opposition, women can function well in military command and operations. Were we ever again to expect brutal battlefield casualties, we would surely rotate the women to safer areas of service. Women want the choice to serve, but even the most militant feminists won't argue that women should be conscripted and *forced* to fight and die, as men often are.

Egalitarian ideals sent Israeli and Soviet women into combat in the 1940s, but neither nation had the stomach to continue sending women to their deaths.[28] So far as I know, no human community regularly sacrifices its women to its enemies as long as it has men available to sacrifice instead.

WHY MEN RISK THEIR FORTUNES

Men tend to love risky adventures, more so than women. The upside is that men excel as inventors, explorers, entrepreneurs, and industrialists. The downside is that the idiot who plays the horses and gambles away the family savings is almost always a man. Asked why gamblers are almost always men, feminist Gloria Steinem suggested that a woman who marries takes a big enough gamble to last her the rest of her life. Yet a man also gambles when he marries, for it is through his wife and family that he gains his emotional bearings.

Try another explanation. Across the ages, the man who gambled and won might gain access to several women—through sanctioned polygyny or unsanctioned trysts—spreading his gambling inclinations to many offspring. A female who gambled and won could only slightly improve her progeny, while a loss would be as catastrophic for her as it would be for a man. So nature rewards male genes for taking risks, more than female genes.

Men take more risks than women not just in Western culture, but in every culture observed anywhere in the world.[29] Risk is a guy thing.

PHYSICAL CONFRONTATION

MEN ARE not always chivalrous, of course. We look next at some of the harsher aspects of gender confrontation.

BATTERING

Physical battering does not occur in your typical marriage, surely, and most of us can be thankful that we will never experience it. But it does occur. Figures vary widely, but 11 to 12 percent of men physically confront their wives, according to one of the better surveys by researchers Murray Straus and Richard Gelles.[30] About 3 to 4 percent of these are seriously aggressive acts, such as punching or biting, while the rest are more ordinary acts such as grabbing, pushing, or slapping. The *most* serious offenses, in which a man beats, chokes, threatens, or actually attacks with a weapon, occur in less than 1 percent of relationships.[31]

Men who batter tend not to be your normal, average citizens. A check against police records revealed that almost 80 percent of those subject to restraining orders had criminal records, and almost half had prior convictions for multiple assaults against other men as well as women.[32]

Now the oddly surprising findings: Women physically assault their husbands just as often, according to these same surveys, often using physical implements but causing less serious injury. A review of the more than thirty available studies reveals that *all* find about as many women as men who physically assault their mates.[33, 34] So 11 to 12 percent of women physically confront their husbands, with 3 to 4 percent being seriously aggressive.

We hear little about women hitting men. Battered husbands are more deeply shamed by being battered, and file police complaints only one-twelfth as often as do battered wives.[35] Some people who read about women assaulting their mates choose not to believe it. Some object to the mere mention of these figures, considering them highly offensive without knowing quite why. *A man hitting a woman is a moral abomination, while a woman hitting a man seems more a lapse of proper manners or an awkward joke.* If the figures offend, it is because they can dilute our outrage about men hitting women by noting that women sometimes hit too.

It is human nature to hold men responsible, whether they are the ones doing the hitting or they have simply allowed things to get so out of hand that their wives hit them. When a man gets hit, we may think, "What did he do to her?" or, "Did he strike her first?" Yet women who hit their mates are found to have similar motives as men,[36] usually striking from intense anger or rage and on impulse. We are not normally too concerned about battered husbands, and few take it seriously.[37] It is hard to be as outraged about a woman hitting the man, even when the injury is the same.

Counting assaults from either partner, some 16 percent of couples report some physical conflict, with 6 percent of these being more severe incidents. The figures suggest that *only* men hit in a quarter of these cases, *only* women hit in a quarter, and in the remaining half of the cases physical confrontation *goes both ways.*[38]

Severe injury occurs infrequently and estimates are harder to attain.[39] One-quarter of 1 percent of the married women in the Straus and Gelles survey reported needing medical care for a domestic injury,[40] and fewer men than women required medical attention.[41] So overall, as many as fifty couples engage in some form of physical confrontation for every injury requiring medical attention.[42] Why so many physical confrontations compared to relatively few serious injuries? Most men who physically confront control their strength, and most women are not strong enough to injure, and do not intend to anyway. Most of the men and women who physically confront each other do so to underscore an argument and to get their way, like quarreling siblings, and not to eliminate the opponent.

Unfortunately, a few *are* trying to eliminate the opponent. At the extreme fringe of what might euphemistically be called "marital misconduct," women murder their husbands or have them murdered about three-quarters as often as men murder their wives.[43] So even here, in the meanest and ugliest aspects of troubled relationships, we see something close to a balance between the sexes.

CRIME AND PUNISHMENT

Governments occasionally conduct surveys to find out how seriously we consider various crimes, to help set appropriate punishments. A U.S. Department of Justice survey finds that Americans rate a wife stabbing her husband to death as 40 percent less severe than a husband stabbing his wife to death.[44] Any murder is immoral, of course. Yet we consider it more understandable when women murder men, but totally abhorrent when men murder women.

Chivalrous sympathies also influence formal punishment. Figures compiled by Warren Farrell show that women offenders serve about half as much time in prison as do men who commit the same violations.[45] Compared to men, women are given probation more often. When they are incarcerated, they receive shorter sentences and serve less of their sentences before being paroled. Women who murder are only one-twentieth as likely to be sentenced to death as are men who murder.[46] The emotional reasons are understandable. Our natural inclination to protect women curbs our inclination to punish them. Even moderate feminists, such as Carol Tavris, argue that women are punished too severely and deserve more consideration.[47] And to many, the argument *feels* right. The law may be written evenly, but our chivalrous feelings guide its administration.

Our inclination to punish males more harshly applies to children as well. Faced with equally disruptive behavior from boys and girls, teachers are three times as likely to reprimand the boys as girls.[48] And boys are more often reprimanded in a harsh and public manner and receive heavier penalties, while girls get softer reprimands in private and lighter penalties.

The issue is perplexing. We have an *abstract* moral standard that says that all of us should be treated the same, and also an *innate* moral standard that wants us to support women and hold men accountable. Perhaps the heavens see equal worth in the souls of men and women, and judge it just as wrong, therefore, to harm one as to harm the other. But as human beings, we operate within the moral standards nature has programmed into us.

WOMEN COMMAND
OUR ATTENTION

CHIVALRY INFLUENCES not just our feelings and actions, but also what we think and say about men and women. Women who are mistreated feel justified in airing their grievances, while men mistreated by women feel inadequate and ordinarily keep it to themselves. Women are more openly critical toward men, as we have seen, than men are toward women.

The imbalance in the number of complaints voiced by men and women biases our impressions. Take the widespread belief that women usually do more of the work overall while men watch more TV. I often hear about women who have jobs outside the home and then do a second shift of housework and childcare while their husbands watch football. So I, too, naturally assumed women are busier. A University of Maryland study tracked over five thousand Americans and found that we have about equal free time—men have forty-one hours of free time a week and women have forty hours.[49] A University of Michigan study, looking at jobs, commuting, childcare, housework, and yard work, found that the average husband works sixty-one hours per week while wives average fifty-six hours.[50] With these findings in mind, I can think of any number of men I know who work all the time, while their wives have more manageable schedules. So it balances out. The number of women who are busier than their husbands about equals the number of men who are busier than their wives. We acquire a biased impression because women who hold jobs and do the housework complain about how unfair it is, and publicize their grievances,[51] while overworked men seldom complain about it. It may be little consolation for those women who do more than their fair share, but the findings do show a balance between the sexes.

In arguments over who is being unfair to whom—which is what most marital arguments are about—those who are more comfortable with conflict have an advantage. Typically, a woman accuses first and argues longer and more forcefully. Some men can argue as well as women, but most men try to avoid offending and withdraw in the face of female accusation. *So women's concerns command our attention because women are stronger at presenting their concerns.* And women who complain evoke sympathy, while men who complain about women appear weak or crass and totally unsympathetic. So women's concerns command our attention because we are normally more sympathetic toward mistreated women.

> *A man defending husbands vs. wives or men vs. women*
> *has got about as much chance as a traffic policeman*
> *trying to stop a mad dog by blowing two whistles.*
> —RING LARDNER

We should note our normal emotional reactions and then try to step outside of them. See our normal sympathies as a lens through which we ordinarily view gender. The lens magnifies some concerns, minimizes others, and distorts the relationship between men and women. We must recognize the lens, so we are not taken in by its familiar images. Only then can we look around it to see gender concerns clearly. Our clumsy emotional programming has not the vaguest chance of figuring it out on its own.

CHIVALROUS MISINFORMATION

Our moral sympathies also guide and distort public opinion. Sensational figures that purport to show women suffering from grievous mistreatment spread through the media and into the public consciousness. Christina Sommers in

Who Stole Feminism traces several major findings, from the original research through the misinterpretations and fabrications, showing how chivalrous sensitivities corrupt our understanding of ourselves.[52]

Although the better research finds that 3 to 4 percent of women are physically abused, the figures have been inflated to 7 percent or higher (4 million women or more) by broadening the criterion to include minor incidents in which one is "pushed, grabbed, shoved, or slapped." The larger figures were widely reported in the media, with no indication that they included contact that might sensibly be considered something less than abuse.[53] No mention is ever made that women physically confront men as often as men confront women.

A finding was widely reported that 37 percent of married women are "verbally or emotionally abused" by their husbands. What a startling indictment of men, and of marriage! Yet the 37 percent was attained by including any woman whose husband insulted or swore at her or stomped out during an argument, regardless of whether it occurred once or often, and regardless of whether she was insulting him at the time.[54] A better statement of the finding is that 37 percent of married women get into arguments with their husbands in which angry words are exchanged. Not such a startling story, is it?

Marital arguments usually go both ways or are dominated by women. So it would be just as logical to report that 37 percent of married men are verbally or emotionally abused by their wives. Of course, it could never happen. A tale of verbally abused wives triggers our chivalrous sympathies, whereas the same tale of verbally abused husbands is an awkward aberration. We see men as strong but not always good, while we see women as good but not always strong. A woeful tale of men being verbally abused by women turns everything wrongside out, and our emotions reject it.

Insofar as chivalrous standards govern media programming, the media not only mirrors our innate biases but amplifies them. The inside story is not simply that men mistreat women, which is the familiar story, but that shoddy treatment comes in many forms and most assuredly goes both ways. Unfortunately, it is shamefully easy to finagle the findings in order to tug at our heartstrings.

A widely publicized study by the American Association of University Women argues that schools are failing to meet girls' needs.[55] "When we shortchange girls," the AAUW warns, "we shortchange America." While the top boys get higher test scores in math and science than the top girls, a 1982 U.S. Department of Education study finds that girls outperform boys on average in *all* high school subjects, including math and science.[56] Almost twice as many girls as boys now participate in student government and belong to school honor societies.[57] The AAUW study notes that 80 percent of the high school girls and 71 percent of the boys say teachers think girls are smarter.[58] Of college and university students, 55 percent are female, 45 percent male.[59] So it would be just as easy to argue that schools are failing to meet boys' needs. But would anyone be interested?

Perhaps in one important respect, schools are failing the girls: With fewer boys attending college, educated young women who want to marry will face a critical shortage of educated young men.

A recent Gallup poll finds that 73 percent of Americans believe that society is biased in favor of men and against women.[60] The media reports stories of bias against women but not of bias against men, so our beliefs follow the programming. The media itself merely reflects our innate sensitivity to bias against women and our insensitivity to bias against men.

CHAPTER TWELVE

What Changes and What Stays the Same?

Plus ça change, plus c'est la même chose.
The more things change, the more they stay the same.

May you live in interesting times!
—ANCIENT CHINESE CURSE

SWEEPING CHANGES SEEM to be underway in gender relations, as material prosperity and reproductive choice allow women the freedom to limit their families and pursue career options. Our expectations of love and marriage are also changing. We look for personal fulfillment, more so than did earlier generations, who sought to fulfill their responsibilities and struggled simply to survive. We want more egalitarian relationships that allow us to be and do whatever we want, free from traditional gender patterns. We expect the best, but even the most wonderful expectations can lead to disillusionment and shattered relationships. We must make proper allowances for human nature.

In the midst of so many changes, some aspects of gender relations seem to remain constant regardless of social customs. To the extent that these reflect something inherent in human nature, we do well to take them seriously. Let's look at how gender qualities play out in modern society.

NATURE PROGRAMS US TO FOOL OURSELVES

EVEN IN our modern era of information overload, our gender expectations continue to be shaped as much by our innate programming as by observable reality. In instance after instance, what we *feel* is right and true stands at odds with what is found to be so by close observation. *Evolution has sensitized our minds and emotions in ways that we are only now beginning to understand.* By selecting for combative women and acquiescent men, evolution programs us to grossly misunderstand gender relationships.

Look at the proposition that men dominate women and always have. Why is it so often said and so seldom refuted? Men dominate in public affairs, of course, but in personal arguments women dominate while men withdraw. Women complain that men dominate women, to hold men responsible, while men acquiesce or even support the argument, to avoid confrontations. Thus, the myth that men dominate women prevails because women argue it, and women dominate in such arguments. Ironically, the myth prevails not because it is so, but because it is not so.

Yet the argument does convey a key feature of gender relations. We can agree that the dominant parties ought to be held responsible. So saying that men dominate women means that *men ought to be held responsible for what happens to women.* See this not as a statement of truth, but as a chivalrous moral position advocated by women and generally accepted by men as well.

The argument that men are more privileged and powerful serves a similar function. Men are more privileged and powerful in the important sense that men are freer to venture out into the world and produce what we need to survive and compete. The argument that men are more privileged supports the transfer of assets from the men who produce to the women who need the assets to survive.

WHY CLAIM TO BE OPPRESSED?

The same applies to the accusation that men oppress women and always have. Angry women claim that men oppress women, to shame men into concessions, while men acquiesce or withdraw in order to avoid confronting these angry women. Some men even support the argument, to win favor with the women.

Of course, men do not claim to be oppressed by women and never will. Women are programmed to identify mistreatment and to complain, and gain an advantage by doing so, whereas men are programmed to suppress complaints about women, to avoid losing face. We take complaints from women seriously, but not complaints by men. Could you even imagine reversing the argument? Suppose a man says that men are oppressed by women, in order to shame women into concessions. Instead of shaming women, he shames himself and sounds ridiculous. Women shun him, and men avoid being seen with him. Social propriety allows women to complain publicly about men, but censures men who complain openly about women.

Men have certain advantages in Western society, but women too have certain advantages. On the single most objective measure, resource allocation, men earn more money but women share in it about equally. Men dominate in public realms and women in personal realms. Our arrangements are surely too intricate and too complex to warrant a simplistic conclusion that one sex is oppressing the other.

BIOLOGY AND CULTURE

Some of the sex traits I attribute to our evolution have been traditionally attributed to socialization. It has been argued that males have higher libidos because society expects males to be more sexual, or because society represses female sexuality more than male sexuality. Social considerations do guide and control our actions in many ways, some obvious and others more subtle. But when a particular trait appears regularly throughout the multitude of human cultures and throughout the animal world as well, why try to pin it on social expectation? We would not argue that tomcats pursue female cats because we *expect* them to—even though we do expect them to. The argument is backward and unreasonable. We expect tomcats to pursue because we *see* them doing so, and they would do so regardless of whether or not we expect it of them. And so too with humans. We expect young men to be more interested in casual sex than young women, but they would be that way regardless of whether you or I or a professor at Harvard expected them to be.

Many sex traits involve some combination of nature and culture. Chivalry is social in that we feel men ought to support women and avoid harming them, and we apply social pressures and sanctions to compel men to act as we think they should. A father typically expects his youngsters to treat their mother with respect, and punishes them for upsetting her. Women favor men who treat them well, but condemn those who offend, as do family, friends, and society in general. Yet chivalry is also biological, in that evolution contributes to innate moral sympathies, which then find expression in cultural expectations.

The exact ways men and women broker power varies across cultures and from one era to another. But given that women are more comfortable in confrontations and are more sympathetic, their concerns must carry weight. Superiority in emotional combat is not a whim of our modern era, as if we could wink and make it otherwise. Women were more argumentative than men several generations ago, as the early research shows, and we have no reason to believe it was ever otherwise. And women are not apt to give up their natural power advantage any time soon.

The same applies to chivalrous sympathies. Our outrage against men mistreating women arises out of primal sensitivities programmed by our genes. Is there any society anywhere in which family and friends are more concerned about women using men than about men using women? I have never heard of one. Indeed, it would be hard to even imagine a culture in which family and friends struggle to protect males from sexually exploitative females instead of the other way around.

Evolution, as we have seen, accounts for a wide range of gender qualities that are not easily accounted for by strictly social explanations. It accounts for why men feel obligated to women, bond more strongly, and are more deeply troubled when relationships fail; and for why women appear more dependent, but are freer to leave a relationship. It accounts for why men do not reveal weaknesses and why women want men to open up and reveal weaknesses. It accounts for why women want to express their feelings while men want to fix whatever is wrong and be done with it. It accounts for why men are more competitive than women and why women gossip more and are quicker to take offense. It accounts for why women want communication and caresses before sex, while men want to get to the action as soon as possible. It accounts for why men want sex to reconnect after a quarrel and why women want to reconnect prior to sex.

Evolution provides good explanations for those gender traits that we expect and for those that we do not expect. It would take some clever finagling to try to account for all of this without considering natural selection, and I know of no serious attempt to do so. Surely, culture shapes who we are. But it should be clear by now that our inborn natures also guide our feelings and actions, and so must shape key features of any culture.

If we knew how important genes are,
we would be more careful about whom we let into ours.
—BOB WYRICK

HOW ADAPTABLE ARE WE?

AT ONE time or another, humankind has probably adapted to almost every condition imaginable. Amid the changes now underway in marriage and family relationships, we look here at which of these suit us and bring forth the best in us and which are hostile to our natures.

WHY WOMEN ARE LESS SATISFIED IN MARRIAGES

Many of the same men who panic about getting married later adjust to being married, and most men anchor their personal identity in marriage and family. Over and over, findings confirm that married men are substantially healthier and happier than are men who are unmarried, divorced, or widowed.[1] Women, more than men, question the marriage arrangement and wonder if the deal is as good as it should be. Marriage for many women is a decidedly mixed blessing, scattering its joys and struggles about evenly and conferring neither overall advantage nor handicap. So we arrive at an observation that is a personal concern for some and of wider social concern as well: *All studies agree that women are generally less satisfied with their marriages and family lives than are men.*[2] So women, who have traditionally made homes, are less satisfied living in them.

Why are wives less content than husbands? Ask any man or woman, married or unmarried, young or old, or any marriage therapist, clergyman, social scientist, journalist— or anyone else for that matter—and you will never find a shortage of answers. Yet the usual explanations fall in two general categories—either women are oppressed and suffer from subordinate status in marriages, or women do more work and are exhausted from overwork. Each explanation feels about right, but neither stands up to closer scrutiny. Women are considered subordinate to men, but we have seen how it all turns around when we look at who actually controls the arguments and who usually gives in. And while we hear that women do more than their share of the work, actual observations show that on average husbands work as much as wives. Women who hold jobs outside the home continue to do more of the housework and childcare than their husbands, which is unfair and should be corrected, but that does not really answer the question. Women with outside jobs are on average more satisfied with their marriages than are housewives, who tend to be more depressed[3] and more hostile toward their husbands than women who hold jobs.[4]

Try another explanation. Nature programs the woman, who traditionally required support, to continually question the man's love for her, to experience insecurity at any sign of wavering, and to be upset and find fault as a way of forcing the support she requires. *Insofar as nature commandeers her emotions to monitor his commitment, a woman has the more emotionally wearing job.* She may need a man to support her and her children, but nature has not required her to idealize him or to be wildly appreciative of him.

"When women are unhappy they usually think they need more love, but the objective evidence suggests that they need more independence," notes Francesca Cancian. When men are unhappy, in contrast, they usually think they need more success, but they need more time.[5] An unhappy woman may feel that her relationship is making her unhappy, and it is, but by fretting about it, she is also making herself unhappy. A few observations suggest how this works. I have seen more than one woman who was upset about a man who showed her too little attention, who then separated, and found herself reasonably content with no attention at all. It is not just that a woman needs more love from a man, for if that were so she would feel worse, not better, when she loses the little love she was getting. Her insecurities push for a stronger commitment, wearing her out, but she recovers when separation allows her a respite.

In recommending more independence, Francesca Cancian means that women need to be more comfortable with the imperfect relationships they have and to trust in their own survival with the man or, if necessary, without him. *Women do not need to push for more assurance of love as if their survival depended upon it, which only makes them unhappy with any relationship.*

Women may also be unintended casualties of our chivalrous natures and customs, which sympathize with women and uphold their complaints. A woman who *feels* she faces more than her fair share of the sacrifices is apt to be unhappy about it, regardless of how fairly or unfairly the sacrifices are actually shared. Questions of fairness are often a matter of opinion, of course, with few objective standards for comparison. Even when men and women participate in the same activities, we do not necessarily judge them the same. The same few rounds of quick sex might leave him feeling great and her feeling used. Yet the objective criteria available, such as hours worked or financial resources allocated, show men to be generally chivalrous and relationships to be reasonably fair.

Recognizing the balance might help women feel more appreciative toward their mates and toward men in general. Recognizing their own substantial contributions might help men feel more adequate about themselves and about their involvement with wife and family.

Women who are angry talk to friends about their feelings, more than angry men do,[6] and recent findings indicate that friends can influence our attitudes.[7] Talking to friends who uphold marriage can help you resolve conflicts and solidify commitments. Talking to companions who are critical of marriage can leave you more distressed and more distant from your husband. As the traditional cultural support for marriages weakens, social opinion can and will contribute to additional dissatisfactions with marriage.

♀ Choose carefully whom you talk to about your personal concerns, so that you might benefit from your friends and gain balance instead of being swept along by a current of resentment. If you have acquaintances who are hostile toward relationships, realize they can sour you to your own relationship.

WHAT ABOUT PATRIARCHY?

Traditionally, men have been considered the heads of households, in what might today be considered a sexist arrangement. But look beyond the appearances and consider the real power differences. In arguments, when interests conflict, women usually dominate while men defer, placate, or withdraw. So, to the extent that men appear dominant, we can figure it is because women allow them to appear that way. Look at why. Traditionally, the man was expected to commit himself to the support of his wife and children. In return, so far as he upheld his responsibilities, he was honored as the head of the family. See the trade-off? In exchange for supporting his wife, doing what she and the children require of him, deferring to her when she is upset with him, and losing when he tries to argue against her, he was honored as the head of the family. Such arrangements have benefits for each spouse. He gets the honor, and she benefits from his support. So the supposedly patriarchal arrangement benefits women at least as much as men.

In marriages in which the woman openly heads the family, where is the trade-off? She is officially in charge, and she wields the covert emotional power as well, leaving him with no respect and no voice. What is in it for him? Or for her, since she has no reason to respect him?

View patriarchy as an artfully crafted but fragile arrangement, honoring men who stay and support their families, and thus encouraging them to do so. The advantage is intact marriages, holding men and women together for their mutual benefit and for the benefit of the children. The traditional Christian support for men as heads of households would seem to help balance intimate relationships, upholding men who stay involved and contribute.

A ream of research finds that marriages in which husbands and wives participate equally are the most satisfying, supporting our egalitarian ideals. Wife-dominated marriages are the least satisfying, and husband-dominated are in the middle.[8] That is, marriages in which women openly dominate their husbands tend to be more troubled and less fulfilling than those in which men appear to dominate. Men do not find wife-dominated marriages satisfying, which should be obvious, but women do not find them satisfying either.

♀♂ So strive for equal participation. But if you must err, and want to survive, it might be better to err on the side of men talking slightly more and women listening more.

In the traditional Western wedding, the bride promised to "love, honor, and obey." The time when women were expected to obey is long gone—as if the average man was ever able to command his more volatile wife to obey him if she did not want to do so. But what about the honor? In the rebellion against patriarchy, that too is being lost. Honor confers respect for contributions, and men who are honored have more reason to stay and contribute than men who are scorned. "Honor your husband" can be translated loosely as, "Curtail your superior firepower, listen to him and try to understand his concerns, so that he may have a real voice in the family." Otherwise, female emotions dominate and males withdraw, creating an imbalance that neither one finds satisfying.

Were men naturally more powerful in marital squabbles, an increase in female power would promote equality. But flawed ideology leads to flawed policy. Insofar as women are naturally more powerful, additional female power undermines the traditional balance of marital relationships. Men withdraw in the face of female accusation, leaving marriages emotionally barren and strictly matriarchal. The challenge is to strike a proper balance, so that men and women can both participate and gain the best from one another.

In America in the mid-nineties, 30 percent of children are born to single females.[9] Instead of fathers, these children have sperm donors—whose only real investment is the few hours or weeks it takes to talk a woman into accepting the donation. Of the 70 percent of children born into intact marriages, half will grow up in broken homes, with 90 percent of these in the custody of their mothers. So more than 60 percent of children born today will be raised in matriarchal arrangements with no father or only an absent father. Of the just under 40 percent raised in two-parent homes, mothers typically spend considerably more time with the children and call the shots. Can anyone seriously believe that the average American family is patriarchal? Consider patriarchy an endangered species of family, in need of protection.

Traditionally, a woman and her family have been responsible for ensuring that a man who shared her pleasures would marry her and provide for her and their children. The arrangement selects for the more responsible men, and it pressures any man who wants a woman to act responsibly, initially to win favor and then to support her and her family. A woman today who bears illegitimate children and raises them on welfare is most assuredly not doing her part to socialize a man of her own and guide him to responsible citizenship. These strictly matriarchal arrangements flourish today because the government transfers the resources from working men and women and their families to pay the bills.

The number of unmarried mothers translates into a corresponding number of unmarried men without family responsibilities. It results in more unsocialized youngsters who grow up to become violent young men and unwed teenage moms. In the long run, fatherless households lead to broad social disintegration, equally harming men, women, children, and the whole community.

Only a century ago, the extended family was the norm. Before that, children were often raised communally, with the help of assorted grandparents, uncles and aunts, and older siblings, and with the rest of the community stepping in when necessary. Today, with so many children raised by televisions and shopping malls, the two-parent family is the best option we have available. To strengthen the two-parent family, we surely must strengthen its weakest link—which is the position of a father in the family.[10]

WHO IS MINDING THE CHILDREN?

Although our childcare practices are socially acquired and vary across cultures, some of our basic feelings seem to be more deeply ingrained. Modern couples may agree that the woman will pursue her career and the man will do his share of the childcare, which seems fair. Yet once the baby is born, the traditional feelings usually take over. She yearns to be with her baby and feels torn about going back to work, while he is totally stressed by the additional responsibilities and cannot get out into the world soon enough to earn a living and provide for his family. Such emotional reactions seem to be remnants of our primitive cultural heritage. In earlier hunter-gatherer cultures, mothers would gather food and carry their infants with them or leave them with their relatives. Back home, women tended their small children in communal arrangements, with other adults. Men were under pressure to provide, and clans might survive or perish according to how seriously the men fulfilled their obligations.

New practices do not always fit with our inborn natures. The fifties practice of isolated suburban mothers tending small children, bored and lonely, gave rise to what Betty Friedan called "the problem that has no name." The isolation of the suburban housewife is a far stretch from our earlier communal arrangements, and feels unnatural. Yet leaving your infant in commercial childcare tended by strangers is just as unnatural—making it the "solution" that is now the problem.[11] A more natural solution might be childcare close to work, where mom can duck in and stay in touch. Or, perhaps, extended family networks could take up some of the slack.

What about the new, sensitive man who contentedly stays home and tends the infant while his wife works? To a fast-track career woman, a husband who doubles as a nanny would be a godsend. Yet few men are volunteering for baby duty, and those who do often feel at loose ends or turn decidedly morose. Not all women are suited for childcare, of course, but men tend to be particularly ill-suited for it. Among our ancestors, it was the fate of old men and invalids to be left with the women while the "real men" banded together to take on the outside world. Staying at home with an infant meant *failing* to support the family, and it had another evolutionary drawback. A man who stayed at home while his wife ventured into the outside world had no assurance that her next child was also *his* next child. The very temperament that would allow a man to be comfortable at home while his wife ventures forth would have amounted to genetic suicide over the centuries. So, today, the man who stays at home with the children while his wife goes out can feel totally unmanned, without knowing quite why.

Just as we understand how women are troubled by leaving small children to go to work, we should be willing to understand how much men are troubled by *not* leaving to go to work. Women can and do get used to leaving their children, and perhaps men can adapt to staying home alone and tending the babies. We can do what we have to do in spite of our temperaments. We just cannot always feel as good about it as we would wish.

ACCOMPLISHED WOMEN AND "WHY ARE THERE NO GOOD MEN OUT THERE?"

Wives working outside the home created some strains for traditional husbands a generation ago, but most men are reasonably well adjusted to it now. The second income supplements the family finances, easing some of the pressures, and for many families it is now a necessity rather than an option. Wives work in almost 60 percent of marriages in the United States.

What happens when the wife is more accomplished and earns significantly more money? As of 1994, 22 percent of working women out-earned their husbands,[12] and more are likely to do so in the coming years. Indeed, girls now outnumber boys in colleges, and 68 percent of freshman girls plan to get graduate degrees, compared to 65 percent of the boys.[13] It might seem like a blessing for financially strapped men, but it has a downside. When the man earns more money or at least as much, he provides an essential contribution that gives him a place in the family. When the woman earns more, what does the man provide that is so essential? Her higher income does not reduce her emotional power. If anything, it makes her more powerful! So the high-earning woman is the economic head of the family and the emotional powerhouse as well, while the man is neither. Is it so surprising that some men find that intimidating?

A sexual relationship is traditionally seen as a contribution a female provides for a male and for which she expects to be compensated. As we have seen, compensation for females is not merely a Western custom, but extends across cultures and is seen in many animal species as well. The expectation that men compensate women for romantic favors carries over into family finances. When the man earns more money, what he earns should become hers as well simply because she is his wife. But when she earns more money, what she earns seems to remain hers until she chooses to share it with him.[14] How many of us feel that the man has earned a share of a woman's wealth simply because he shares her bed? So her higher earnings introduce an additional strain into family finances, which are troublesome enough even under more traditional arrangements.

Women traditionally want men who can command resources, and highly successful women are no exception. Indeed, successful women are found to set higher expectations for their husbands than less successful women.[15] Highly successful women who make more than $50,000 a year and hold professional positions report wanting mates who have professional degrees, high social status, high intelligence, and high incomes, more so than less successful women. College women who expect higher earnings after college report a stronger preference for men with high earnings than do women who expect more modest incomes. Clearly, earning more money *raises* a woman's financial expectations for her husband, rather than lowering them.

How is a somewhat average man expected to compensate an exceptional woman who earns more? He might tend the children and do the housework, but is that enough? And would he be comfortable with himself doing that? A woman who wants to be compensated for her romantic favors is not usually inclined to pursue a man whom she must compensate.

A highly accomplished woman might lower her standards, choose a mate from among the less accomplished men available, make whatever allowances it takes to be together, and learn to love him. Or, she might go on daytime television and proclaim that there are no good men out there. Females are choosy, as Darwin observed, and a fair number of highly successful women rate themselves above the available men. As more women earn high incomes, the chances diminish that they will find enough high income men to go around.

> *I married beneath me. Of course, all women do.*
> —LADY ASTOR

Divorce rates are higher in marriages where wives earn more than their husbands.[16] In contrast, men who earn more and enjoy a higher professional status than their wives have more stable marriages. A financially successful man commands respect from his wife, who has practical reasons to stay. Note the contrast: Financially successful men have more stable marriages because they adequately support their wives, whereas financially successful women have less stable marriages, because they have the independence to leave. These findings are consistent with our earlier observation that men bond more strongly and that women leave relationships more often than men.

Clearly, women who are socially and financially able to leave are more apt to do so. And so it has been across the ages.[17] In hunter-gatherer societies women often had independent resources, and divorce rates were relatively high. In early agricultural societies, in which men controlled the wealth of the land, marriages were stable and divorce was rare. Divorce began to rise in the industrial revolution, as women took jobs, and it continues to climb as women gain more financial independence.

A recent poll queried single Americans as to whether they want to be married.[18] The vast majority of younger men and women—somewhere around 90 percent—look forward to marriage. But within the critical twenty-five to thirty-four-year-old age span, 87 percent of the single men but only 70 percent of the single women want to be married. Thus *twice* as many women as men in this age group want to stay single. Even adjusting for more women in this population, that should leave enough men to go around—if the women would settle for the available men.

Of the reasonably attractive women over thirty who tell me there are no good men out there, all have one thing in common. Every one can acknowledge having had one or more men who wanted to marry her, but who did not meet her standards.

A man whose job involves social or artistic contributions may get by with a lower paycheck, as long as both he and his wife value his contributions. So a man need not earn as much, as long as he is considered to be as talented or successful as his wife in some meaningful ways.

High-salaried men usually marry, and so transfer the benefits of their earnings to their wives. High-salaried women, however, are not eager to support freeloaders, and tend not to spend money foolishly chasing unsuccessful men. So while women share in the wealth men acquire, the transfer does not operate the other way around.

THERAPIST AS GURU

Ordinarily, we figure that a healthy individual should be able to show reasonable judgment, and participate and find satisfaction in enough of what life might offer.[19] So a competent therapist might address whatever seems to muddle your judgment or prevent you from living a meaningful life.

Relationships, of course, are one of the more important features in most of our lives. So therapy often aims to improve an unsatisfactory relationship or get you away from an unsatisfactory partner, depending on which course seems more promising. Are you messing up what could be a reasonable relationship, or is your partner as impossible as you feel he or she is? Would it be good judgment to stay and work on it, or to write this one off to experience and cut your losses? Any answers, of course, rest on an understanding of what is right or normal, or at least manageable, and what is bad enough to be intolerable. So the answers necessarily involve moral standards and personal sympathies.

No man is a hero to his wife's psychiatrist.
—ERIC BERNE

Therapists tend to see women as more connected and more intimate, while men relate less through feelings and more by sharing activities and doing things for those they love.[20] The challenge is to remain impartial. It is easier to be sympathetic with upset women than with their husbands or boyfriends who are upsetting them. Therapists are vastly more inclined to push an upset woman to dump her dead-beat husband, than to push a stressed out man to dump his deadweight wife. Insofar as men are responsible for women and not the other way around, helping men leave trouble-some women is immoral while helping women leave trou-blesome men is seen as admirable.

Popular titles, such *Women Who Love Too Much,*[21] *Smart Women, Foolish Choices,*[22] and *Men Who Hate Women and the Women Who Love Them,*[23] challenge women to be more inde-pendent and to cast off men who mistreat them or fail to meet their expectations. The advice appeals to our sympa-thies toward women and our normal inclination to hold men responsible.

When are cantankerous individuals considered abusive? We judge by gender. Men who scold women are often judged to be verbal batterers, while women who scold men are just upset and expressing their feelings. So women are justified in leaving irate men who are verbally abusive, while men are not justified in leaving because irate women are merely expressing their feelings.

CHAPTER THIRTEEN

Lust and Anger As Gender Follies

E ACH GENDER HAS its own favorite appetites—men tend toward lust and women toward anger.

As we have seen, male genes benefit from men being sexual opportunists. So nature inclines males to find an interested woman immensely appealing, and to feel that being with her would be paradise on Earth (or as close as one can come to it). Female genes, in contrast, benefit from women holding men accountable, thus compelling men to provide for them and their children. So nature inclines women to see themselves as mistreated or ignored, and to feel they have every right to express their anger and be heard. To be blunt, *men's genes benefit from getting laid while women's genes benefit from making men pay for it.*

Lust and anger are clearly apportioned by gender. Women can be nymphomaniacs and men can be anger-mongers, of course, but it is not typical. Men are eager for casual sex while women prefer relationships. Women are more inclined to accuse and complain while men are stressed by confrontation and try to avoid it. We can see these traits as weaknesses: Men have a weakness for casual sex, while women have a weakness for casual anger.

Most men curtail their lust and most women curtail their anger, out of a sense of propriety and concern for relationships. When we do not, lust and anger carry each sex into its own typical follies.

ILLUSIONS

An average young man will undress with almost any willing young woman, abandoning normal judgment and seemingly oblivious to the consequences to himself or to those around him. Women find such opportunism hard to understand, or consider it truly irrational. Men see it as irrational as well, when they are watching some other man fall into it or are far enough away from it to look back at themselves and grimace. We joke about how a man is "thinking with his little brain instead of his big brain." It's just a guy thing.

A man is more easily seduced than a woman. The University of Hawaii study, reviewed earlier, suggests that an attractive woman who has her mind set on seduction may need as little as five minutes to talk a young man into it. It is surely fair to say that men use less judgment than women when getting into sexual involvements. Many use no judgment at all.

A man does not judge an interested woman by the same standards he would use to judge anyone else. A woman sees in an instant when another woman is coming on to her man, and considers her trashy. The typical man figures the woman is just being nice, and hardly understands what all the fuss is about.

How irrational can a typical man be? Switch the gender positions and look at it the other way around. Suppose a man tells a woman that she turns him on and he wants to sleep with her, and she concludes, therefore, that he must love her. We would figure that she has no judgment (and never had), or that she has just lost all common sense and is temporarily insane. At the minimum she is a menace to herself and needs protection. Now switch it back around. When a woman tells a man he turns her on and she wants to sleep with him, he feels extraordinarily flattered. And yes, at least for the moment, he is so full of himself that he is sure she must be in love with him. He is also temporarily insane, of course. It's a guy thing. But the condition is so typical and so familiar that we try to make allowances and work around it.

It is anger rather than lust that can carry women to folly. Women feel they have a right to be comfortable and secure, and feel personally cheated when they are not. So women feel justified, therefore, in expressing their anger against the men who are failing to provide for them. An average woman is apt to take offense where none is intended, more so than a man, and to consider herself mistreated amid the usual strains of a relationship. She is more apt to exaggerate her complaints rather than understate them, as a man might, and she has no idea how troublesome her anger is to those around her. She can expect men to fix her concerns without herself specifying the problems. It's a girl thing. Men find so much anger hard to understand and consider angry women irrational. Women occasionally consider the anger irrational as well, when they see how it trashes relationships.

LIBERATED APPETITES

Each gender has its own views of personal liberation from social straightjackets. A man was traditionally limited to a single woman (or to a few at most), and was required to marry and support a woman along with as many children as she might bear. So not surprisingly, liberation for a young man can mean freedom to pursue casual relations with various women without the responsibility of marrying and supporting them. The male appetite for casual sex was the chief beneficiary of the sexual revolution of the sixties.

What is liberation for women? The sexual revolution freed women as well as men, and many women continue to experiment with free sex and multiple partners. But casual sex is not as extraordinarily appealing to women as it is to men. Many women go along with it simply for convenience, but later consider men insensitive and complain about being used. Women are also freer now to work outside the home, and that too can be appealing. But women work as much for the income as for a love of the job, and working mothers miss their children. Many working women are worn out, and now complain about doing it all instead of having it all.

Expressing anger is now becoming more acceptable, which is especially appealing when everything else fails. Women have always been quicker to make accusations than men, but traditionally it was considered improper for a woman to express her anger too forcefully or too publicly. Women are now freer to complain about men, publicly and without censure, while men run for cover. The female appetite for angry accusation seems to be the principal beneficiary of our more openly expressive standards of conduct.

Women are not great believers in free sex, often wanting stable relationships and correctly recognizing that free sex reduces the pressure to commit. Men are not great believers in free anger, correctly recognizing that men usually lose in angry exchanges with women.

An appetite for casual sex should not be taken to mean that men are better off in casual relationships. Men, as we have seen, are more often harmed by casual relationships than are women. Men are intrigued by casual sex, but do better with stability and commitment. Similarly, an appetite for casual anger should not be taken to mean that women are better off complaining. Women who unleash their anger get swept up in their own justifications, and fail to develop compassion or depth of character. Women who stay balanced and see both sides will surely have healthier relationships and more fulfilling lives.

SEXAHOLICS AND RAGEAHOLICS

Lust and anger can be seriously addictive. Men can get a powerful rush from casual sex but feel empty afterward, and so look for more sex to fill the void. Another night, another babe, another rush, but the same old familiar blahs the next morning.[1]

Women can feel righteous and powerful expressing their anger. "Choosing to be angry . . . means you're feeling alive," observe Sandra Thomas and Cheryl Jefferson in *Use Your Anger*.[2] Yet when the anger is spent, you feel just as empty and insignificant as ever, and look for further grievances to justify more anger, to fill the void. Overall, women who are often angry report being depressed more often and more seriously than women who are seldom angry.[3] Anger, in turn, poses as a convenient way out of persistent depression. "I have become even more angry . . ." Gloria Steinem explains, because "the alternative is depression."[4]

In the language of addictions, more men than women are sexaholics, while more women than men are rageaholics. Lust and anger can mask our emptiness and boredom, but only temporarily. Mostly, they waste our time and expend energy we might use doing something more productive.

In the Christian tradition, gender follies are sins that incline us to treat our opposites as less than fully human. Lustful men see women as sexual objects, to satisfy an appetite, while angry women see men as villains, to accuse and condemn rather than to understand.

AN ERA FOR EACH

American society seems to be providing each gender an era for its appetites. The sexual revolution of the sixties introduced an era of casual sex, which continued for two decades but slowed somewhat with the fear of AIDS. An era of casual anger is now upon us, and will continue for some time. It too promises to be personally and socially challenging. The joy of sex of an earlier era is giving way to the joy of anger.

One can hardly escape the sense that American women are becoming increasingly hostile toward men. What is changing? Women are traditionally more critical than men, but in earlier eras their criticism stayed mainly in and around the home and among family and close friends. The traditional pattern was for men to dominate in business and public affairs while women dominated in personal relations and at home. Women now hold influential public positions, in universities and in the media, and are carrying their anger toward men into the broader public consciousness. No longer as dependent on men to provide for them, women express their anger more openly.

In a 1970 survey, women were most likely to call men "basically kind, gentle, and thoughtful." In a similar survey in 1990, women more often described men as only valuing their own opinions, trying to keep women down, preoccupied with getting women into bed, and not paying attention to household affairs.[5] Recent research suggests that overall, our contemporary stereotypes of women are generally more moral than our stereotypes of men.[6] Is that a surprise? Women are more often seen as socially sensitive, friendly, and concerned about others, whereas men are seen as dominant, controlling, and independent. Our current views mirror somewhat the English and American attitudes in the early Industrial Revolution, when women were thought to create homes of "peace and concord, love and devotion," while men strived in their work realms of "selfishness and immorality."[7]

In *Who Stole Feminism?*,[8] philosopher Christina Sommers shows how anger is taking control of the feminist movement. Pioneer feminists were "equity" feminists, as are many women today, *wanting the same equal and fair treatment for women as for everyone, with no special privileges.*[9] But the more visible feminists today are "gender" feminists, who exaggerate their grievances and see themselves as eternally mistreated, regardless of circumstances. The movement might be called "anger" feminism, as anger guides its thinking and supplies its power advantage. Anger feminism casts itself as social innovation, but it is merely using the traditional female anger advantage against the more civil men and women who stand in its way.

Anger feminism can appeal to women in the same way the playboy philosophy can appeal to men. Each allows us to act on some of our most primitive appetites, and each justifies itself as liberation from social repression. The free love movement of the sixties was supposed to end possessiveness and herald in a new era of brotherly love. So much for self-serving idealism. And now the feminist anger movement is supposed to overturn patriarchy and usher in a more just civilization. "Your anger is a source of power and enlightenment," proclaim Thomas and Jefferson in *Use Your Anger,* subtitled *A Woman's Guide to Empowerment.* "If we [women] all care enough to be justifiably angry, we can transform our world."[10] As in the era before, the idealism here is self-serving. As Yogi Berra might have said, it's déjà vu again—with the lessons not learned the first time around.

What simplistic philosophies! No longer must we look at the consequences of our actions, or temper our conduct out of concern for our companions. Men and women need only unleash their respective lust and anger, and all will come up roses!

Lust and anger are genetically adaptive, but can lose their advantages in our technological world. A young lad who ogles the nude foldouts pumps his genes not into the next generation but into oblivion, and finds the experience quite satisfying. But hey, whoever said his genes were that smart? A young lass with too much of an attitude scares off suitors and can remain childless. But hey, whoever said her genes were that smart? Among our ancestors, lecherous men had no pornographic videos to waste their energies on, and almost all women married as attractive youngsters and well before a shrewish temperament might outweigh their youthful appeal. Our "lech" and "bitch" inclinations are genetically adaptive, but can turn somewhat maladaptive in unforeseen circumstances.

NO SOLID COALITIONS

It should be noted that neither men nor women form solid same-sex coalitions. Men commonly compete against their fellow men for power, prestige, and the available women. The successful men take as much as possible while the losers grub for the leftovers. And women too compete against one another for the resources that men might provide, turning their anger against other women as easily as they turn it against men. It shows up clearly in the workplace, as we'll see in the next chapter.

CHAPTER FOURTEEN

Gender Conflict at Work

MANY OF THE contrasts between the sexes that we have seen in personal relationships continue into public activities. We look here at clear contrasts in how men and women tend to deal with competition and conflict in workplace relationships.

TWO TYPES OF POWER IMBALANCES

MEN AND women each stand out in their preferred topics of conversation. Men stand out in "information" talk while women control most of the "feelings" talk. In conversations about facts, men compete for air time, to show themselves informed, while women want to fit in rather than stand out. Men appear more confident, while women speak more tentatively, according to observations compiled by Deborah Tannen in *Talking from 9 to 5*.[1] Women tend to present their positions as suggestions rather than as imperatives ("We might consider . . ." versus "We should . . ."). And women use more qualifiers ("Do you know what I mean?"). Yet when women do speak more like men, they can be seen as bossy or boasting, thereby diminishing their credibility instead of improving it.

So men often dominate in classrooms and business meetings and almost anywhere else one might build himself up or thrust himself forward and show he knows what is going on. Male assertiveness begins early. Seeking confirmation, I asked a middle school teacher if the boys in her classes raise their hands more often to answer questions. "No," she replied, "the girls raise their hands. The boys *wave* their hands and shout, 'I know, I know, I know! Teacher, I know!'"

Teachers tend to call on the boys more than the girls, which has been interpreted as unconscious sexism. Yet to maintain control of the class, a teacher must control the most boisterous students. The boys tend to be rowdier than the girls, and quicker to go off task and disrupt classrooms. Teachers call on the boys to keep them on task, so that they contribute to the class rather than wrecking it.

♀ Women should speak up more. And we should all be more careful to slow down and listen, so that women can contribute and not be drowned out by competitive men.

Conversely, when it comes to personal judgments, women dominate. Women control conversations about what is right or wrong in personal relations and who is being fair or unfair to whom. Men try to stay out of trouble. Yes, women can be quite critical of men, but that is only half the problem. Men are so oversensitive that a mere smidgen of female anger totally silences them. I have seen a single irate woman accuse a room full of men of being sexists, thereby silencing them all, much like a scolding school marm might silence a roomful of misbehaving schoolboys. Most of these men were tenured professors, of equal or higher rank than the woman who silenced them. Surely these men had opposing opinions. Actually, they had strong opinions, and expressed them afterward, congregating in small, furtive groups and complaining bitterly about what a hostile bitch she was and how impossible it was to get anything done with her around. Yet none of the men challenged her directly, and that is my point here. *Men stew and steam but do not openly confront hostile women.* Women consider it unfair that men try to exclude them from conversations, and indeed it is unfair. Good communication stays out in the open and allows input. But remember that men stay away from angry women not out of simple arrogance, but because men are totally out-gunned by female hostility.

The change from boldly assertive to totally immobilized must seem puzzling, but it makes perfect evolutionary sense. Men are highly competitive because successful men acquire more mating opportunities, thus passing on their competitive genes. So in a real sense, men are competing with one another for favor among the women. Men who offend women are the biggest genetic losers, and men most certainly do not compete to *lose* favor with women. So where pushing oneself forward offends, the same men who ordinarily are so assertive meekly acquiesce, to avoid being blackballed.

In mixed-gender situations, women complain openly about men, but men watch their words to avoid offending. *A woman who attacks men is unappealing, but she commands your concern. A man who attacks women is not only unappealing but morally retarded, and he sabotages his own standing.* The result is now a workplace in which women accuse openly while men resent being accused, but keep quiet, fearing censure and loss of position.

♀♂ Men might muster some courage and learn to argue with angry women. And fair-minded women might speak up for men when chivalry prevents them from defending themselves.

"IMPRESS YOU" AND "ACCUSE YOU" ARGUMENTS

IN ARGUMENT, information talk and feelings talk become "impress you" talk and "accuse you" talk. "Impress you" arguments aim to show you how much I know, how smart I am, how brilliant my plan is, and that it is in your best interest to listen to me and go along with my brilliant plan. My winning depends on getting you to feel good about what I am saying. So "impress you" arguments appeal to mutual interests, offer compromises, and are humorous or at least pleasant; and they can also include the smoke and mirrors that are standard fare in sales.

"Accuse you" arguments aim to convince you that you have offended and are out of line; that you are unfair or otherwise wrong and unacceptable; and that you must back down or face further censure. "Accuse you" arguments are loaded with anger, and are meant not to appeal to your interests, but to weaken your will and lower your standing so you can no longer oppose. I also call these "bust you" arguments, because they aim to break your will and bust you down to a lower standing.

"Impress you" arguments are standard fare among men, who are continually competing to impress one another and to impress women. Men tend to restrain their anger in the workplace, correctly recognizing the risks it carries for their future careers. Men are relatively intolerant of other men who take offense too easily or accuse too freely. Women also use the "impress you" style of argument, although there is a downside. Some audiences are unimpressed with women who push themselves forward and try to be too impressive. A critical difference is that women feel freer to make accusations when they're upset or offended.

"Accuse you" arguments are highly stressful, but usually win in personal confrontations over "impress you" arguments. *When a woman is upset by something a man says, public sympathies go strongly with her and against him because he offended her.* Men withdraw when women accuse, correctly recognizing that anything they might say is unlikely to impress.

Because of this, it is often the more competitive men who dominate in information conversations and the more hostile women who dominate in conversations about who is being mistreated or oppressed. The most competitive men do not necessarily represent our broader interests, and neither do the most hostile women! What does it take to hear from everybody else?

GENDER STYLES IN WORKGROUPS

I would not pretend to cover workstyles adequately in a book on personal relations, but I will offer some highlights.

Men and women create characteristic work group atmospheres. Men are persistently competitive but typically banter and rib each other, in a sort of ritual combat, which women seldom do and do not always understand. Ribbing challenges you to override your own personal sensitivities to be a good sport—or lose face. By accepting ribbing, men confirm that they are team players who will live up to expectations and not allow personal feelings to stand in the way. Ribbing bonds men together and builds morale. *Ritual banter over insignificant matters prepares men to take it all in stride when they clash over more serious concerns.*

Women in groups often try to cooperate and get along, with ample pleasantries,[2] avoiding anything that might cause hurt feelings. Not surprisingly, women can feel awkward and out of place around the competitive banter and ritual insults typical of males. Women are more reluctant to be too forward, for fear of offending someone, and women themselves take offense when another woman acts too forward. When conflict does occur, women tend to take it more personally.[3] When challenged or threatened, women tend to become upset more than men and are quicker to anger. Note the contrast: By taking ribbing, men show they are team players who get along by going along. *By taking offense, women set the standards of what is acceptable or unacceptable conduct around them, as they do in personal relationships.*

The mix of male and female styles can be irritating for everyone. Women are troubled by men who compete to forge ahead instead of considering others' feelings. And men are troubled by women who are hurt and offended instead of playing the game by the rules and taking it all in stride.

CONFLICT WITH WOMEN
IS MORE STRESSFUL

GIVEN OUR different styles, we might expect men and women to be more comfortable working around those of the same gender. We might expect men to prefer working for men, and women to prefer working for women. Yet that is not what we find.

A 1996 Gallup poll of working Americans finds that 37 percent of men and 54 percent of women prefer working for a man.[4] Only 17 percent of men and 22 percent of women prefer working for a woman (while the remainder have no preference). So about twice as many men prefer working for a man rather than a woman, and the preference among women for male bosses is slightly higher still. Moreover, the general preference for male bosses is apparently increasing. The current preference for men as bosses is 4 percent higher among men and 10 percent higher among women than it was a mere three years ago.

What is going on? Personal relationships often succeed or fail on the basis of how we resolve conflict, and we might expect the same of workplace relations as well.

To better understand these preferences, I polled a hundred men and a hundred women whose work positions involved significant conflict with both men and women.[5] Those surveyed were from all walks of life, from high-salaried lawyers and executives, through professors, psychologists, teachers, nurses, and middle managers, to waiters and waitresses, secretaries and clerks.[6] Interviewees were asked, "In your experience, is conflict more stressful (troublesome, intimidating) when it is with men, or when it is with women? Or is it the same?" They were also asked, "Why?"

Of the men, roughly 50 percent reported being more stressed by conflicts with women than by similar conflicts with men.[7] Just over 15 percent felt conflict is more stressful with men. The remaining almost 35 percent said there is no difference or it depends on the person or the situation. Thus, men tend to be more stressed in conflict with women. Their reasons fell in two main categories: Women take conflict more personally and are more easily upset and angered than men; and following conflict, women tend to stay angry longer, hold grudges, and retaliate, whereas men usually try to reconcile. A few mentioned that women are not as clear about what they want, making conflict resolution more difficult.

One man saw it both ways, feeling that women are good to work with because they are more personal and more caring, but also harder to resolve conflict with because personal feelings get in the way. Several men noted that after open conflict in meetings, men tend to make eye contact and joke with their rivals, to reestablish the relationship and convey respect, whereas women often avoid eye contact, leave mad, stay mad, and make trouble later.

A few mentioned chivalry as an obstacle. A popular professor rated female administrators as the most stressful aspect of his job, noting that women can openly berate him, while he feels he is too much of a gentleman to berate women in return. "It is shameful to lose to these women," he noted, "but it is disgraceful to attack back."

The survey of women produced similar findings. About 60 percent of the women reported more stress in workplace conflicts with women than with men.[8] Just over 15 percent said that conflict is more stressful with men. The remaining 25 percent said it depends upon the person or the situation.

Thus, by a considerable margin, women too find conflict more stressful when it involves other women.

The two most common reasons the women gave are the same ones the men gave: Women often personalize relationships and become upset and angry when things go wrong; and women tend to hold grudges and "do not forget," acting to pay you back long after an incident should have been over. In addition, several women noted that women gossip more and can turn a whole office against you.

Several of the younger and more attractive women felt that older women had gone after them out of obvious jealousy. Several of the women volunteered that they themselves have gone after other women at work for strictly personal reasons. An interview of a thousand women published by the American Management Association found that over 90 percent felt they had been undermined by another woman at work.[9]

Conflicts also flare over ideology. A clergywoman mentioned a close woman friend from seminary who now refuses to talk to her, judging her insufficiently supportive of the feminist cause. She thought it would be unusual for a man friend to change so completely and snub her over a matter of conscience.

Conflict is judged to be more stressful with women regardless of one's job status. I was surprised by the number of professional women with feminist identities who reported being more stressed by conflicts with women than by those with men. A few commented on the apparent contradiction. A good-natured lawyer joked that conflict with women is more stressful because she does not expect as much from men. Several women felt that women can be good to work with, but a few are hostile beyond belief.

Women were generally open about stating their opinions, while several of the men were reluctant and asked that their opinions be held in strictest confidence. Men who admit being troubled by women bosses might be condemned as sexists, jeopardizing their careers. Women, in contrast, are fearless. Immune to censure, women speak their minds.

WHY IS IT MORE STRESSFUL WITH WOMEN?

Several of my respondents assumed that women were naturally gentler, and were simply overreacting in competitive surroundings. A reporter in Florida commented that, "Many women at the paper feel they have to take on male qualities, and they become really hard and harsh." A female minister told me, "It's a man's world, and women feel they have to be tough just to prove themselves." Guys are surely competitive, but hostility is more of a girl thing. *Insofar as women are more emotionally combative at work, they are showing the same qualities in work relationships that they show in personal relationships.*

Are women more combative because women are powerless, as anger feminists suggest? Are women angry because it is their only way to be heard? Anger is one way to be heard, of course. But nothing in my survey indicates that anger is reserved for the weak or that women mellow as they gain real power. My survey suggests that conflict is often *more* stressful with women professionals and supervisors than it is with secretaries and waitresses. Indeed, most of us are considerably more stressed by conflict with those who have power over us than with our subordinates. Do not expect workplace stress to subside anytime soon. More realistically, if trends continue, we might expect hostilities to increase as women gain more formal power.

Why do women hold grudges more than men, and spread angry gossip about rivals? Whatever the causes, the tendencies show up early and are seen in youngsters four to fourteen who play together.[10] Boys tend to confront one another directly when conflict arises. In sharp contrast, girls often gossip about girls who are absent from the group and allege offenses that an absent girl supposedly committed against a girl who is present, introducing suspicions that lead to conflict.

Remember that boys are observed to be generally better than girls at resolving disputes in games.[11] Girls often end their games when disputes arise, to preserve the peace, whereas boys argue over the rules, even seeming to enjoy their legalistic jousts. Conflict among girls tends to continue longer, sometimes over several weeks or more, while boys usually settle their arguments and resume playing. So boys gain an early advantage in managing conflict by relying on rules, and girls need to catch up if they are to become competitive as women.[12]

Carol Gilligan suggests that women rely more on feelings and social sensitivities than on formal rules, and are not less adept than men at principled reasoning but merely different in their reasoning.[13] While her findings have been challenged,[14] she obviously struck a personal chord with many women. Yet so far as women do rely more on sensitivities, it leaves them with fewer ways to resolve conflict. Rules are public and principles can be argued, while sensitivities are personal and subjective, and so are less amenable to challenge and debate.

The different ways men and women express themselves can surely cause misunderstandings, as Deborah Tannen argues. Yet were misunderstanding the main obstacle, each sex would be more stressed in conflict with its opposites, which is not the case. Both men and women are found to be more stressed by women. Clearly, *in conflict management at work, gender temperament is far more important than gender misunderstandings.*

Are women too nice, as *Time* magazine chivalrously asks?[15] Men are typically more competitive, continually jockeying for position. But men also recognize that everyone else is out for himself (or herself) as well. So when interests clash, men consider it business and try to mend relationships afterward and stay on good terms. Women tend to be more considerate and to reveal more of themselves, expecting friendship. But when others violate the trust or infringe on their territory, women feel totally betrayed. The betrayal triggers anger and hostility.

♀ Be more assertive, looking out for your own interests instead of being so nice; but also more assertive, in the sense of carefully promoting your own interests instead of relying on your anger to do it for you.

Several men reported having excellent women colleagues and supervisors, and observed that *those women who are good to work with are even-tempered and have conflict-management styles similar to men.* That is, these women are not easily upset or angered, they focus on the task at hand and put personal feelings aside; and they do not hold grudges. Some of these women made a point to rib their coworkers, and themselves took ribbing gracefully, refusing to be offended.

It goes without saying that not all women managers personalize conflict—many are truly professional in confrontations. And not all men are management-material—some are emotional volcanoes. The observation here is only that women *tend* to personalize conflict more so than men.

Women's preference for male managers is slightly stronger than men's preference, and women are slightly more stressed by conflict with women than men are. So why are women even more troubled by women than men are? When women confront other women, the chances are higher that at least one, and possibly both, will personalize the conflict rather than seeking to resolve it. The odds are greater that one or both will act as expressers and that neither will be a fixer.

Where is workplace conflict headed? Some of my acquaintances suggest that the present hostilities can escalate only so far, and that rational heads must eventually prevail and calm the storms. Perhaps, but only if we can speak openly and reach for our common interests.

BUT SHOULD WE MENTION IT?

While many recognize that conflict with women tends to be more stressful, it has been considered improper and perhaps sexist to mention it. Great! *If we are not allowed to even state the problem, how on Earth are we to manage it?* How can women managers understand what they do that causes unnecessary stress, and try to improve their performances? How can the men and women who work for women better adjust to the relationships? We have a long way to go, and politically correct blinders take us about four inches in front of our own noses. Surely a more practical generation of men and women will want to understand the problem and try to fix it, and not just censure those who are candid enough to mention it.

The Gallup poll did not ask why we tend to prefer male bosses, but the report blames it on "gender bias." The pollsters thus cast the problem not as something women bosses are doing, which might be corrected, but as yet another social injustice that women should take personally. As long as we cannot speak openly about women personalizing conflict, even top analysts and national journalists remain clueless. It is too easy to blame workplace preferences on mythical biases. Simple social propriety censors the information we need to interpret the problem and to take steps to fix it.

Continuing to ignore the problem is costly and foolish. Those who personalize conflict make workplaces unnecessarily stressful for everyone around them. And women who are otherwise highly qualified may not advance as far as they would if they learned to manage conflict instead of personalizing it.

Training programs are available that identify how women overpersonalize work conflict and teach better ways to handle it.[16] Improved conflict management would benefit women managers, benefit the men and women who work for them and around them, and benefit whole organizations.

♀♂ We should all acknowledge that being offended and angry vastly increases the stress level of the workplace, and we should work together to find solutions. Schools and workplaces should provide training programs to help women identify tendencies to personalize conflict and to learn to manage better.

The finding that women personalize conflict more than men need not adversely affect those women who manage well. If anything, the information should make managerial women even more valuable. Establish your credentials, show you can handle conflict, and you'll stand out ahead of those who personalize it.

The finding that women personalize conflict can act like a Rorschach ink blot test. Some take offense that it is being said at all, while others use it to gain insight and figure out how to resolve conflict more amicably.

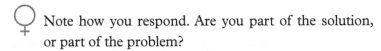 Note how you respond. Are you part of the solution, or part of the problem?

WHY MEN MANAGE CONFLICT

Managers deal continually with conflict, as personal interests and project requirements compete and clash. Indeed, administrators typically face snafus, complaints, confrontations, snubs, and outright insults, in amounts that might be considered highly offensive. The challenge is to avoid taking it personally and treat it all as part of the job. Good administrators manage conflict in a calm and reasonably objective way, not allowing their personal feelings to get in the way.

Why do many men naturally manage conflict, while women more often personalize it? It may be a straight carryover from personal relations, in which women are more combative while men are more stressed by conflict. Also remember that men orient more toward status advancement and are more hierarchical than women. Hierarchy requires individuals to subordinate themselves to higher-ranking members, and it holds higher-ranking members accountable. Others in your organization usually have some say over your future, and gaining position or simply maintaining it involves staying on good terms. Men who express anger toward their companions usually lose status, and smart men work to control themselves. To maintain their positions, men button their mouths and put up with the sort of aggravation and insult that women fly off against. "Real men" are expected to show anger at common enemies, but not against coworkers and teammates.

Women who express anger might lose status too, but not as much, or they might actually gain advantage by dominating their rivals. *Hostile women are tiresome but not frightening, while hostile men seem truly dangerous.* Work situations do not seem to penalize female anger as much as male anger.

Why are men so afraid of losing standing? Evolution surely sensitized men toward preserving status, more than it did women. High status typically meant more mating opportunities, but any man had to maintain *some* position in his group or fall off the face of the Earth. A man who crossed his companions could lose all standing and any chance of mating. He could be beaten up, killed, banished, imprisoned, or simply shunned and prohibited from taking a mate. Better to accept lowly status if he must, stay on good terms, and try to improve his situation later on. In contrast, a woman who crossed her companions could still mate and have children. So the evolutionary penalties for expressing anger appear to be far more severe for men than for women. Nature would therefore select for stronger inhibitions in men, but allow women more latitude to express their anger.

It may seem paradoxical that men, who are more often violent and surely more lethal, are also less contentious and more willing to compromise. Yet these seeming opposites go together. Because violence is so lethal among men, nature selects more strongly for caution in conflict and reconciliation afterward.

We might say that men tend to make good administrators for the same reason men make good soldiers. Men subjugate themselves to ugly jobs and accept unlimited indignities, to maintain status and avoid failing. Women recognize when they are being used and abused, and have the sense to object.

CHIMPANZEE POLITICS

Frans de Waal observes a parallel in chimpanzee conflict.[17] Male chimps compete for rank amid shifting alliances, but continually compromise to preserve the peace. Males also typically reconcile with their rivals immediately after conflict occurs, with elaborate greetings and mutual grooming activities, avoiding the perils of lingering animosities. Such reconciliation is truly imperative, as a male on the losing side might actually be killed by his rivals.[18]

Female chimpanzees have more stable friendships and often serve as mediators and power brokers for the more competitive males. Indeed, females are even observed to confiscate stones or sticks from males who are using them to bluff rivals.[19] But females have no compelling reason to reconcile with their own rivals, de Waal notes. So when they do clash, the females may simply stay away from each other, appearing to hold grudges. As with humans, the chimpanzee males are more openly competitive but also better at the compromise and reconciliation that makes competition tolerable.

Chimpanzee males also appear more ambitious and political in their relationships, while the females are more personal.[20] When two chimps fight, a third chimp may intervene to tip the balance of power. De Waal notes that females often intervene to support their friends and family, siding with those they play with, hang out with, and groom. So females intervene out of feelings of friendship and loyalty. In contrast, males who intervene often do so to strengthen alliances and impress followers, thereby supporting their own ambitions. In quarrels, the dominant male often intervenes to support the weaker of the two combatants, maintaining the peace and thereby gaining the respect of the colony. The frequency with which the males make and break strategic alliances indicates opportunistic policy, suggesting that male chimps act rationally to their own political advantage and not out of sympathy for friends and antipathy for rivals. We thus see the same patterns in chimps that we see in ourselves: Females act more on feelings, while males act on policies to forward agendas.[21]

Some people contend that women, who nurture our young, are therefore especially inclined toward peaceful accommodation and could bring salvation to a world run by competitive men. Perhaps nurturing youngsters *should* incline females to resolve conflict more amicably, but clearly it does not. Nor does it elsewhere in the animal world. A mama bear nurturing her cubs is especially quick to attack any intruder who might threaten them.

Over the ages, managing strategic coalitions has surely been more vital for male genes than for female genes. The more political men rule tribes and villages, gaining access to more women. Men with better organized armies survive and conquer, spreading their genes along with their ways of life. It is easy to see why men might naturally be more fascinated with the politics of managing organizations.

WHO SHOULD MANAGE CONFLICT?

Whatever their origins, conflict management abilities ought to be considered in any work situation.

Recall the Gallup poll showing that preferences for men bosses are stronger now than they were a mere three years ago. Why is public opinion hardening against women bosses? We cannot fault the media, which is generally sympathetic toward women in authority. Television and cinema now portray women as wise and progressive administrators, physicians, police officers, and starship commanders. So what is going on?

The trouble would seem to lie in our real-world experiences. As more women are promoted to supervisory positions, more subordinates must contend with women supervisors who personalize conflict. The increasing public preference for men bosses would seem to reflect the painful experiences of both men and women in confrontations with our new generation of more powerful women.[22]

Some people advocate preferences and quotas, on the grounds that women are underrepresented in management. Yet women themselves tend to be more stressed by conflict with women bosses, and feel their workplace interests are better represented by men. Arbitrarily promoting women to supervisory positions increases workplace stress and creates unnecessary hardships for working women as well as for men. Insofar as personalizing conflict is holding women back, it makes more sense to fix the problem first and then see what happens. Surely women who manage conflict reasonably well can be promoted on their own merits, without government action forcing them upon anyone.

♀♂ Women (and men as well) should be assessed on essential administrative qualities, and those who do not have naturally even temperaments could learn to moderate themselves or could be steered away from high-conflict positions.

Men and women working together as equals requires some adjustments. Everything in our blood tells us to support women and hold men responsible when women are upset. Evolution has so programmed our sympathies that it is almost impossible to do otherwise and still consider ourselves decent people. And yet, to treat men and women impartially, we need to counter our innate programming, which so skews our responses. Workplace anger lowers morale and imperils our abilities to reason together.

♀♂ Organizations should actively seek to curtail those women (or men) who unleash their anger at work. Organizations should support men and women who challenge angry coworkers, recognizing that doing so is stressful but necessary to build a productive working atmosphere.

Why are men and women uncomfortable with women in authority? Women already assert a great deal of emotional power, as we have seen. Formal authority then amplifies the emotional power imbalance, making an upset woman in authority totally overwhelming.

Among the Iroquois of northeast America, women chose the men who ruled the tribes. When a chief died, "the senior woman of the clan . . . in consultation with the other women of the clan, selected the man from her clan who was to be given the name of the deceased chief and so his position."[23] In America, about as many women vote as men, and women seem to be relatively comfortable with men as leaders. Women who have emotionally stressful relations with women bosses may be overly cautious about women as political leaders. Perhaps women who gain conflict management skills will become more attractive as leaders.

CHIVALROUS PROTECTION

Just out of seminary and applying for a job, an unmarried acquaintance of mine was questioned thoroughly on his sexual activities. Was he sexually active? Were any of the women he dated angry at him? Over what? Had he ever been attracted to anyone at work, and how did he handle it? What did he consider to be his greatest weakness with women? And so on. The committee was concerned about possible sexual activities between clergymen and parishioners, and they wanted to do everything imaginable to screen out potential problems. My friend felt like he had been through the inquisition, and he wished the committee had focused more on what was between his ears and less on what was between his legs. But he understood why the church was so concerned, and he chose to cooperate because he was a team player and wanted the job.

A committee may not worry much about a clergy-woman having improper sexual relations, but she might be too easily upset to be a calming influence or too combative herself to hold a congregation together. Imagine a committee grilling a woman applying for a job: "How often are you upset at people around you? What do you do when you are upset? Have you been angry with anyone for what you considered to be insensitive statements? What did you say or do when you were angry? Has anyone ever considered you touchy? Do you feel that women are mistreated in American society, and do you blame men? How might your anger interfere with your ministry?. . ." And so on. I doubt any committee would be inclined to grill a woman candidate like this. If it did, she would surely object, and she might sue for sexual discrimination. You cannot grill a woman as closely as you can a man, and you most surely cannot grill a woman on troublesome aspects of the female temperament.

Chivalrous standards require everyone to be more careful with women than we are with men. And men must be inordinately careful, as men who upset women are stigmatized by it regardless of who was or was not being reasonable. Chivalry makes it harder to screen out troublesome women or to control them before they trash morale and reduce productivity.

Recent workplace law makes sexual harassment a civil offense, and harassment litigation is now a growing industry.[24] Only about 5 percent of these lawsuits concern demands for sexual favors, while the rest allege hostile environments.[25] Yet about 90 percent of sexual harassment lawsuits are filed by women against men. The prevalence of women suing men does not mean that men are more hostile or that women are subject to more hostility. Women are observably more hostile, but that hardly matters. Women litigate against offending men because women ought to be treated civilly, whereas men do not litigate against offending women because men ought to be able to take care of themselves. The special female-only prerogative to sue our opposites makes men yet more mistrustful of women.

MORAL CLIMATES AND PRODUCTION CLIMATES

Women are making tremendous inroads in ethical and moral institutions. Many universities now have feminist curricula and feminist administrators, which advocate for women but can be unnecessarily harsh toward men.[26] Seminaries too have feminist agendas, which support women but accuse men.[27] Seminaries that were 80 percent male only twenty years ago are now typically 30 percent male and 70 percent female,[28] as qualified young men see the disrespect and look for friendlier climates elsewhere. Men are so readily outgunned that even a sprinkling of female anger nudges them quietly out the doors.[29] Indeed, holding the men may be the most critical challenge for moral and religious institutions over the next several decades. Laws and law enforcement are becoming more protective of women and more punitive toward men who harm women.

On the other hand, women managers still seem to face a glass ceiling as corporations fail to promote women into their highest ranks. Perhaps only 5 or 10 percent of senior management are women, as opposed to 20 to 45 percent of middle management (depending on whose figures you read).[30] Of the principal managers who found small corporations and take them public, 96 percent are men, and only 4 percent are women.[31] So why are women so successful in some areas and not in others?

Success would seem to depend on the nature of the institutions. Women are most successful in what might be termed moral or ethical institutions, which are concerned about what is right and good and fair. Women gain advantage there because they are more combative and more sympathetic, dominating arguments and garnering more support, while men withdraw. In the strictly for-profit institutions, these same traits work against women. Corporate boards want managers who can control conflict and build alliances, and are wary of women who personalize conflict. Boards also want to be able to control executives and sack those who fail to meet expectations, and are wary of women who must be treated gently and might litigate against them. Men who take risks and build alliances grow small firms into competitive corporations and remain in charge.

Women will gain further inroads in the job market as they gain work experience. Women can also gain by arguing that women are being unfairly excluded, thereby personalizing the issue and turning corporate promotions into moral imperatives.

CHAPTER FIFTEEN

Together We Stand

MEN AND WOMEN report being about equally satisfied with their lives, which should not be too surprising given that we share so many of the same or similar activities. A recent poll showed that 55 percent of men and 54 percent of women considered themselves very satisfied with their lives, and another 38 percent of men and 40 percent of women rate themselves somewhat satisfied.[1]

QUALITY OF LIFE

LOOK AT where we stand as a people. Overall, are Americans continuing to prosper? Based upon the usual standard of gross domestic product (GDP), we appear to be better off year after year. But the GDP gauges how much money changes hands, which is actually a poor measure of prosperity. Some changes that involve painful trade-offs are counted only as gains. When a mother with young children takes a job outside the home, her additional income contributes to the GDP. And when she places her children in daycare, that also contributes, as do her commuting expenses, the work clothes she must buy, and the fast food she takes home because she no longer has the time to cook. But the loss of her service to her children is not subtracted out, since it did not produce a salary. Some activities that most of us would count as obvious losses are instead tallied as gains. Each divorce adds to the GDP, since a divorcing couple must pay the lawyers and support two households instead of one. Rising crime adds to the GDP, as stolen items must be replaced, security systems installed, and criminals tried and imprisoned.

A recent article in the *Atlantic Monthly* suggests an indicator of prosperity that adds in the value of family life, leisure hours, community, and so on, and subtracts out what causes additional hassles.[2] According to this indicator, prosperity in the United States increased substantially from 1950 to 1970, but has dropped off by about 45 percent since then. So if life seems more hurried and less pleasant now than it was a generation ago, it's probably because it is. Similarly, an index of social health developed at Fordham University suggests that the social climate also has deteriorated steadily since the 1970s, as families and communities continue to unravel.[3]

The moral and political climate of our generation has been so dominated by special interests that we have all but ignored the important issues that affect us all. While we each argued for our own favorite factions, a significant share of our mutual prosperity simply slipped away from us and is now gone. Modern gender politics adds to the confusion. Anger feminism is just one more faction pushing its own agenda, but sex and gender concerns should be bringing us together, not tearing us apart.

ILLUSIONS ARE COSTLY

By sympathizing with women and censuring men, our chivalrous sensitivities invite us to totally misunderstand ourselves. Take the position that men have created literally everything that is wrong with Western civilization, and then consider the corollary: Men have also created everything right and good about Western civilization.

Both are almost true, it could be argued, because nearly all of the explorers, inventors, entrepreneurs and industrialists, statesmen, and military leaders who shaped our civilization were men. The argument that men ruined everything is now commonplace in universities, and is considered socially acceptable. The corollary, that men produced the benefits of modern civilization, is considered chauvinistic and offensive, and unsuitable to mention in mixed company. By permitting only half of the truth to be heard, social propriety produces the illusion that men harm society more than they uphold it. We would do better with a higher regard for truth, and a more evenhanded approach that appeals to reason rather than to unreasonable emotions.

How do you go about improving upon something if you do not know who or what makes it work? Imagine a girl and a boy on a teeter-totter, going up and down, up and down. Now imagine that a magician makes the boy disappear, giving the illusion that the girl can operate the teeter-totter on her own. Suppose you mistake the illusion for reality. You build a teeter-totter with only one seat on it, figuring that the girl will have more fun if she does not have to worry about getting some boy to cooperate with her. Foolish illusions lead to foolish actions. The girl sits on the teeter-totter and waits, wondering why it is not working, while the boy wanders off and gets into some mischief. Perhaps we might blame the boy, as he is surely not helping matters. But then, whoever thought the teeter-totter would operate without him?

A moral climate that is unsupportive of either gender can hardly sustain an advanced civilization. As it plays into the next generation, the failure to uphold men will harm men, women, and children, and the whole culture, about equally. What will inspire our young boys toward responsible manhood? Who will guide them? Women can continue to complain about how terrible men are and how badly women are treated, but that can hardly produce more responsible men. A society that fails to honor its men will find itself with a new generation of rogue men who are truly without honor.

Moral institutions in which women complain about men become matriarchal, as men fall silent or go elsewhere. It happens every day in families, and it can happen just as easily in universities and churches. Men must be supported and also somewhat protected from female hostility if they are to stay and contribute. We agree that women should be sheltered from harsh men, but what would be the rationale for sheltering men from harsh women? We would have to go outside our innately chivalrous sensitivities, turn our whole understanding of gender backward, and recognize that men need protection from hostile women. Is that too much to expect?

COOPERATION

It is a mistake to take our traditional gender arrangements for granted. The quality of life we grew up with was based on the arrangements of that time, and it is just as easy to lose that quality as it is to improve upon it. Women count on a standard of material prosperity that has been traditionally produced by men, and men find meaning and identity in families, which have been traditionally held together by women. Yes, women who work do supplement our prosperity, and men can sometimes hold families together. But neither men nor women can casually abandon our traditional responsibilities and then expect that the job will still get done.

We each have areas of relative strengths. Women are stronger in emotional arenas, and thus are at the heart of relationships and families and at the heart of our social and moral concerns as well. Men, who are less emotional, are stronger at the compromise and accommodation by which task groups are organized and managed. So which we judge to be the stronger sex depends on which areas we consider. In earlier years, women were considered the "weaker sex," perhaps to remind men to support women or to give men the confidence to face emotional women. Surely by now, that odd convention must seem but an expedient illusion.

Nobody will ever win the battle of the sexes, and here's why: Either gender that manages to run over its opposite must live with the consequences. Our lives are woven together too closely for any of us to live comfortably in the close presence of companions who suffer and resent each other. We rely on one another too deeply and in too many ways to work only for our own interests and expect a satisfactory quality of life.

Society does not do well by simple selfishness, and any group that argues its own agenda at the expense of everyone else is acting selfishly. Thinking in terms of women versus men will not benefit us as a community, any more than it will benefit two individuals who are trying to make a go of marriage. We must think of ourselves as a community, figure out what might be best for us all together, and then work to set it in motion. How do we build a more livable community? Chances are we will do it working together for our common benefit, or we will not do it at all.

Our genes orient us strongly toward helping ourselves, somewhat less toward helping family and favored friends, and hardly at all toward helping the broader community. So we must find the wisdom and the strength to override some of our genetic inclinations, in our public actions and in our personal relationships. Being realistic about human nature helps us build upon our strengths and make allowances for the rough edges. We must understand ourselves, understand our opposites, and work to bring out the best in each other. Only through serious cooperation can we create order and meaning out of the chaos and conflict that our genetic legacies produce.

RECOMMENDED READING

ON MARRIAGES

Howard Markman, Scott Stanley, and Susan Blumberg, 1994. *Fighting for Your Marriage*. San Francisco: Jossey-Bass.

Catherine Johnson, 1992. *Lucky in Love: The Secrets of Happily Married Couples and How Their Marriages Thrive*. New York: Penguin.

ON HUMAN EVOLUTION

Helen Fisher, 1992. *The Anatomy of Love: A Natural History of Love, Marriage, and Why We Stray*. New York: Fawcett Columbine.

Jared Diamond, 1993. *The Third Chimpanzee: The Evolution and Future of the Human Animal*. New York: Harper Perennial.

Robert Wright, 1994. *The Moral Animal: The New Science of Evolutionary Psychology*. New York: Pantheon Books.

ON MANAGING GENDER FOLLIES

FOR MEN: Patric Carnes, 1992. *Out of the Shadows: Understanding Sexual Addiction*. Center City, MN: Hazelden.

FOR WOMEN: Susan Jeffers, 1989. *Opening Our Hearts to Men*. New York: Fawcett Columbine.

NOTES

PART ONE: LOVE MEANS RESOLVING CONFLICT

1. Howard Markman, "Backwards into the Future of Couples Therapy and Couples Therapy Research." *Journal of Family Psychology*, 4, 1991, 416–425.

Chapter One: Women As Sturdy Combatants

1. J. Gottman and R. Levenson, "The Social Psychophysiology of Marriage." In P. Noller and M. Fitzpatric (eds.), *Perspectives on Marital Interaction* (Clevedon, Avon, England: Multilingual Matters, 1988), 182–202; D. Baucom et al., "Gender Differences and Sex Role Identity in Marriage." In F. Fincham & T. Bradbury (eds.), *The Psychology of Marriage: Basic Issues and Applications* (New York: Guilford, 1990).
2. John Gottman, "A Theory of Marital Dissolution and Stability." *Journal of Family Psychology*, 7, 1, 1993, 57–75.
3. John Gottman, "The Social Psychology of Marriage" (Unpublished manuscript), 21: cited in Markman, 1991, 422.
4. D. Zillman, *Hostility and Aggression* (Hillsdale, NJ: Erlbaum, 1979).
5. Asked if they were over a hot conflict two hours later, 15 women but only 8 men at an alcohol counselors presentation said "yes" while 8 women and 16 men said "no." Asked at a singles workshop if they were over an argument an hour later, 5 women but only 2 men answered "yes," while 8 women and 12 men said "no."
6. J. Gottman and R. Levenson, "Assessing the Role of Emotion in Marriage." *Behavioral Assessment*, 8, 1986; 31–48; Gott-

man and Levenson, 1988; J. Gottman, "How Marriages Change." In G. Patterson (ed.), *Family Social Interaction: Content and Methodological Issues in the Study of Aggression and Depression* (Hillsdale, NY: Erlbaum, 1990), 75–101.

7. See: A. Christensen and C. Heavey, "Gender and Social Structure in the Demand/Withdraw Pattern of Marital Conflict." *Journal of Personality and Social Psychology*, 59, 1, 1990, 73–81.

8. See M. Komarovsky, *Blue Collar Marriage* (New York: Random House, 1962); L. Rubin, *Worlds of Pain: Life in the Working Class Family* (New York: Basic Books, 1976).

9. G. Margolin and B. Wampold, "Sequential Analysis of Conflict and Accord in Distressed and Nondistressed Marital Partners." *Journal of Consulting and Clinical Psychology*, 49, 1981, 554–67; C. Notarius and J. Johnson, "Emotional Expression in Husbands and Wives." *Journal of Marriage and the Family*, 44, 1982, 483–489; H. Raush, L. Barry, W. Hertel, and M. Swain, *Communication, Conflict and Marriage* (San Francisco: Jossey-Bass, 1974); C. Schaap, *Communication and Adjustment in Marriage* (Lisse, the Netherlands: Swets & Zeitlinger, 1982).

10. M. Komarovsky, *Dilemmas of Masculinity* (New York: Norton, 1976); L Rubin, *Intimate Strangers: Men and Women Together* (New York: Harper & Row, 1983); H. Kelly, J. Cunningham, J. Grisham, L. Lefebvre, C. Sink and G. Yablon, "Sex Differences in Comments Made During Conflict Within Close Heterosexual Pairs." *Sex Roles*, 4, 1978, 473–479.

11. Beginning with early observations by L. Terman, P. Buttenweiser, L. Ferguson, W. Johnson, and D. Wilson, *Psychological Factors in Marital Happiness* (New York: McGraw-Hill, 1938).

12. An analysis of marital case records by Agustus Napier tallies two wives dominating to each husband who dominates: *The Fragile Bond: In Search of Equal, Intimate, and Enduring Marriage* (New York: HarperCollins, 1990).

13. J. Gottman, "Why Marriages Fail." *Family Therapy Networker*, May/June, 1994, 40–48.

14. Chance accounts for 50% of the cases, and the 85% figure (35% better than chance) accounts for 70% of the remaining

cases. That leaves only 30% to be accounted for by gender-unrelated traits.

15. Harriet Lerner, "The Taboos Against Female Anger." *Menninger Perspective,* Winter, 1977, 5–11.

16. Harriet Lerner, *The Dance of Anger* (New York: Perennial Library, 1985), 5.

17. Celia Halas, *Why Can't a Woman Be More Like a Man?* (New York: Macmillan, 1981): see Carol Tavris, *Anger: The Misunderstood Emotion* (New York: Simon and Schuster, 1989), 195–196.

18. Sandra Thomas and Cheryl Jefferson, *Use Your Anger: A Woman's Guide to Empowerment* (New York: Simon & Schuster, 1996), 6.

19. Such as: Herb Goldberg, *The Hazards of Being Male* (New York: New American Library, 1976); and Jack Nichols, *Men's Liberation* (New York: Penguin, 1975).

Chapter Two: The Nature of Gender

1. W. Gallagher, "How We Become What We Are." *Atlantic Monthly,* Sept. 1994, 38–55.

2. John Archer, "Sex Differences in Social Behavior: Are the Social Role and Evolutionary Explanations Compatible?" *American Psychologist,* 51, 9, 1996, 909–917; ___, "Darwinian and Non-Darwinian Accounts." 52, 12, 1997, 1383–84. Evolution often works in cooperation with socialization.

3. The science of evolution involves multiple competing and overlapping principles. Traits can be selected because they benefit an individual or a genetically related kin group. Single genes can influence multiple traits, and single traits are often influenced by multiple genes. Genetically carried propensities show themselves in some circumstances but not in others.

4. Susan Rogers, "Female Forms of Power and the Myth of Male Dominance: A Model of Female/Male Interaction in Peasant Society." *American Ethnologist,* 2, 1975, 727–56: see Helen Fisher, *The Anatomy of Love: A Natural History of Love, Marriage, and Why We Stray* (New York: Fawcett Columbine, 1992), 216.

5. Martin Whyte, *The Status of Women in Preindustrial Societies* (Princeton: Princeton University Press, 1978): see Fisher, 1992, 217.

6. Anne Moir and David Jessel, *Brain Sex: The Real Difference Between Men and Women* (New York: Dell, 1991); John Leo, "Differences Emerge Between Male, Female." Universal Press Syndicate, Feb. 21, 1995.

7. Moir & Jessel, 1991, 48: cited in K. Peterson, "Battle of the Sexes Starts in the Brain." *USA Today*, Mar. 14, 1995, section D.

8. Current thinking holds that secondary sex traits often arise from sexual selection, by male competition for females and female choice of males.

9. From G. P. Murdock's *Ethnographic Atlas:* analyzed by Robert Wright, *The Moral Animal: The New Science of Evolutionary Psychology* (New York: Pantheon, 1994), 90.

10. Robert Wright, "Our Cheating Hearts." *Time,* Aug. 15, 1994, 44–52. Obviously, this presumes approximately as many men as women.

11. Donald Symons, *The Evolution of Human Sexuality* (New York: Oxford University Press, 1979): cited in Wright, 1994, 38 & 62.

12. David Givens, *Love Signals: How to Attract a Mate* (New York: Crown, 1983); Timothy Perper, *Sex Signals: The Biology of Love.* (Philadelphia: ISI Press, 1985): cited in Fisher, 1992, 25 & 32.

13. Warren Farrell, *Why Men Are the Way They Are* (New York: McGraw Hill, 1986), 124–131.

14. Whyte, 1978: see Fisher, 1992, 32.

15. Frans de Waal, *Chimpanzee Politics: Power and Sex Among Apes* (Baltimore: Johns Hopkins University Press, 1982, 1989), 186. The percentages were tallied by student Ronald Noë.

16. Analyses by Charles Sibley and Jon Ahlquist, reviewed by Jared Diamond, *The Third Chimpanzee: The Evolution and Future of the Human Animal* (New York: HarperCollins, 1992), 23. Estimates vary slightly on the amount of genetic information that is identical.

17. R. Clark & E. Hatfield, "Gender Differences in Receptivity to Sexual Offers." *Journal of Psychology and Human Sexuality,* 2, 1989, 39–55; see D. Buss & D. Schmitt, "Sexual Strategies Theory: An Evolutionary Perspective on Human Mating." *Psychological Review,* 100, 1993, 227; and Wright, Aug. 1994, 51.

18. M. Oliver and J. Hyde, "Gender Differences in Sexuality: A Meta-Analysis." *Psychological Bulletin*, 114, 1993, 29–51.

19. H. Ehrlichman & R. Eichenstein, "Private Wishes: Gender Similarities and Differences." *Sex Roles*, 26, 1992, 399–422: cited in Archer, 1996, 917.

20. D. Symons and B. Ellis, "Human Male-Female Differences in Sexual Desire." In A. Rasa, C. Voge, and E. Voland (eds.), *The Sociobiology of Sexual and Reproductive Strategies* (London: Chapman & Hall, 1989), 131–146: see Archer, 1996, 913.

21. UCLA and Council on Education Study, 1997: reported by Margot Hornblower, "Learning to Earn." *Time*, February 24, 1997, 34.

22. Symons, 1979.

23. See Wright, 1994, 42–49.

24. Among the rare exceptions, such as sea horses and sea snipes, the males invest more than the females in each offspring, thus supporting the principle that the sex that invests more will be choosier. Here the exceptions prove the rule: See R. Wright, "Feminists, meet Mr. Darwin." *The New Republic*, Nov. 28, 1994, 36; and J. Grier and T. Burk, *Animal Behavior* (St. Louis: Mosby–Year Book, 1992), 356–357.

25. Sara Hardy, "Empathy, Polyandry, and the Myth of the Coy Female." In R. Bleier (ed.), *Feminist Approaches to Science* (New York: Pergamon, 1988).

26. Wright, Nov. 1994, 34–46.

27. George Williams, *Adaptation and Natural Selection: A Critique of Some Current Evolutionary Thought* (Princeton, NJ: Princeton University Press), 1966; Robert Trivers, "Parental Investment and Sexual Selection." In B. G. Campbell (ed.), *Sexual Selection and the Descent of Man, 1871–1971* (Chicago: Aldine, 1972).

28. Initial findings by A. Bateman, "Intra-Sexual Selection in *Drosophila*." *Heredity*, 2, 1948, 349–68.

29. Trivers, 1972, 153.

30. Charles Darwin separated selection into natural selection, by survival of the fittest, and a second process, sexual selection, by which mates choose and are chosen. Currently, the term *natural selection* is often used to refer to both survival and mate selection.

31. David Buss, "Psychological Sex Differences: Origins Through Sexual Selection." *American Psychologist*, 50, 3, 1995, 164–168.
32. Alice Eagly, "The Science and Politics of Comparing Women and Men." *American Psychologist*, 50, 3, 1995, 145–158.
33. Buss, 1995.
34. David Buss, *The Evolution of Desire* (New York: Basic Books, 1994): cited in Beth Azar, "Modern Mating: Attraction on Survival?" *APA Monitor*, July or Aug, 1996, 30.
35. Fisher, 1992.
36. The early Kinsey findings are terribly skewed by sampling biases, and he does not claim to have representative samples.
37. Bronislaw Malinowski, *The Sexual Life of Savages in North-Western Melanesia:An Ethnographic Account of Courtship, Marriage and Family Life Among the Natives of the Trobriand Islands, British New Guinea* (New York: Harcourt, Brace, 1929), 319.
38. M. Shostak, *Nisa: The Life and Words of a !Kung Woman* (New York: Vintage, 1981), 271.
39. Fisher, 1992, 34–35.
40. Symons, 1979, 138–41; C. Badcock, *Oedipus in Evolution: A New Theory of Sex* (Oxford: Basil Blackwell, 1990), 142–60; Wright, 1994, 68.
41. R. Thornhill, "Sexual Selection in the Black-Tipped Hangingfly." *Scientific American*, 242, 6, 1980, 162–172.
42. Warren Farrell, *The Myth of Male Power* (New York: Berkley Books, 1994), 34.
43. Suggested by P. Draper and H. Harpending, "A Sociobiological Perspective on the Development of Human Reproductive Strategies." In K.B. MacDonald (ed.), *Sociobiological Perspectives on Human Development* (New York: Springer-Verlag, 1988), 349.
44. L. Silverstein, "Primate Research, Family Politics, and Social Policy: Transforming 'Cads' Into 'Dads'." *Journal of Family Therapy*, 7, 3, 1994, 267–282.
45. Trivers, 1972, 145.

PART TWO: THE BINDS THAT TIE

Chapter Three: Pursuers and Distancers

1. T. Fogarty, "Marital Crisis." In P. Guerin (ed.), *Family Therapy:Theory and Practice* (New York: Gardner Press, 1976);

___,"The Distancer and Pursuer." *The Family*, 7, 1979, 11–16. D. Wile, *Couples Therapy: A Non-Traditional Interpretation* (New York: Dryden Press, 1981); A. Christensen and C. Heavey, "Gender and Social Structure in the Demand/ Withdraw Pattern of Marital Conflict." *Journal of Personality and Social Psychology*, 59,1, 1990, 73–81. Augustus Napier, "The Rejection–Intrusion Pattern: A Central Family Dynamic." *Journal of Marriage and Family Counseling*, 4, 1978, 5–12.

2. Deborah Tannen, *You Just Don't Understand* (New York: Ballentine, 1990).
3. See E. Pettit and B. Bloom, "Whose Decision Was It?" *Journal of Marriage and the Family*, 46, 587–595; A. Zeiss, R. Zeiss, and S. Johnson, "Sex Differences in Initiation of and Adjustment to Divorce." *Journal of Divorce*, 4, 2, 1980, 21–33.
4. In 1986, women filed 61.5% and men filed 32.6% of divorces, with the remainder filed jointly. Women without children filed a higher proportion (65.7%) of divorces than those with children (56.9%), suggesting that children bind women to marriages. Associated Press Wire Service, June 7th, 1989, from the National Center for Health Statistics.
5. *Time*, June 6, 1988, 35.
6. C. Hill, Z. Rubin and L.A. Peplau, "Breakups Before Marriage: The End of 103 Affairs." *Journal of Social Issues*, 1, 1976, 147–168.
7. E.J. Kanin, K.D. Davidson, and S.R. Scheck, "A Research Note on Male-Female Differentials in the Experience of Heterosexual Love." *Journal of Sex Research*, 1970, 6, 64–72.
8. Hill, 1976.
9. Elaine Walster and G. William Walster, *A New Look at Love* (Reading, Mass: Addison-Wesley, 1978).
10. C.W. Hobart, "The Incidence of Romanticism During Courtship." *Social Forces*, 36, 1958, 364.
11. Kanin et al, 1970.
12. Hobart, 1958, 364; L. Peplau, Z. Rubin, and C. Hill. "Sexual Intimacy in Dating Relationships." *Journal of Social Issues*, 33, 1977, 86–109; Zick Rubin. 1973. *Liking and Loving: An Invitation to Social Psychology*. (New York: Holt, Rinehart & Winston.)

13. In a survey of 83,000 women, reported by *Ladies' Home Journal,* Jan. 1983.
14. The difference between *feeling* love versus *meaning* it is from professor Peter Ossorio, at the University of Colorado, 1972.
15. Charles Darwin, *The Descent of Man, and Selection in Relation to Sex,* 1871: (Princeton, NJ: Princeton University Press, 1981—facsimile edition). ___, *Expressions of the Emotions in Man and Animals,* (1872: Chicago: University of Chicago Press edition, 1965).
16. In Monty Python's *The Meaning of Life* (MCA Home Video, 1986).
17. Tannen, 1990, 86.
18. T. Wills, R. Weiss, and G. Patterson, "A Behavioral Analysis of the Determinants of Marital Satisfaction." *Journal of Consulting and Clinical Psychology,* 42, 1974, 802–811.
19. John Gottman, "Predicting the Longitudinal Course of Marriages." *Journal of Marriage and Family Therapy,* 17, 1, 1991, 4.
20. M. Street, "What Men Will Never Tell You." *Ladies' Home Journal,* Apr. 1994, 106.
21. Cited by *Washing Post* columnist William Raspberry.
22. Robert Fulghum. *All I Really Need to Know I Learned in Kindergarten* (New York: Villard, 1990), 56.
23. David Buss, "Sex Differences in Human Mate Preferences: Evolutionary Hypotheses Tested in 37 Cultures." *Behavioral and Brain Sciences,* 12, 1989, 1–49; and Buss, 1994, chapter 2.
24. Buss, 1994.
25. Farrell, 1986, especially 17–90.
26. L. Peplau and S. Gordon, "Women and Men in Love: Sex Differences in Close Relationships." In V. O'Leary, R. Unger, and B. Wallston (eds.), *Women, Gender, and Social Psychology* (Hilllsdale, NJ: Erlbaum, 1985); J. Robertson and L. Fitzgerald, "The (Mis)treatment of Men: Effects of Client Gender Role and Life-Style on Diagnosis and Attribution of Pathology." *Journal of Counseling Psychology,* 37, 1990, 3–9; S. Shields, "Functionalism, Darwinism, and the Psychology of Women: A Study in Social Myth." *American Psychologist,* 30, 1987, 739–754.

27. G. Williams, *Adaptation and Natural Selection: A Critique of Some Current Evolutionary Thought* (Princeton, NJ: Princeton University Press, 1966).

28. F. Fujita, E. Diener, and E. Sandvik, "Gender Differences in Negative Affect and Well-Being: The Case For Emotional Intensity." *Journal of Personality and Social Psychology*, 1991, 61, 3, 427–434.

29. Strong sex differences are found in throwing distance and accuracy, and in cognitive spacial rotation abilities necessary to aim moving projectiles at moving targets. R. Ashmore, "Sex, Gender, and the Individual." In L. Pervin (ed.), *Handbook of Personality: Theory and Research* (New York: Guilford Press, 1990) 486–526; and Buss, 1995, 166.

30. Cited in Steven Naifeh, *Why Can't Men Open Up?* (New York: Warner Books, 1985).

31. Reported by P. Adelmann, *Psychology Today*, May 1989, 69.

32. Study reported on National Public Radio, 1980.

33. J. Gottman, May/June, 1994.

Chapter Four: Expressers and Fixers

1. L. Rubin, *Just Friends: The Role of Friendship in our Lives* (New York: Harper & Row, 1985).

2. Tannen, 1990, 49–73.

3. Tannen, 1990, 96–122.

4. G. Murdock, "The Common Denominator of Cultures." In G. Murdock, *Culture and Society* (Pittsburg: Pittsburg University Press, 1945); R. Wright, 1994, 236–262.

5. K. Hill and H. Kaplan, "Trade-Offs in Male and Female Reproductive Strategies Among the Ache, parts 1 and 2" (esp. 282–83). In L. Betzig, M. B. Mulder, and P. Turke (eds.) *Human Reproductive Behavior: A Darwinian Perspective* (New York: Cambridge University Press, 1988).

6. Frans de Waal, "Sex Differences in the Formation of Coalitions Among Chimpanzees." *Ethology and Sociobiology*, 5, 1984, 239–55; J. Goodall, *The Chimpanzees of Gombe: Patterns of Behavior* (Cambridge, Mass.: Harvard University Press, 1986).

7. Quoted in Symons, 1979, 162: see Wright, 1994, 248.

8. B. Low, "Cross-Cultural Patterns in the Training of Children: An Evolutionary Perspective." *Journal of Comparative Psychology*, 103, 1989, 311–319: reported in Archer, 1996, 915.

9. Figures based on corporate executives, cited in C. Casamassima, "Battle of the Bucks." *Psychology Today*, March/April, 43, 1995.

10. E.W. Burgess and P. Wallin, *Engagement and Marriage* (Philadelphia: Lippincott, 1953), 270: 37.5% of men vs. 22.3 % of women report frequently conceding to avoid losing the fiancé's affection.

11. Catherine Johnson, *Lucky in Love* (New York: Penguin Books, 1992), 97–100.

12. Citation could not be located.

13. Thomas Hargrove and G. Stempell III, "Poll: More Men than Women Eye Marriage." Scripps Howard News Service, July 29, 1993.

14. J. Smith, J. Mercy, and J. Conn, "Marital Status and the Risk of Suicide." *American Journal of Public Health*, 78, 1, 1988, 79: as cited in Farrell, 1994, 169.

15. Comment credited to psychiatrist and media analyst Frank Pittman.

16. I believe Groucho made this quip after being rejected by a club because he was Jewish.

17. Elaine Hatfield and G. William Walster, *A New Look at Love* (Lanham, MD: University Press of America, 1978); see also A. Cohen and I. Silverman, "Repression–Sensitization as a Dimension of Personality" in B. A. Maher, Ed., *Progress in Experimental Personality Research, Vol. 1* (New York: Academic Press, 1964).

18. A. Skolnick: as summarized in *Psychology Today*, Dec., 1987, 6.

19. C. Johnson, 1992, 63.

PART THREE: THE MIX AND MISMATCH OF SEXUAL INTERESTS

1. See Hatfield and Walster, 1978, for a comparison of romantic and companionate love.

2. T. Houston, S. McHale, and A. Crouter, "When the Honeymoon Is Over." in R. Gilmore and S. Duck (eds.), *The*

Emerging Field of Personal Relationships (Hillsdale, NJ.: Lawrence Erlbaum, 1986).

Chapter Five: Imbalanced Sexual Interests

1. B. Zilbergeld and P. Kilmann, "The Scope and Effectiveness of Sex Therapy." *Psychotherapy,* 21, 1984, 319–26.
2. H.S. Kaplan and C. J. Sager, "Sexual Patterns at Different Ages." *Medical Aspects of Human Sexuality,* June, 1971, 10–23.
3. Karen Shanor, *The Shanor Study: The Sexual Sensitivity of the American Male* (New York: Dial Press, 1978), 253.
4. Buss, 1994.
5. Jared Diamond, "Why Women Change." *Discover,* July 1996, 131–137; ___ *The Third Chimpanzee* (New York: Harper-Perennial, 1992), 133–135.
6. Reported by David Buss, 1994, 187.
7. Cited in R. Bell, Premarital Sex in a Changing Society (Englewood Cliffs, NJ: Prentice-Hall, 1966), 137.
8. A. Kinsey, W. Pomeroy, C. Martin, and P. Gebhard, *Sexual Behavior in the Human Female* (Philadelphia: Saunders, 1953).
9. My observation is that this seems to happen in about half of such cases.

Chapter Six: Wish Lists

1. Ray Bergner and Laurie Bergner, "Sexual Misunderstandings: A Descriptive and Pragmatic Formulation." *Psychotherapy,* 27, 3, 1990, 464–467.
2. W. Waller, *The Family: A Dynamic Interpretation* (New York: Holt, Rinehart and Winston, 1951): supported in a review by J. R. Eshleman, *The Family* (Boston: Allyn and Bacon, 1985), 326–27.
3. Kaplan and Sager, 1971.
4. Ibid.
5. M. S. Weinberg, R. Swensson, and S. Hammersmith, "Sexual Autonomy and the Status of Women: Models of Female Sexuality in U.S. Sex Manuals from 1950 to 1980." *Social Problems,* 30, Feb. 1980, 312–24. Summarized in Eshleman, 1985.

Chapter Seven: The Politics of Pleasure

1. Anthony Pietropinto and Jacqueline Simenauer, *Beyond the Male Myth* (New York: Times Books, 1977). Cited in J.S. Hyde, *Human Sexuality* (New York: McGraw-Hill, 1992), 354-55.

2. H. J. Rose, *Handbook of Greek Mythology* (New York: E.P. Dutton, 1959). Other accounts portray Teiresias as a lesser God who lived on earth for several years as a woman, but the conclusion is the same.

3. C. Kerényi, *The Heroes of the Greeks*, trans. H.J. Rose (New York: Grove Press, 1960), 100. Used by permission of Grove/Atlantic, Inc.

4. Joyce Brothers, *What Every Woman Ought to Know About Love and Marriage* (New York: Random House, 1984), 128.

5. Eugene Linden, "Bonobos." *National Geographic*, 181, 3, 46–53, March, 1992.

6. Karen Wright, "Evolution of the Big O." *Discover*, June 1992, 53–59.

7. Based on a survey of 3,679 women. Mark Bellis, et al, *Company*, 1989, April, 60–92.

8. Suggested by John Alcock, "Ardent Adaptionism." *Natural History*, April 4, 1987: cited in K. Wright, 1992.

9. D. Rancourt-Laferriere, "Four Adaptive Aspects of the Female Orgasm." *Journal of Social and Biological Structures*, 6, 1983, 319–33.

10. R. Robin Baker and Mark Bellis, "Human Sperm Competition: Ejaculate Manipulation by Females as a Function for the Female Orgasm." *Animal Behavior*, 46, 1993, 887–909. Female orgasm retains more sperm in the cervix when it occurs between 1 minute before and 40 minutes after male ejaculation. See also R. L. Smith. "Human Sperm Competition." In R. L. Smith (ed.), *Sperm Competition and the Evolution of Mating Systems* (New York: Academic Press, 1984).

11. Randy Thornhill, S. Gangestad, and R. Comer, "Human Female Orgasm and Mate Fluctuating Asymmetry." *Animal Behavior*, 50, 1995, 1601–1615; see also F. Bryant Furlow and R. Thornhill, "The Orgasm Wars." *Psychology Today*, Jan–Feb 1996, 42–46.

12. David Buss, "Parental Uncertainty and the Complex Repertoire of Human Mating Strategies." *American Psychologist*, 51, 2, 1996, 161–162.

13. Ruth Westheimer, *Dr. Ruth's Guide for Married Lovers* (New York: Warner Books, 1986), 78.

Chapter Eight: Fantasies

1. Douglas Kenrick: cited in Wright, Aug. 1994, 48.
2. J. Markert, "Romancing the Reader: A Demographic Profile." *Romantic Times*, 18, Sept. 1984.
3. Symons, 1979, esp. chapter 7: "The Desire for Sexual Variety."
4. D. Buss and D. Schmitt, "Sexual Strategies Theory: An Evolutionary Perspective on Human Mating." *Psychological Review*, 100, 1993, 204–232.
5. Gilbert Bartell, "Group Sex Among the Mid-Americans." *Journal of Sex Research*, 1970, 6, 113–130; Brian Gilmartin, "That Swinging Couple Down the Block." *Psychology Today*, 1975, 8 (9), 54.
6. Kanin et al., 1970, 64–72.
7. See research presented in Chapter 3: "Pursuers and Distancers."
8. C. Muehlenhard and S. Cook, "Men's Self-Reports of Unwanted Sexual Activity." *Journal of Sex Research*, 24, 1988, 58–72: Cited in: "Can a Man Be Raped?" Time, June 3, 1991, 53.
9. "Sex in America Today." *Parade*, Aug. 7, 1994, 4–6.
10. Pioneered by marital behavior therapist Richard Stuart. Personal communication, Aug. 1, 1995.
11. R. Baron and D. Byrne, *Social Psychology: Understanding Human Interaction*, 2nd ed. (Boston: Allyn, 1977): cited in J. McCary and S. McCary, *McCary's Human Sexuality*, 4th ed. (Belmont, Calif.: Wadsworth, 1982), 205.

PART FOUR: GENUINE UNDERSTANDING

Chapter Nine: Soul Mates

1. Johnson, 1992, 43.
2. Robert Wright, "Can Machines Think?" *Time*, March 25, 1996, 50–56.

3. Diane Ackerman, "The Fears That Save Us." *Parade*, Jan. 26, 1997, 18–20.

4. See David Chalmers, *The Conscious Mind* (Oxford University Press, 1996); Colin McGinn *The Problem of Consciousness: Essays Toward a Resolution* (Blackwell Publishers, 1993).

Chapter Ten: Listen to Me!

1. Tom Rusk, *The Power of Ethical Persuasion:Winning Through Understanding at Work and at Home* (New York: Viking Penguin, 1994).

2. Markman, 1991; K. Lindahl and H. Markman, "Communication and Negative Affect Regulation in the Family." In E. Blechman (ed.), *Emotions and Families* (New York: Plenum, 1990), 99–116.

3. Howard Markman, Scott Stanley, and Susan Blumberg, *Fighting for Your Marriage* (San Francisco: Jossey-Bass, 1994).

4. Janet Lever, "Sex Differences in the Games Children Play." *Social Problems*, 23, 1976, 478–487; See also Markman et al, 1994, 43–48.

5. Markman et al, 1994, 44–46.

6. Markman et al, 1994, 5–7.

7. Gottman, 1991, 4. The reported r=.92 correlation between the husband's heart rate and deteriorating satisfaction over the next three years accounts for 84% of the variance, which might appear slightly lower on a second sample.

8. Richard Driscoll, *Mental Shielding to Brush Off Hostility* (Knoxville Tenn.: Frontiers Press, 1994).

9. See reviews in P. Zimbardo and M. Leippe, *The Psychology of Attitude Change and Social Influence* (Philadelphia: Temple University Press, 1991), 100–107; S. Strong, "Social Psychological Approach to Psychotherapy Research." In S. Garfield and A. Bergin (eds.), *Handbook of Psychotherapy and Behavior Change,* 2nd ed. (New York: John Wiley and Sons, 1978), 122–24.

10. See findings in chapter 2, "Women as Sturdy Combatants."

PART FIVE: WHERE TO FROM HERE?

Chapter Eleven: Surprisingly Chivalrous

1. C. Southwick, "An Experimental Study of Intragroup
   Agonistic Behavior in Rhesus Monkeys (*Macaca mulatta*)."
   Behavior, 28, 1967, 182–209.
2. Richard Lore and L. Schultz, "Control of Human Aggression." *American Psychologist*, 48, 1, 1993, 20.
3. R. Lore and K. Flannelly, "Rat Societies." *Scientific American*,
   106–116, May 1977.
4. Donald Grayson, "Differential Mortality and the Donner
   Party Disaster." *Evolutionary Anthropology*, 1993, 151–159.
   I did not include here the five men who died, before the
   encampment, from violent confrontations.
5. The one exception was a 12-year-old boy, who might have
   been performing exhausting physical tasks along with the
   the men.
6. Laura Ingalls Wilder, *The Long Winter* (New York: Harper-
   Collins, 1953) 227, 252, & 308.
7. J.P.W. Rivers, "Women and Children Last: An Essay on Sex
   Discrimination in Disasters." *Disasters*, 6, 1982, 256–267;
   ___, "The Nutritional Biology of Famine." In G.A. Harrison
   (ed), *Famine* (Oxford: Oxford University Press, 1988),
   56–106.
8. In the U.S., three times as many men as women are murdered
   each year, primarily by men. U.S. Department of Justice,
   Federal Bureau of Investigations, *Crime in the United States*,
   1988, 11: as reported by Farrell, 1994, 214. In a *Time* tally of
   464 people shot in a single week, 84% were men: "7 Deadly
   Days," *Time*, July 17, 1989, 31.
9. L. Wolf, "Human Evolution and the Sexual Behavior of
   Female Primates." In J. Loy and C. Peters (eds.), *Understanding Behavior* (New York: Oxford University Press), 1991,
   136–137; K. Stewart and A. Harcourt, "Gorillas: Variation in
   Female Relationships." In B. Smuts et al., eds., *Primate Societies* (Chicago: University of Chicago Press, 1987); Frans de
   Waal, *Chimpanzee Politics* (Baltimore: Johns Hopkins Univer-
   sity Press, 1982), 168; J. Goodall. *The Chimpanzees of Gombe:
   Patterns of Behavior* (Cambridge, Mass: Harvard University
   Press, 1986), 453–66; R. Wright, 1994, 51.

10. de Waal, 1982: as cited in E. Linden, "A Curious Kinship: Apes and Humans." *National Geographic*, 181, 3, 35, March, 1992.

11. B. Smuts, "Male Aggression Against Women: An Evolutionary Perspective." *Human Nature*, 3, 1992, 1–44; ___, "The Evolutionary Origins of Patriarchy." *Human Nature*, 6, 1995, 1–32.

12. de Waal, 1982: in Fisher, 1992, 222.

13. Based on social security contributions, which are not paid on higher earnings and thus may slightly underestimate the percent men earn as compared to women. As of 1985, men contributed $75 billion, women $38 billion. U.S. Dept. Of Health and Human Services, Social Security Administration, Office of Research and Statistics, *Earnings and Employment Data for Salary Workers Covered Under Social Security by State and County, 1985*, compiled by L. Fribush, publication #13–11784, Oct. 1988, 1: as cited in Farrell, 1994, 350.

14. An average of $470 per year is spent for husbands versus $767 for wives among married couples without children (with $553 not categorized by sex). Figures vary slightly for unmarried men and women with and without children. See: U.S. Bureau of the Census, *Statistical Abstract of the United States: 1994 (114th edition)*. Washington, DC, 1994, 462. "Apparel and services" is the only category broken down by sex.

15. Andrew Kadar, "The Sex-Bias Myth in Medicine." *Atlantic Monthly*, Aug. 1994, 66–70. Feminist rebuttals offered opposing interpretations, but none even tried to challenge any of Kadar's basic figures: see Letters, *Atlantic Monthly*, Dec. 1994, 16. Warren Farrell argues that better medical care contributes to women living longer than men (1994, 180–198).

16. J. Vaessey and K. Howard. "Who Seeks Psychotherapy." *Psychotherapy*, 30, 4, 1993, 546–553.

17. In 1987, the National Institude of Health spent 13.5% of its budget to research female-only diseases, and 6.5% on male-only diseases. In 1993, the NIH spent $213 million studying breast cancer, and $51 million researching prostate cancer (a third more women are killed by breast cancer than men by prostate cancer—46,000 women vs. 35,000 men a year—and

at slightly younger ages): see Kader, 1994. Yet more research is done on men than on women. New medications are often tested first on men, to avoid exposing women to unnecessary risks, and then further tested on both sexes once deemed sufficiently safe.

18. Men contributed $75 billion, women $38 billion as of 1985. U.S. Dept. Of Health and Human Services, Social Security Administration, Office of Research and Statistics, *Earnings and Employment Data for Salary Workers Covered Under Social Security by State and County, 1985,* compiled by L. Fribush, publication #13–11784, Oct. 1988, 1: as cited in Farrell, 1994, 350.

19. The average benefit was $8,200 per year for men, and $6,200 per year for women as of 1990. U.S. Department of Health and Human Services, Social Security Administration, *Social Security Bulletin Annual Statistical Supplement* (Washington, D.C.: USGPO, 1991), 149. The average man retiring at 65 who lives his expected 7 more years receives $57,000; the average women who lives her expected 14 more years receives $87,000: as cited in Farrell, 1994, 350.

20. R. Ropers, "The Rise of the New Urban Homeless." *Public Affairs Report,* (Berkley: U. of California at Berkley, Institute of Government Studies, 1985), Oct–Dec, 26, #5 & 6, 1; and J. Wright, *Address Unknown; The Homeless in America* (New York: Aldine De Gruyter, 1989): as cited in Farrell, 1994, 208–209.

21. Wright, 1994, 62.

22. Wright, 1994.

23. Figures as of July, 1992. U.S. Department of Health and Human Services, NIOSH (Morgantown, West Virginia). Cited in Farrell, 1994, 106.

24. M. Wilson & M. Daly, "Competitiveness, Risk Taking, and Violence: The Young Male Syndrome." *Ethology and Sociobiology,* 6, 1985, 59–73: summary in Buss, 1995.

25. Indications are that hunting injuries were common among the Neanderthals, who lived throughout Europe just prior to modern man but do not appear to be our direct ancestors. Rick Gore, "Neandertals." *National Geographic,* 189, 1, Jan. 1996, 2–35.

26. Wilson and Daly, 1985, 59–73.

27. Jane Goodall, *The Chimpanzees of Gombe* (Cambridge, Mass.: Harvard Universty Press, 1986); see also Diamond, 1992, 191–94; and Linden, "Apes and Humans," 1992, 33–34.

28. John Barry and Evan Thomas, "At War Over Women." *Newsweek*, May 12, 1997, 38–39.

29. J. Brown, "A Note on the Sexual Division of Labor." *American Anthropology*, 72, 1970, 1073–78; K. Hawkes, "Why Do Men Hunt? Benefits for Risky Choices." In E. Cashdan (ed.), *Risk and Uncertainty in Tribal and Peasant Economies*, (Boulder: Westview Press, 1990), 145–166.

30. Murray Straus and Richard Gelles, "Societal Change and Change in Family Violence from 1975 to 1985 as Revealed by Two National Surveys." *Journal of Marriage and the Family*, 48, 1986, 465–479: see review by Christina Sommers, *Who Stole Feminism?* (New York: Touchstone, 1994), 188–208.

31. In Straus and Gelles survey, 14 out of 3,500 women, or .4% of the sample, reported these most serious offenses (Straus and Gelles, 1986, 471): see also Sommers, 1994, 196–97, for figures confirming these findings.

32. A. Klein, "Spousal/Partner Assault: A Protocol for the Sentencing and Supervision of Offenders" (Quincy, Mass.: Quincy Court, 1993), 5–7. Batterers had an average of 4.5 prior crimes against persons.

33. The review is limited to studies using proper sampling and does not include those using self-selected samples.

34. M. Straus, "Physical Assaults by Wives: A Major Social Problem." In R. Gelles and D. Loseke (eds.). *Current Controversies on Family Violence* (Newbury Park, CA: Sage, 1993), 71. Studies based on self-selected samples were not included. See also R. Gelles, *The Violent Home: A Study of Physical Aggression Between Husbands and Wives* (Beverly Hills, CA: Sage, 1974); K. Lane and P. Gwartney-Gibbs, "Violence in the Context of Dating and Sex." *Journal of Family Issues*, 6, 1985, 45–59; M. Laner and J. Thompson, "Abuse and Aggression in Courting Couples." *Deviant Behavior: An Interdisciplinary Journal*, 3, 1982, 229–244; E. Jouriles and K. O'Leary, "Interspousal Reliability of Reports of Marital Violence." *Journal of*

Consulting and Clinical Psychology, 53, 1985, 419–421; J. Makepeace, "Life Events, Stress, and Courtship Violence." *Family Relations*, 32, 1983, 101–109; L. Nisonoff and I. Bitman, "Spouse Abuse: Incidence and Relationship to Selected Demographic Variables." *Victimology*, 4, 1979, 131–140; A. Sack, J. Keller and R. Howard, "Conflict Tactics and Violence in Dating Situations." *International Journal of Sociology of the Family*, 12, 1982, 89–100; S. Steinmetz, "The Battered Husband Syndrome." *Victimology: An International Journal*, 2, 1977–78, 499–509; and R. McNeely and G. Robinson-Simpson, "The Truth about Domestic Violence." *Social Work*, Nov.–Dec., 1987.

35. Suzanne Steinmetz, *The Cycle of Violence. Assertive, Aggressive, and Abusive Family Interaction* (New York: Praeger Press, 1977).

36. Steinmetz, 1977.

37. The National Coalition of Free Men is one of the few organizations that takes husband battering seriously: contact at (516) 482–6378.

38. The figures add properly when 8% are mutual confrontations, 4% are only men hitting (8% + 4% = 12% total men hitting) and 4% are only women hitting (8% + 4% = 12% total women hitting).

39. See Sommers, 1994, 188–208 for an account of how the figures on battering are exaggerated and misinterpreted.

40. The Straus and Gelles survey found that 7.3 % of the 137 women who were seriously assaulted (or .25% of all women) reported they required medical attention. M. Straus, "Physical Assaults by Wives: A Major Social Problem." In R. Gelles and D. Loseke (eds.). *Current Controversies on Family Violence.* (Newbury Park, CA: Sage, 1993). Confirmed by phone conversation with Murray Straus, Nov. 29, 1995, and Jan. 11, 1996. In a 1992 survey by the Family Violence Prevention Fund, nurses reported from 2 incidents per month in small hospitals to 8 in large hospitals, confirming generally low rates of domestic assault injuries requiring medical attention (reported in Sommers, 1994, 203).

41. The Straus and Gelles survey found that 1% of the 95 men seriously assaulted required medical attention (or .04% of the sample). Straus, 1993. Some 38% of domestic casualties in

one inner city emergency room were men, vs. 62% women: "Domestic Violence Victims in the Emergency Department," *Journal of the American Medical Association*, June 22–29, 1984, 3260 (as cited in Sommers, 1994, 201). An estimate of half as many men as women requiring medical attention based on these later figures would be considered high for the general population. The 11 injuries (10 women and 1 man) located by the Straus and Gelles survey are not sufficient for a reliable comparison.

42. Based on the 16% of couples who reported assaults, vs. the .29% (.25% of women +.04% of men) who reported injuries requiring medical attention.

43. J. Mercy and L. Saltzman, "Fatal Violence among Spouses in the United States," 1976–85. *American Journal of Public Health*, 79, 5, 1989, 595–9. Wolfgang reports similar rates between husbands and wives from 1948–52, in *Patterns in Criminal Homocide* (New York: Wiley, 1958). These figures are for the United States and do not pertain in other nations (where women have less access to lethal weapons).

44. U.S. Department of Justice, Federal Bureau of Investigation, Bureau of Justice Statistics, *National Survey of Crime Severity* (Washington, D.C.: US-GPO, 1985): as cited in Farrell, 1994, 214.

45. See figures presented in Farrell, 1994, 240–283.

46. An estimated 2% of men who murder receive a death sentence, compared to 0.1 % of women. U.S. Dept. of Justice, Bureau of Justice Statistics, *Profile of Felons Convicted in State Courts*, Jan. 1990, publication #NCJ-120021, 9: cited in Farrell 1994, 240. Since 1954, no woman has been executed for killing only men.

47. See Tavris, *The Mismeasure of Woman*, 110–115, for the standard argument that women are treated too harshly and should be given special considerations and exemptions. The argument that women are punished more harshly than men is based on anecdotes, and not on figures that actually compare punishments for women vs. men.

48. D. Sadker, Myra Sadker, and D. Thomas, "Sex Equity and Special Education." *The Pointer*, 26, 1, 1981, 36: reviewed in Sommers, 165–166. See also John Nicholson, *Men and*

Women: How Different Are They? (Oxford: Oxford University Press, 1984), 90.

49. J. Robinson, University of Maryland, 1985. Cited in Marsha Mercer, "Americans May Have More Free Time Than They Realize." Scripps-Howard News Service, Aug. 7, 1991.

50. F. T. Juster and F. Stafford, "The Allocation of Time: Empirical Findings, Behavioral Models, and Problems of Measurement." *Journal of Economic Literature*, 29, June 1991, 477: as cited in Farrell, 1994.

51. A. Hochschild, *The Second Shift: Working Parents and the Revolution at Home.* (New York: Viking, 1989).

52. Christina Hoff Sommers, *Who Stole Feminism? How Women Have Betrayed Women* (New York: Touchstone, 1994).

53. Sommers, op. cit, 188–200.

54. Sommers, op. cit, 196–197.

55. *A Call to Action: Shortchanging Girls, Shortchanging America* (Washington DC: American Association of University Women, 1991). See Sommers, op. cit., 157–187.

56. *The Condition of Education* (Washington DC: National Center for Education Statistics, U.S. Department of Education, 1985) 50 & 52: in Sommers, 1994, 161.

57. *Digest of Education Statistics* (Washington, DC: U.S. Department of Education, 1992), 136: in Sommers, 1994, 160.

58. Sommers, op. cit, p. 148.

59. *The Condition of Education* (Washington DC: National Center for Education Statistics, U.S. Department of Education, 1991), 44. As cited in Sommers, op cit, p. 160.

60. Gallup poll. Reported by Sheri Prasso, "Most People Prefer Men as Bosses, Poll Finds." Associated Press wire service, week of March 25th, 1996.

Chapter Twelve: What Changes and What Stays the Same?

1. Nicholson, 1984, 57: see research summaries by: J. Bernard, *The Future of Marriage* (New Haven, CT: Yale University Press, 1982); and M. Johnstone and S. Eklund, "Life-Adjustment of the Never-Married: A Review with Implications for Counseling." *Journal of Counseling and Development*, 6, 1984, 230–236.

2. J. Veroff, E. Douvan, and R. Kulka, *Inner American: A Self-Portrait from 1957 to 1976* (New York: Basic Books, 1981) p.178. Discussed in R. Bellah et al., *Habits of the Heart*, (New York: Harper & Row, 1986), p.111.

3. Nicholson, 1984, 58.

4. Universty of Tennessee Woman's Anger Project, Sandra Thomas principal investigator, showed that housewives are generally angrier than women who work outside the home: cited in Thomas and Jefferson, 1996, 71.

5. Francesca Cancian, *Love in America: Gender and Self-Development.* (Cambridge, England: Cambridge University Press, 1987) 81.

6. Sandra Thomas and collaborators: *Women and Anger.* New York: Springer, 1993.

7. D. Julien, H. Markman, S. Léveillé, E. Chartrand, and Jean Bégin, "Networks' Support and Interference with Regard to Marriage: Disclosures of Marital Problems to Confidants." *Journal of Family Psychology*, 8, 1, 16–31.

8. Bernadette Gray-Little, and N. Burks, "Power and Satisfaction in Marriage." *Psychological Bulletin*, 933, 1983, 513–38; R.G. Corrales, "Power and Satisfaction in Early Marriage." In R.E. Cromwell and D.H. Olson (eds.), *Power in Families* (New York: Wiley, 1975); R. Centers, B.H. Raven, and A. Rodrigues, "Conjugal Power Structure: A Reexamination." *American Sociological Review*, 36, 1971, 264–278; R.O. Blood Jr. and D.M. Wolfe, *Husbands and Wives: The Dynamics of Married Living* (Glencoe, IL: Free Press, 1960).

9. In 1992, according to the National Center for Health Statistics, 29% of American children were born to single women (almost 22% among whites and 68% among blacks). The 30% here is a conservative projection to 1998.

10. See Daniel Amneus. *The Garbage Generation: The Consequences of the Destruction of the Two-Parent Family and the Need to Stabilize It by Strengthening Its Weakest Link, the Father's Role.* (Alhambra, CA: Primrose Press, 1990).

11. Suggested by Wright, Nov. 1994.

12. C. Casamassima, "Battle of the Bucks." *Psychology Today*, March/April, 1995, 43.

13. UCLA and Council on Education study, 1997. Reported by Margot Hornblower. "Learning to Earn." *Time,* February 24, 1997, 34.

14. See Casamassima, 1995, 67.

15. M. Wiederman and E. Allgeier, "Gender Differences in Mate Selection Criteria: Sociobiology or Socioeconomic Explanation?" *Ethology and Sociobiology,* 13, 1992, 115–124; M. Townsend, "Mate Selection Criteria: A Pilot Study." *Ethology and Sociobiology,* 10, 1989, 241–253. Reviewed in Buss, 1994, 46.

16. A.J. Cherlin, 1978. "Women's Changing Roles at Home and on the Job." *Proceedings of a conference on the national longitudinal surveys of mature women in cooperation with the employment and training administration.* Department of Labor special report, #26; P.C. Glick, 1975. "Some Recent Changes in American Families." *Current Population Reports.* Social Studies Series P-23, #52. Washington, D.C.: U.S. Bureau of the Census: see Fisher, 1992, 193.

17. See Fisher, 1992, 275–291.

18. Thomas Hargrove and G. Stempell III, "Poll: More Men Than Women Eye Marriage." Scripps Howard News Service, July 29, 1993.

19. The conceptualization is taken from Peter Ossorio, "Pathology." In Keith Davis and Thomas Mitchell (eds), *Advances in Descriptive Psychology Vol 4,* (Greenwich, Conn.: JAI Press, 1985,) 151–203.

20. Carol Tavris, *The Mismeasure of Woman* (New York: Simon & Schuster, 1992), 249–263.

21. Robin Norwood, *Women Who Love Too Much: When You Keep Wishing and Hoping He'll Change* (Los Angeles: J.P. Tarcher, 1985).

22. Connell Cowan and Melvyn Kinder, *Smart Women, Foolish Choices* (New York: Clarkson N. Potter, 1984).

23. Susan Forward, *Men Who Hate Women and the Women Who Love Them* (New York: Bantam, 1987).

Chapter Thirteen: Lust and Anger As Gender Follies

1. See Patric Carnes, *Out of the Shadows: Understanding Sexual Addiction* (Center City, MN: Hazelden, 1992).

2. Thomas and Jefferson, 1996, xix.

3. Women's Anger Study: see Thomas and Jefferson, 1996, 107.

4. Gloria Steinem, at CUNY, October, 1992: reported by Sommers, 1994, 21.

5. From Roper surveys, summarized by D. Crispell, "The Brave New World of Men." *American Demographics*, January, 1992, 38.

6. Alice Eagly, "The Science and Politics of Comparing Women and Men." *American Psychologist*, 50, 3, 1995, 145–158; A. Eagly & A. Mladinic, "Are People Prejudiced Against Women? Some Answers from Research on Attitudes, Gender Stereotypes, and Judgments of Competence." In W. Stroebe & M. Hewstone (eds.), *European Review of Social Psychology*, *Vol. 4*, 1–35. (New York, Wiley, 1994); A. Eagly, H. Mladinic, & S. Otto, "Are Women Evaluated More Favorably Than Men? An Analysis of Attitudes, Beliefs, and Emotions." *Psychology of Women Quarterly*, 15, 1991, 203–216.

7. R. Bellah *et al. Habits of the Heart: Individualism and Commitment in American Life* (New York, Perennial Library, 1985), 87.

8. Sommers, 1994.

9. Sommers, 20.

10. Thomas and Jefferson, 1996, xix & 351.

Chapter Fourteen: Gender Conflict at Work

1. Deborah Tannen. *Talking from 9 to 5*. (New York: William Morrow and Co., 1994), esp. 21–42.

2. Tannen, 1994, esp. 66–70.

3. Tannen, 1994, esp. 57–63.

4. Prasso, 1996.

5. Those whose positions did not expose them to conflict with both genders were not counted in the interview.

6. Sample included African-Americans and Hispanics and a single Asian respondent.

7. Of the 100 men surveyed, 51 reported being more stressed by conflict with women, 16 were more stressed with men, and 33 said it is the same or it depended on the individual.

8. Of the 100 women surveyed, 62 reported being more stressed with women, 16 were more stressed with men, and 22 said it is the same or depends on the individual.

9. Tara Roth Madden, *Women vs. Women: The Uncivil Business War* (New York: American Management Association, 1997).

10. Marjorie Harness Goodwin, "Children's Arguing." In S. Philips, S. Steele, and C. Tanz, *Language, Gender, and Sex in Comparative Perspective* (New York: Cambridge University Press, 1987), 200–248; M. Goodwin, "He-Said-She-Said: Formal Cultural Procedures for the Construction of a Gossip Dispute Activity." *American Ethonologist*, 7, 1980, 674–695: see Tannen, 1990, 108.

11. Janet Lever, "Sex Difference in the Games Children Play." *Social Problems*, 23, 1976, 478–487; ___, "Sex Differences in the Complexity of Children's Play and Games." *American Sociological Review*, 43, 1978, 471–483.

12. Suggested by Jean Piaget, *The Moral Judgment of the Child* (New York: The Free Press, 1965—originally published in 1932), and Lawrence Kohlberg, "Stage and Sequence: The Cognitive-Development Approach to Socialization." In D. A. Goslin, ed., *Handbook of Socialization Theory and Research* (Chicago: Rand McNally, 1969).

13. Carol Gilligan, *In a Different Voice* (Cambridge, Mass.: Harvard Unversity Press, 1982).

14. See Tavris, 1992, 83–90; Sommers, 1994, 152–154.

15. "Are Women Too Nice At the Office?" *Time*, Oct. 3, 1994, 60–61. Synopsis of Deborah Tannen's *Talking from 9 to 5*.

16. Estlle Davison-Crews, "Females in the Workplace: Acknowledging, Preventing Betrayal." *AORN Journal*, 51, 4, 1990, 1028–1034; ___, "Covert Actions by a Coworker: Identification, Consequences, Solutions." *AORN Journal*, 56, 5, 869–872; in Donna Smith, "We Women Can Be Our Own Worst Enemies." *The Oak Ridger*, Feb. 19, 1994.

17. In Linden, "Apes and Humans," 1992, 35.

18. This was the eventual fate of Luit, one of the ranking Arnhem males. Frans de Waal, *Peacemaking Among Primates*, (Cambridge, Mass.: Harvard University Press, 1989.)

19. de Waal, 1989, 38.

20. de Waal, 1989, 194–199.

21. See J. Bond and W. Vinacke, "Coalitions in Mixed-Sex Triads." *Sociometry*, 24, 1961, 61–75; J. Dearden, "Sex-Linked Differences of Political Behavior: An Investigation of Their

Possibly Innate Origins." *Soc. Sci. Inform.*, 13, 19–25. In de Waal, 1989, 198.

22. The workplace conflict survey I conducted included only those with significant conflict with both sexes, which accounts for its slightly stronger results.

23. Elizabeth Tooker, "Women in Iroquois Society." In M. Foster, J. Campisi, & M. Mithune (eds), *Extending the Rafters: Interdisciplinary Approaches to Iroquoian Studies* (Albany, NY: SUNY Press, 1984), 112.

24. Harassment suits filed with the EEOC more than doubled between 1989 and 1993, from 5,600 to 11,900. W. Olson, *The Excuse Factory* (New York: Free Press, 1997): in Jonathan Rauch, "Offices and Gentlemen." *The New Republic*, June, 1997, 22–28.

25. Olson, ibid.

26. See Daphne Patai and Noretta Koertge, *Professing Feminism: Cautionary Tales from the Strange World of Women's Studies* (New York: Basic Books, 1995); Katie Roiphe, *The Morning After: Sex, Fear, and Feminism on Campus* (Boston: Little Brown, 1993).

27. Information is from 10 men and 2 women, from 9 separate seminaries, all of whom report atmospheres unmistakably hostile toward men.

28. These figures were reported to me in 1995 for Episcopal, Methodist, Presbyterian, and Unitarian seminaries.

29. In an average class of 40 students, seminarians tell me there might be only two or three relentlessly hostile women. Yet that is enough to intimidate the men and prevent anyone from talking freely.

30. Figures are from a survey by the Catalyst think tank, as cited in Bonnie Erbe, "Why Aren't Women Corporate CEO's?" Scripps Howard News Service, March 6, 1996; and from *Women's Research Network News*, Winter, 1994, 5.

Chapter Fifteen: Together We Stand

1. Estimate of corporate CEO's is by Tony Petrelli, past chairman of the Regional Investment Bankers Association (RIBA), which handles 85% of initial public offerings of companies under $15 million dollars.

2. Louis Harris and Associates, Commonwealth Fund Survey of Women's Health (New York: Commonwealth Fund, 1993): reviewed by Sommers, 1994, 246–251.

3. C. Cobb, T. Halstead, and J. Rowe, "If the GDP Is Up, Why Is America Down?" *Atlantic Monthly,* Oct. 1995, 59–78.

4. Marc Miringoff, Institute for Innovation of Social Policy, Fordham Graduate Center in Tarrytown, New York: as cited in Nick Ravo, 'Warning sign' seen as study finds a decline in social health of nation. New York Times News Service, Oct. 14, 1996.

REFERENCES

Archer, John (1996). Sex Differences in Social Behavior: Are the Social Role and Evolutionary Explanations Compatible? *American Psychologist*, 51, 9, 909–917.

Buss, David (1994). *The Evolution of Desire: Strategies of Human Mating*. New York: Basic Books.

Buss, David (1995). Psychological Sex Differences: Origins Through Sexual Selection. *American Psychologist*, 50, 3, 164–168.

Casamassima, C. (1995). Battle of the Bucks. *Psychology Today*, March/April, 43.

de Waal, Frans (1982, 1989). *Chimpanzee Politics: Power and Sex Among Apes*. Baltimore: Johns Hopkins University Press.

Eshleman, J.R. (1974). *The Family*. Boston: Allyn and Bacon.

Farrell, Warren (1986). *Why Men Are the Way They Are*. New York: McGraw Hill.

Farrell, Warren (1994). *The Myth of Male Power*. New York: Berkley Books.

Fisher, Helen (1992). *The Anatomy of Love: A Natural History of Love, Marriage, and Why We Stray*. New York: Fawcett Columbine.

Gottman, J. and R. Levenson (1988). The Social Psychophysiology of Marriage. In P. Noller and M. Fitzpatric (eds.), *Perspectives on Marital Interaction*. Clevedon, Avon, England: Multilingual Matters, 182–202.

Gottman, John (1991). Predicting the Longitudinal Course of Marriages. *Journal of Marriage and Family Therapy*, 17, 1, 3–7.

Gottman, John (1994). Why Marriages Fail. *Family Therapy Networker*, May/June, 40–48.

Hatfield, Elaine and G. William Walster (1978). *A New Look at Love*. Lanham, MD: University Press of America.

Hill, C., Z. Rubin and L.A. Peplau (1976). Breakups Before Marriage: The End of 103 Affairs. *Journal of Social Issues*, 1, 147–168.

Hobart, C.W. (1958). The Incidence of Romanticism During Courtship. *Social Forces*, 36.

Johnson, Catherine (1992). *Lucky in Love: The Secrets of Happy Couples and How Their Marriages Thrive*. New York: Penguin Books.

Kadar, Andrew. (1994). The Sex-Bias Myth in Medicine. *Atlantic Monthly*. Aug., 66–70.

Kanin, E.J. et al. (1970). A Research Note on Male-Female Differentials in the Experience of Heterosexual Love. *Journal of Sex Research*, 6, 64–72.

Kaplan, H.S. and C.J. Sager (1971). Sexual Patterns at Different Ages. *Medical Aspects of Human Sexuality*, June, 10–23.

Luria, Z., S. Friedman, and M. Rose (1987). *Human Sexuality*. New York: John Wiley and Sons.

Linden, Eugene (1992). A Curious Kinship: Apes and Humans. *National Geographic*, 181, 3, March, 2–45.

Markman, Howard (1991). Backwards into the Future of Couples Therapy and Couples Therapy Research. *Journal of Family Psychology*, 4, 422.

Moir, Anne and David Jessel (1991). *Brain Sex: The Real Difference Between Men and Women.* New York: Dell.

Nicholson, John (1984). *Men and Women: How Different Are They?* Oxford: Oxford University Press.

Olson, K. *The Excuse Factory* (New York: Free Press, 1997).

Prasso, Sheri. Most People Prefer Men as Bosses, Poll Finds. Associated Press wire service, week of March 25th, 1996.

Sommers, Christina Hoff (1994). *Who Stole Feminism? How Women Have Betrayed Women.* New York: Touchstone.

Symons, Donald (1979). *The Evolution of Human Sexuality.* New York: Oxford University Press.

Tannen, Deborah (1990). *You Just Don't Understand.* New York: Ballentine.

Tannen, Deborah (1994). *Talking from 9 to 5.* New York: William Morrow and Co.

Trivers, Robert (1972). Parental Investment and Sexual Selection. In B. G. Campbell (Ed.), *Sexual Selection and the Descent of Man, 1871–1971.* Chicago: Aldine.

Tavris, Carol (1992). *The Mismeasure of Woman.* New York: Touchstone.

Thomas, Sandra and Cheryl Jefferson (1996). *Use Your Anger: A Woman's Guide to Empowerment.* New York: Simon & Schuster.

Trivers, Robert (1972). Parental Investment and Sexual Selection. In B. G. Campbell (Ed.), *Sexual Selection and the Descent of Man, 1871–1971.* Chicago: Aldine.

Whyte, Martin (1978). *The Status of Women in Preindustrial Societies.* Princeton: Princeton University Press.

Wilson, M. and M. Daly (1985). Competitiveness, Risk Taking, and Violence: The Young Male Syndrome. *Ethology and Sociobiology,* 6, 59–73.

Wright, Karen (1992). Evolution of the Big O. *Discover,* June, 53–59.

Wright, Robert (1994). *The Moral Animal: The New Science of Evolutionary Psychology.* New York: Pantheon.

Wright, Robert (1994). Feminists, Meet Mr. Darwin. *The New Republic,* Nov. 28, 34–46.

Wright, Robert (1994). Our Cheating Hearts. *Time,* Aug. 15, 44–52.

INDEX

ABOUT THE AUTHOR

RICHARD DRISCOLL, PH.D., trained at the University of Colorado, and now specializes in relationships, conflict management, and inner guidance. He has written three previous books and twenty professional articles.

Dr. Driscoll is married to Nancy Davis Driscoll, P.h.D, who is also a psychologist, and they are in private practice together. The have over forty years of combined professional experience working with relationships, and over fifty years of personal experience being married (to each other). As a husband and wife team, they conduct workshops on gender and relationships. They have three children, and live in Tennessee.

Information about workshops and speaking engagements may be attained through Westside Psychology, at (423) 690-0962.

Mental Shielding to Brush Off Hostility can be ordered directly at (800) 769-0962.